D1196648

Furiously Funny

UNIVERSITY PRESS OF FLORIDA

Florida A&M University, Tallahassee
Florida Atlantic University, Boca Raton
Florida Gulf Coast University, Ft. Myers
Florida International University, Miami
Florida State University, Tallahassee
New College of Florida, Sarasota
University of Central Florida, Orlando
University of Florida, Gainesville
University of North Florida, Jacksonville
University of South Florida, Tampa
University of West Florida, Pensacola

☞ Furiously Funny

Comic Rage from Ralph Ellison to Chris Rock

Terrence T. Tucker

University Press of Florida
Gainesville · Tallahassee · Tampa · Boca Raton
Pensacola · Orlando · Miami · Jacksonville · Ft. Myers · Sarasota

Copyright 2018 by Terrence T. Tucker
All rights reserved
Printed in the United States of America on acid-free paper

This book may be available in an electronic edition.

23 22 21 20 19 18   6 5 4 3 2 1

A record of cataloging-in-publication data is available from the Library of Congress.
ISBN 978-0-8130-5436-0

The University Press of Florida is the scholarly publishing agency for the State University
System of Florida, comprising Florida A&M University, Florida Atlantic University, Florida
Gulf Coast University, Florida International University, Florida State University, New College
of Florida, University of Central Florida, University of Florida, University of North Florida,
University of South Florida, and University of West Florida.

University Press of Florida
15 Northwest 15th Street
Gainesville, FL 32611-2079
http://upress.ufl.edu

To my wonderful wife, Mary,
who makes every day worth it

Contents

Acknowledgments

You would think that an acknowledgments page in a book about humor and rage would be funny or "deep." I thought about listing everyone from my pre-K teachers to the customers at a gas station where I used to work. No go. But it would have been worth it. Instead, all I have to give is thanks. This project owes a great debt to a number of significant people. First, the confidence of Professors Gordon Hutner and Yolanda Pierce made both the conception and the execution possible. Not only have their comments proved invaluable, but their concern for my work and life beyond this book has provided vital perspective. Critical input has also come from the brilliant Dale Bauer, the prolific Tracy Campbell, and the unflappable Andrew Kimbrough. One of these days I'll be as funny and charismatic and giving as you all have been. I thank the members of my writing group, who selflessly took the time to read and respond to numerous drafts. Both Rachel Simon and Matthew D. Towles, the prides of their respective Illinois and Virginia, have been excellent colleagues and better friends, especially when we're arguing about the Civil War.

At the University Press of Florida I particularly want to thank Amy Gorelick for getting the process started and encouraging changes that expanded the scope of the book. Thanks to my "neighbor" Sian Hunter for taking the baton and carrying it to the finish line with tenacity. Thanks to Marthe Walters and Ann Marlowe for being patient and thoughtful shepherds.

Finally, my family has been an incredible source of strength and inspiration. My mother, whose love of English is part of the Ford/Price family's commitment to education as a practice of freedom, has been the engine driving my pursuit. She's the funniest person and the best teacher I know. Thank you to my grandparents and my aunts for their encouragement and their example. Thanks to family for keeping me thinking and keeping me fed. The spaghetti's on me next time. Big thanks to my family in Lexington and Atlanta for all the great conversations and for keeping me grounded, especially about when and how to get my hair cut. This project was written with the family that comes after me in mind: my children Zoe and Xavier, my younger brother Tony, my nephews and nieces, my cousins and godchildren. Thanks to everyone for keeping me laughing.

Introduction

A Joke to the Eye

I was a Negro for twenty-three years; I had to give that shit up.
No room for advancement.

Richard Pryor, *Pryor Convictions, and Other Life Sentences*

In Richard Pryor's infamous 1967 "flameout," he walked offstage at a Las Vegas nightclub and initiated a transformation that reshaped his consciousness and identity. The shift he notes above reveals his dissatisfaction with his initial attempts at comedy, as a "Negro," a term used in this context as an African American who uses colorless, apolitical comedy to achieve financial success. Despite his upbringing in Peoria, Illinois, about which he eventually spun tales of going to brothels and his father dying "fucking," Pryor started out by structuring his comedy after that of Bill Cosby. Cosby, who would go on to become one of the most influential figures in the last two decades of the twentieth century, had already cemented his reputation as an apolitical comic by the end of the 1960s with six consecutive Grammys for his comedy albums and his costarring role in the television show *I Spy*. Pryor's respect for Cosby moved beyond comic material. After witnessing Cosby perform, Pryor concedes in his autobiography, *Pryor Convictions, and Other Life Sentences*, "I decided that's who I was going to be from then on. Bill Cosby. Richard Cosby" (72). Pryor initially adopted Cosby's routine because of the promotion of middle-class values that appealed to audiences by minimizing racial and class difference. When Pryor emerged from his self-imposed exile, however, he returned with a style that revolutionized the comic, racial, and political landscape.

Pryor's style featured the revelation of the underground tradition of African American humor. Beneath mainstream African American humor, from Bert Williams's own literal performance in blackface to *Amos 'n' Andy*'s metaphorical representations, an uncensored African American comedic tradition was evolving in front of predominantly African American audiences in the nightclubs that became known as the Chitlin' Circuit. There, artists removed their masks to reveal the specific pain, fear, and frustration other African Americans found familiar. There, African American artists constructed responses to racist attack by exposing white folly, highlighting American hypocrisy, and celebrating African American difference. When Pryor definitively ripped off the mask of African American humor in front of white audiences, he exposed a tradition that was willing to openly confront whites. His contribution came in the transformation of despair and self-destruction into comic observations on the human condition. Part of Pryor's significance to this study is his inclusion of a broad range of emotions that move his comic routines beyond entertainment.

Pryor's inclusion of the rage that permeated African American expressions from music to literature to political ideology rejected attempts to render his comedy easily consumable or appropriated by his white audiences. White audiences ceased to be passive, uncritical spectators; rather, they were forced to confront the continued legacy of racial oppression that was the subtext of Pryor's riffs on the police or the differences between blacks and whites. Pryor's volatile mixture of humor and ideology, of rage and history, and of politics and pathos is at the core of what I refer to in this book as comic rage.

I define comic rage as an African American cultural expression that utilizes oral tradition to simultaneously convey humor and militancy. In this vernacular, stereotypes about African Americans (Aunt Jemimas, Bad Niggers) and methods of perpetuating those stereotypes are exploded and interrogated to reveal hypocrisies in the construction of American identity, history, and culture. Comic rage centralizes African American experience and, fueled by militant rage, uses a comic lens to examine the complexities and inconsistencies in the American national narrative. Pryor's discussion of differences between blacks and whites, then, rejected the historical promotion of whiteness as normal, "cool," or desirable. Pryor's routine becomes significant because assumptions about whiteness, in addition to fostering black self-hatred, have had significant ramifications across the American legal, political, and cultural spectrum.

At a time when voices of African American rage are considered divisive and African American humor is mistaken as a sign of racial progress, comic rage is a vital source of cultural expression that actively reveals the perpetuation of white supremacist hegemony through its mixture of tones and inversion of traditional discourse. The works in this study share a comic vision that realigns the discourse on race through an unequivocal frustration at stereotypical ideas about African Americans—as well as at some African American responses to stereotypes, which are equally limiting. Most often, the changes we see are intimately connected with the historical moment, becoming more assertive as black cultural production reflected a more militant response to white oppression. Creative responses became increasingly couched in the language and tradition of African American folk culture. Because the key ingredients are humor and rage, the gulf—in terms of tradition, evolution, and expression—can seem too contrasting. Yet comic rage regularly appeared in post–World War II moments, as African Americans began to challenge overtly the impact of white supremacist hegemony in the United States.

What results is an important African American art form similar to jazz and blues, namely the merging of African American comedic tradition with African American militant political thought manifested through activism and literature. African American humor acts as a site where blacks resist nihilistic threat, while African American political thought and activism constructively channel African American rage at white supremacist assault. By fusing the two, primarily through the use of African American vernacular tradition, comic rage re-visions constructions of blackness by challenging previous perceptions and exploring the complexities and contradictions of race on both sides of the color line. Moreover, the boldness with which comic rage is expressed often results in its defiant presence in mainstream American culture. According to Siva Vaidhyanathan in "Now's the Time: The Richard Pryor Phenomenon and the Triumph of Black Culture," "Pryor showed the same African American experiential groundings, regardless of his audience. He spoofed misguided liberals as well as dangerous rednecks, even though his audience was often filled with white liberals. Pryor riddled all authority figures with the full arsenal of his comic tools: parody, tricksterism, hyperbole, double-edged vernacular, and rapid-fire revelations of hypocrisy" (42). In the same vein, Pryor's characterizations of various figures in the African American community, specifically the black underclass, stood in contrast to efforts by many African Americans to promote only a middle-class image in order to indict racist oppression. Works of comic rage like Pryor's produce material that confronts both whites and blacks.

The works that populate this book, then, explode the race-relations dichotomy of white subject and black object. In doing so, works of comic rage act in the tradition of Julia Kristeva's "abjections." In *Powers of Horror*, Kristeva points out that the abject sits alongside traditional ideas of being: "It lies there, quite close, but it cannot be assimilated. It beseeches, worries, and fascinates desire, which, nevertheless, does not let itself be seduced" (1). I extend Kristeva's discussion of being to include traditional narratives and discourse, particularly as they relate to race and to how they are manifested in literature and ideology. While the abject stands "detached and autonomous," it does, according to Kristeva, share "one quality of the object—that of being opposed to *I*" (1). In this book, the "I" represents mainstream (white) narratives that African Americans—through art and literature, protest and behavior—resist. Although works of comic rage, emerging and pulling from African American cultural tradition, share the tradition's resistance efforts, they reject the object's inevitable status of being "ceaselessly and infinitely homologous to [the *I*]" (2). So, works of comic rage might reject the respectability politics of the black bourgeoisie by depicting images of African American life that run the risk of confirming stereotypes of blackness and, in the same moment, ridicule whites for allowing those images to sit at the center of the mainstream's enactment of policy, backlashes against black progress, and reinforcement of racist hierarchies.

Thunder and Lightning: The Roots of Comic Rage

According to Mel Watkins in *On the Real Side*, "Reports of white Americans' astonishment at the uninhibited display and heartiness of blacks' 'cackling laughter' can be found throughout early American writings" (16). Beginning in the nineteenth century, white fascination with African American humor would prompt an appropriation of that humor, specifically through the blackface minstrel tradition. Humor became one of the first African American cultural expressions to be co-opted and exploited to confirm white conceptions of blackness. White cultural production of African American humor was represented in the stories of Joel Chandler Harris, which encouraged a nostalgic image of the antebellum South. In these stories African American slaves were cast as sympathetic, peaceful individuals who seemed happier under the power of white southern rule. Harris's stories were complemented by the still popular minstrel show, which presented African Americans as buffoonish caricatures. In contrast to Harris, Thomas Dixon, whose novel *The Clansman* was eventually made into the infamously racist film *The Birth of a Nation*, offered a disdainful view of Reconstruction in novels that portrayed the South in disarray, with African Americans exerting political and economic power that left white Southerners unable to recover after their loss to the North in the Civil War. Through the "heroic" efforts of paramilitary terrorist organizations like the Ku Klux Klan, which helped to build white racial unity across class lines, order was restored to the South.

Despite the limited use of humor in early African American literature as a result of the mainstream's appropriation of it, Watkins maintains that the development of African American humor was ongoing throughout this period: "The distinctive character of authentic African American humor—sometimes ironic, evasive, and oblique, sometimes playful and purely entertaining, and sometimes aggressively militant—was well established by the early nineteenth century" (81). A similar attack on post-Reconstruction America was being waged through Charles Chesnutt's attempts to subvert the nostalgic productions of the antebellum South that were justifying the violent and racist erosion of African American rights. Darryl Dickson-Carr argues, "The short stories of Charles W. Chesnutt, written as they were in the local color tradition and possessing subtle satirical messages, constitute the sole consistent body of ironic and often satiric literature by an African American in the nineteenth century" (9). Chesnutt's short stories seem a candid response to Joel Chandler Harris's stories, which played on the nostalgia of the Old South through the figure of the lovably inferior and content African American slave.[1] The best-known example comes in "The Passing of Grandison." In "Black America and the Mask of Comedy," Richard K. Barksdale informs us that the story "is in the tradition of comic ridicule, so effectively communicated through the Black man's folk literature. Chesnutt's account of how Grandison, an apparently loyal slave, carefully plots his escape

and effectively ridicules both young and old masters is related with dis-
ciplined narrative control and suspense" (352). From his first collection
to his most famous novel, *The Marrow of Tradition* (1901), Chesnutt de-
stroyed the nostalgic images of antebellum slavery that white Southerners clung to and replaced them with a clear demonstration of black humanity, intelligence, and anger.

However, I focus especially on satire in relation to comic rage for two
reasons. The first is that the close resemblance between satire and comic
rage is emblematic of the symbiotic relationship between American and
African American humor. Louis B. Wright notes in "Human Comedy in
Early America" that "Americans . . . have used satire as an instrument
of reform and have sometimes laughed out of existence shortcomings
in society that provoked the scorn and ridicule of writers. Mark Twain,
one of the greatest American writers, was a master of satire; for many
generations before his time, however, American writers had been employing this instrument with comic effect" (17). The second is that the
dominance of satire in the 1920s and 1930s, which saw the advent of the
Harlem Renaissance and particularly George Schuyler's novel *Black No
More* (1931), impacted perceptions of comedy that eventually initiated
the development of comic rage. In his essay "The Harlem Renaissance,"
Blyden Jackson remarks that Schuyler's novel "invokes his comic muse
principally for the ends of satire, and of satire with a venomous edge"
(300). At the heart of satire is a desire for reform, specifically a return to
preset moral values that have been eroded by corruption, vice, and folly.

Comic rage goes beyond this, urging a re-visioning of society at large
by questioning the truth and legitimacy of the very values the satirist
bemoans are being ignored.[2] In fact, works of comic rage often argue
that the corruption and hypocrisy are a significant part of the acquisi-
tion of power, buried underneath the rhetoric of the morals and values
promoted to the masses. Even as Horatian satire exposes the corruption
through finesse, and Juvenalian through tragic lament, both maintain
a moral standard to which they wish their readers and their society to
subscribe. Neither questions the morals and values they promote. This,
perhaps, is the very purpose of satire. Leonard Feinberg suggests, for
instance, "One of the reasons why we get more pleasure from satire than
from a sermon, even when the satire is making exactly the same point as
the sermon, is that we have an uncomfortable feeling that the minister

expects us to do something about it" (7). Despite Horace's moral instruction and Juvenal's dark forecast, says Feinberg, satire's "essential quality is entertainment." While it is imperative that comic rage be entertaining in order to be effective, it is fearless in its condemnation and ridicule. Fueled by militant rage, it often elicits action from its audience, either physical or psychological, and is thus closer to Feinberg's sense of a sermon.

The satire to which works of comic rage often come closest is the Menippean, which is made primarily of prose narrative, especially the degenerative model.[3] In *African American Satire*, Dickson-Carr argues that in this model "virtually all hegemonies are ridiculed, often through the use of appalling grotesqueries and exaggerations" (17). We can see elements of Menippean satire in comic rage and vice versa. In identifying the beginnings of the African American satiric literary tradition with Menippean satire, the evolution to comic rage becomes much clearer. Aside from the centrality of expressing—as opposed to containing—frustration, comic rage's desire to tear normative values to tatters separates it from classical satirical forms. Comic rage subverts the limitations that plague satire. Feinberg suggests, for example, a "disadvantage of satire that *some truths are simply too uncomfortable to admit*, or to live with for more than a brief period at a time" (266). It is, in fact, those "uncomfortable truths" that comic rage revels in telling at length. Moreover, comic rage is intentionally not escapist, and creates a space, for both writer and reader, where rage can be constructively expressed and the effect of white supremacy can be effectively counteracted. Also, while "African American culture is itself a product of the intercourse between sub-Saharan African and various European cultures" and African American satire "draws from both these traditions" (18) as Dickson-Carr believes, the center of comic rage includes a full-throated embrace of African American folk life and the cultural traditions that have emerged in defiance of white supremacist hegemony's attempt to devalue, exploit, or distort those traditions.

The most common misconception I have encountered in telling people about this project is that this book might be considered a work primarily about comedy. Such is not the case. This book is, first and foremost, about militant rage and the *comic expression of militant rage* in African American texts in the late twentieth and twenty-first centuries. Indeed, tendencies to focus exclusively on humor highlight the virtual absence of discourse on African American rage. Historically, America has treated African American expressions of rage with disdain and fear. In her book of essays *Killing Rage*, bell hooks accurately posits, "To perpetuate and maintain white supremacy, white folks have colonized black Americans, and a part of that colonizing process has been teaching us to repress our rage, to never make them the targets of any anger we feel about racism" (14). African American rage, like humor, has been distorted to maintain destructive stereotypes about African Americans. While humor has been used to portray African Americans as lovable but buffoonish caricatures, depictions of African American rage have contributed to ideas about African Americans as figures of dangerous criminality and uncontrolled violence. Representations of African American rage often cast it as the greatest threat to law and order in American culture. As hooks notes, "Lecturing on race and racism all around this country, I am always amazed when I hear white folks speak about their fear of black people, of being the victims of black violence. They may have never spoken to a black person, and certainly never been hurt by a black person, but they are convinced that their response to blackness must first and foremost be fear and dread" (14). Unlike humor, mainstream expressions of rage have a long history in African American literature.

The delicate fusing of humor and militancy, and the emergence of comic rage as a powerful force in African American literature, developed over time. Beginning with David Walker's *Appeal* (1829), rage in African American literature revealed the violent effects of racist oppression on African Americans as well as calling for collective action that ranged from emigration to revolt. Nevertheless, though Walker's *Appeal* is clearly a text filled with rage, the moments of humor that lambaste American proclamations of liberty are just as vital. Initial representations were seen through irony, highlighting the absurdity of slavery in a newly formed country that openly proclaimed itself unparalleled in providing equality for all. The ironic, near sarcastic allusion to the "rumors" that Thomas Jefferson had children with one of his slaves in the first African American novel, William Wells Brown's *Clotel* (1853), situates humor as a useful form for early African American writers. Frederick Douglass, however, virtually births comic rage into existence in his famed 1852 speech "What to the Slave Is the Fourth of July?" In it Douglass rhetorically questions whether his very invitation to speak is an elaborate joke. Arguing that America's celebrated Independence Day is a constant reminder for blacks of American hypocrisy, he dismisses classic debate principles of logical and moral appeals that would turn opinion against slavery. Instead he declaims:

> At a time like this, scorching irony, not convincing argument, is needed. Oh! had I the ability, and could I reach the nation's ear, I would to-day pour out a fiery stream of biting ridicule, blasting reproach, withering sarcasm, and stern rebuke. For it is not light that is needed, but fire; it is not the gentle shower, but thunder. We need the storm, the whirlwind, and the earthquake. The feeling of the nation must be quickened; the conscience of the nation must be roused: the propriety of the nation must be startled; the hypocrisy of the nation must be exposed; and its crimes against God and man must be proclaimed and denounced. (257–58)

For Douglass, the case was so obvious and so easily made that the reason for slavery's existence moved beyond logic. Douglass, then, sees a furious humor as the only alternative in effectively exposing the absurdity and hypocrisy of American slavery. What becomes important, however, is that none of Douglass's rage is relinquished in the use of humor. His belief that "a fiery stream of biting ridicule, blasting reproach, withering sarcasm, and stern rebuke" is necessary to end slavery is a veritable call for the simultaneous presence of both rage and humor.

Scholarly opinions on the turn-of-the-century author Sutton Griggs range from casting him as the first militant black writer to describing him as accommodationist and servile. Griggs authored five novels from 1899 to 1908, and most consider his first, *Imperium in Imperio*, his best. In the story of the Imperium, a secret black organization that plots to establish Texas forcibly as an independent black state, Griggs's novel could be seen as too fantastical to be taken seriously. Yet the Imperium bears a strong resemblance to the guerrillas trained in Sam Greenlee's *The Spook Who Sat by the Door* (1969) and Guitar Barnes's Seven Days group in Toni Morrison's *Song of Solomon* (1977). Griggs attempts to unify black America's disparate strategies and ideologies, represented in *Imperium* through the main characters Belton Piedmont and Bernard Belgrave. *Imperium* undercuts the promotion of a singular African American ideology, recognizing the necessity of a variety of positions and ideas. This stands in opposition to mainstream expectations that African Americans must espouse only one position or support only one ideology.[4]

The presence of humor and rage in black vernacular tradition is inherent because of the tradition's establishment of a dual meaning in its language. In particular, although the adoption of English was essential for the slaves when they came to America, African oral traditions and languages were fused with English to provide an important method of communication and critique. As Lawrence Levine notes in *Black Culture and Black Consciousness*, "For all of its horrors, slavery was never so complete a system of psychic assault that it prevented the slave from carving out independent cultural forms. . . . If North American slavery eroded the Africans' linguistic and institutional life, it nevertheless allowed them to continue and to develop the patterns of verbal art which were so central to their past culture" (30). Eventually the language, which finds its current manifestation in African American Vernacular English, became a mode of resistance. The unfamiliarity of whites with the double meaning of the slaves' references allowed for the ridiculing of masters and overseers in their presence. Black vernacular tradition may thus separate itself from the oppressive intent of slavery-mandated English, but, as Kristeva argues, "it does not radically cut off the subject from what threatens it—on the contrary, abjection acknowledges it to be in perpetual danger" (9). Therefore, comic rage's use of black vernacular tradition acts as a constant threat to oppressive language, specifically white supremacy's consistent use of language to reconfigure itself through rhetoric's ability to fortify stereotypical narratives and foster destructive policies and ideologies.

While humor clearly appears in various slave spirituals and ballads, there remained a significant void in the collection of African American humor until the publication of Langston Hughes's *The Book of Negro Humor* (1966). A partial reason for the dearth of humor in early African American literary works is that, like other black cultural expressions, African American humor has often been misinterpreted by the white mainstream. An important parallel to humor is African American music. For instance, in his 1845 *Narrative*, Frederick Douglass argued, "I have often been utterly astonished, since I came to the north, to find persons who could speak of the singing, among slaves, as evidence of their contentment and happiness. It is impossible to conceive of a greater mistake.

Slaves sing most when they are most unhappy" (19). From the spirituals that slaves used in the field or at church services to contemporary rap, music has been a vital mechanism in proclaiming a mixture of black despair and unhappiness at white oppression.

The nostalgic antebellum images of African Americans from which the minstrel tradition is drawn, in conjunction with a paternalistic conception of the white southern role in African American life, fueled the rage and fear at African American empowerment during Reconstruction. In his "Voices at the Nadir" William Gleason argues that the "mythopoeic works" of authors like Page and Dixon "were frequently accepted as truthful chronicles. Moreover, newspapers and magazines in both the South and the North unremittingly pressed the stereotypes of the comic-criminal Negro into the daily American consciousness" (229). The twin distortions of African Americans, the "comic-criminal," as Gleason puts it, produced images of blackness that affected legislation and court decisions for decades. The guileless comic fool cast African Americans as simple-minded and incapable (or unworthy) of wielding power. Watkins argues, "African American humor (along with elements of song and dance) was lifted from its original context, transformed and parodied, then spotlighted for the entertainment and amusement of nonblack audiences" (82). Simultaneously, the cunning and dangerous black criminal was used to justify, if not encourage, terrorist violence by the Klan and lynch mobs. Therefore, much of the Renaissance became about the business of establishing African American images that were radically different from the comic-criminal.

In particular, the Harlem Renaissance writers who committed to representing African American folk culture, specifically those who sought to enact the transference from the oral to the written, revealed a world that was inhabited by laughter and anger concurrently: Langston Hughes, Zora Neale Hurston, and Rudolph Fisher, for example. However, it was not until the publication of George Schuyler's *Black No More* in 1931 that critics of the time recognized Schuyler as, according to his biographer Michael W. Peplow, "the first writer to attack" the color line "with the weapon of ridicule. No black writer before Schuyler underscored the fundamental absurdities of America's 'colorphobia' with such devastating wit and scorn" (108). The story of Dr. Junius Crookman's creation of a process that transforms blacks into whites within three days primarily follows Max Disher, a black insurance man in Harlem who undergoes the treatment and heads south as a white man named Matthew Fisher in search of the white woman who has previously spurned his advances. Eventually joining Knights of Nordica, a clear representation of the Ku Klux Klan, Max/Matthew becomes the second-in-command or the Grand Exalted Giraw, using white fear of Crookman's process to multiply exponentially the Knights' membership. He marries the daughter of the Knights of Nordica leader Rev. Givens, the same woman he had been chasing. Along the way we see the influence of forms and themes of American humor contemporaneous with Schuyler's writing.

Dickson-Carr suggests the novel "is simultaneously the first completely satirical novel written by and about African Americans and the first extended work of science fiction by a black author" (57). Until recently Schuyler has been less celebrated than his Harlem Renaissance peers. Although well received by the same African Americans who were satirized in the novel, including W.E.B. Du Bois and James Weldon Johnson, *Black No More*'s critique, which leaves no one unscathed, angered some members of the literate black community and upper-class socialites. Part of this has to do with Schuyler's willingness to ridicule both ends of the black ideological spectrum, from Du Bois to Marcus Garvey. Dickson-Carr contends the book sees "both the integrationist and nationalist branches of black politics," regardless of their internal differences, as "virtually as problematic as white racist organizations who would destroy African Americans altogether" (65). The most obvious, yet also more complicated, reason for the dearth of work done on Schuyler is his conservative bent, which had become increasingly rigid by the late 1970s. His denunciation of Martin Luther King's conduct of the civil rights campaign, publication of his autobiography *Black and Conservative* (1966), and support of Richard Nixon would alienate him even further from the black political mainstream. Peplow believes that criticisms of Schuyler as an Uncle Tom misunderstand his intent. Beginning with his 1926 article "The Negro-Art Hokum" in the *Nation*, Schuyler constructed a body of work that almost always ran counter to the African American literary and political tradition. Proclaiming in the article that "Negro art 'made in America' is as non-existent as the widely advertised profundity of Cal Coolidge, the 'seven years of progress' of [former New York] Mayor [James J.] Hylan, or the reported sophistication of New Yorkers," Schuyler became a figure vilified for the next few decades. Despite his feelings about the validity of African American art, famously refuted in Langston

Hughes's essay "The Negro Artist and the Racial Mountain," *Black No More* centers on the American obsession with and exploitation of race on both sides of the color line. Schuyler does not limit his derision to black leaders but extends it to whites whose hypocrisy lies at the root of the construction of race. Schuyler's project is to question the very idea of racial identity.

So while Matthew/Max completely internalizes white supremacist thinking while he is black, becoming white raises his consciousness and awakens his critical lens that recognizes the rage when he realizes the falseness of claims of white superiority: "The unreasoning and illogical color prejudice of most of the people with whom he was forced to associate infuriated him. He often laughed cynically when some coarse, ignorant white man voiced his opinion concerning the inferior mentality and morality of the Negroes" (43). It is not Schuyler's intent for Max/Matthew to develop into a character who proudly celebrates his blackness or plots the downfall of whites or emancipation of blacks as in *Imperium in Imperio*. However, his anger soon becomes a weapon that can be used to his own benefit. Peplow contends that this "anger, tempered by cynicism, makes Max the perfect con artist" whose "career is one long 'secret mocking laugh' at the white establishment that never suspects Max is a black man in a white skin" (69). Though Max/Matthew is clearly not a character who will lead African Americans in armed revolt against whites, the novel uses his responses to his new perspective to produce a mixture of anger and laughter that critiques the racist logic that enforces the color line and the exploitation of the black and white working classes. The novel's spread of satiric invective among blacks and whites lays the foundation for comic rage's impulse to challenge hypocrisies and inconsistencies regardless of color. So while black America is painted in one of the least flattering portraits of the Renaissance, white America is often cast in a worse light. There is no subject capable of escaping its gaze. Underneath the novel's reductio ad absurdum is a stunning expression of African American fury at color consciousness in America. Though the novel suffers from "the near absence of African American folk humor" (415) as Watkins suggests, I contend that *Black No More* stands as an unprecedented work of African American literary satire, one whose withering attacks, in-depth analysis of race, and uproarious humor form the foundation for the scope and tone of comic rage.

With Pryor we see how, by utilizing the power of humor to dictate the lens through which various topics can be viewed, comic rage enters the mainstream because of the historical moment's willingness to challenge and critique traditional structures and ideas. However, comic rage also entered the mainstream because of the traditional embrace of African American humor, or at least perceptions of African American humor. It also resists the mainstream's tendency to depoliticize African American cultural forms by maintaining African American comedy that engages sociopolitical issues. Specifically, comic rage seeks to connect with the rage of its (black) audience through a humor embedded in the cultural language of that audience. Its rhetoric aids the audience in negotiating oppression as well as challenging traditional, mainstream ideas about African American humor and rage. The audience bears witness to a twin defiance: the first is the expression of a rage shared by the black audience members in an environment that frequently seeks to silence voices of dissent. The second is the rejection of the mainstream perspective by centralizing minority culture without consideration for the gaze of whiteness and, simultaneously, providing an avenue to respond for African Americans who often find themselves voiceless in the face of institutional racism.

The novels of the so-called Wright school, works in the 1940s and 1950s that followed the 1940 publication of Richard Wright's *Native Son* in form and in tone, did possess moments of humor, but they were most often overwhelmed by the formulaic descent of the novels from rage and despair into violence. Thus Ralph Ellison's *Invisible Man* (1952) becomes central to the development of comic rage not only because it stands apart from those works in its consistent separation of black rage from violence but because Ellison's immersion in African American folk tradition allows humor to replace the violence of the protest novel as an expression of rage. The militancy of the Black Arts movement, especially in works by authors like LeRoi Jones/Amiri Baraka and Sonia Sanchez, radicalized African American rhetoric but was augmented by the artists' embrace of the black/folk urban culture that built on Ellison's novel. Consequently, certain artists eventually embraced humor, as previous artists had embraced jazz and blues, to express their dissatisfaction with racism. These efforts signaled the permanent presence of comic rage in African America, beginning with Douglas Turner Ward's play *Day of Absence* (1966).

During the time between Pryor's Las Vegas walkout and the introduction of the fully transformed Richard Pryor in his comedy album *Craps:*

After Hours (1971), he frequently performed at Redd Foxx's club in central Los Angeles, which allowed him to experiment with his more controversial material. Though this period also included the significant cocaine use that became a key part of his act, his time at Foxx's club was important to his transformation for another reason. Christine Acham argues, "Redd Foxx not only gave him the opportunity to experiment with the new material but also initiated his political awakening" (146). Specifically, Foxx's frequent stories about the life of his friend Malcolm X had a profound impact on Pryor, who recalls in his autobiography, "It was the same evolution that I'd go through. Strangely, I hadn't been affected by Malcolm X's death when it occurred. However, after Redd introduced me to him as a person and what he stood for, I missed him terribly" (99). Pryor connects Malcolm's journey from calling whites "devils" to his post-Mecca rebirth with his own eventual renunciation of his use of the term "nigger" after a trip to Africa. Pryor's relationship to Foxx, and through him Malcolm, demonstrates the inherent mixture of humor and militancy that Pryor eventually transformed into extended expressions of comic rage.

As a minister firmly in line with African American sermonic tradition, of which Martin Luther King was likewise a part, Malcolm X used the elements of black oral tradition that produce expressions of comic rage. The verbal dexterity of African American vernacular allowed Malcolm to shift tones within single speeches or allow multiple emotions to coexist. In *Malcolm and Martin and America*, James H. Cone notes, "Malcolm and Martin established an effective *tone* for freedom struggle, combining unwavering militancy with humor and irony" (304). Both were successful because their overt inclusion of humor balanced their calls for social justice and their defiant articulation of dissatisfaction. Cone suggests that expressions of humor were an important response to the hypocrisy of American claims for freedom in a time of segregation and pervasive racial discrimination: "So great were the moral and political contradictions that African Americans were fighting against that humor was sometimes the only response which could keep them sane" (307). Foxx, in reversing Malcolm's pattern, presented a humor that separated itself from other African American comics through a rage and aggressiveness that was usually at or just beneath the surface of his act. His comedy, as a result, was not embraced by mainstream popular culture of the mid-twentieth century.

I extend the rhetorical connections between Foxx and Malcolm to encompass the larger ones that can be drawn between stand-up and literature, specifically through the ways in which comic rage allows the abjected race to aggressively respond to attempts to either expel African Americans from the national hegemony or assimilate them into it. A key work here is John Limon's insightful book *Stand-up Comedy in Theory, or, Abjection in America* (2000). Limon sees "abjection" as the major theme in his examination of stand-up comedy, building on Julia Kristeva's definition to argue, "When you feel abject, you feel as if there were something miring your life, some skin that cannot be sloughed, some role (because 'abject' always, in a way, describes how you act) that has become your only character. Abjection is self-typecasting" (4). Although applying such a definition to stand-up excludes historical moments when societies cast groups in specific roles that result in feelings of abjection, Limon recognizes the disruptive possibilities of stand-up in rejecting such moments. I see the African American presence in stand-up comedy in much the same way previous critics have viewed that presence in other artistic modes such as music, movies, television, and indeed literature. Stand-up, however, occupies a unique space in relation to other art forms. Though linked by our ideas of "text," stand-up is not bound by the requirements of the presence of plot, characters, or story arc in the ways movies, television shows, or literature are, and although its rhetorical strategies are similar to music, stand-up comedy allows artists to present multiple complete narratives, fully develop characters, and explore disparate themes.

In relation to this project, I contend that while comic rage can be expressed in front of white audiences, it is not concerned with appealing to white audiences. Whether they may find critiques of race disagreeable or offensive is not relevant. It is, for whites, the price they pay for appearing. As opposed to Limon's claim that the audience's desire is to focus on the "joke work" of acts like Lenny Bruce and Richard Pryor, African American audience members share in Pryor's wallowing and rage by connecting it to their own rage. Their laughter is celebratory and emerges from familiarity with similar realizations, clarification of previously unarticulated dissatisfactions, and the catharsis of hearing their quiet "truths" made public. Such a premise—unforgiving rage at white constructions of blackness and defiant celebration of blackness itself that should cause prostration—seems antithetical to a theory of abjection.

In Pryor's act, however, he avoids the general paradox that comes with stand-up through "the possibility of forestalling abjection altogether. Pryor's refusal of the usual stand-up posture—the standing up of abjection—is the result," according to Limon, "of his self-identification in an abjected race. He is not the sufferer of abjection, he is the abjection, the body that is repudiated yet keeps returning" (5). Instead of Freud's joke theory in which humor is used to conceal its sources of aggression and sex, comic rage seeks to makes its aggression clear through the primary use of comedy. I do not see works of comic rage, then, as suffering abjection which would cast them aside, but as abjections that break down and recast the traditional American/Western narrative about blackness. Because much of that narrative is invested in the promotion of white bourgeois values, comic rage is ideal by being rooted in and fueled by an African American vernacular tradition that has its roots in the culture of the black working class and underclass, often referred to as black folk culture.

Furiously Funny converses most readily with two other works that trace the production of comic rage in its portrait of slavery and in its critique of contemporary American society. So in *Laughing Mad: The Black Comic Persona in Post-Soul America* (2007) Bambi Haggins focuses her attention on African American comics and their transition from the segregated sites of the civil rights moment through the multicultural ones of the post-soul generation, as well as assessing the attempts to transfer the images they forge in their stand-up routines into the mediums of film and television. Haggins bears witness to the emergence of a black comic persona in the aftermath of the civil rights and Black Power movements. She situates the beginning of the process with the foursome of Dick Gregory, Flip Wilson, Bill Cosby, and Richard Pryor. While Pryor clearly achieved great mainstream success, his stand-up—as opposed to his films—never lost its primary desire to critically confront hegemonic oppression. Unlike Haggins's focus on the personas of the comics she examines, my book's focus is primarily on their stand-up shows and the comedy albums that often emerge from these, because they are works in which the comic can exercise maximum control, in contrast to the multiple actors, directors, editors, and producers that we see involved in the television shows and films Haggins considers. Moreover, I see stand-up not as separate from African American literature but as intimately related. The same expressive culture that drives Ishmael Reed's *Flight to*

Canada fuels Richard Pryor's *Live in Concert* (1979). Pryor and Reed are the most obvious example of the relationship between literature and stand-up that existed openly within the African American community long before the postmodernist collapse of genres. Reed, whose mixture of humor and rage has been unmistakable, serves as a key figure in the book because his work and influence clearly build off the work of George Schuyler and Ralph Ellison, while he also combines his written work with the oral traditions that are easily recognized in Pryor's work.

Most recently, Glenda Carpio's book *Laughing Fit to Kill: Black Humor in the Fictions of Slavery* (2008) describes how authors in the nineteenth and twentieth centuries have used humor to engage the subject of slavery—or, more specifically, the forces that made slavery possible, realigned to create segregation, and that have sustained white supremacist hegemony in post-civil-rights America. Like Carpio's, my work engages a multitude of forms, from novels and plays to stand-up and television in the expression of what she calls "an eviscerating humor, one that is bawdy, brutal, horrific, and insurgent" (7). In addition to Pryor, both of us see Ishmael Reed as a key figure and use his novel *Flight to Canada* (1976) as a central text. Carpio locates her discussion of Reed around his "tragicomic" portrait of slavery, but one whose embrace of HooDoo acts as a force in line with Carpio's embrace of "conjuring" to engage the "complicated dynamics of race and humor to set the denigrating history of antebellum stereotypes against their own humorous appropriation of those images" (15). With the exception of Reed and Pryor, the works in this study target the present or the recent past and deploy comic rage in order to interrogate hegemonic oppression at the contemporaneous moment. While slavery has become a significant site through which we can consider the continued presence of white supremacy, particularly in the genre of neo-slave narrative, the works in my study invest themselves in a direct confrontation that cannot be dismissed as works about "back then." Even the works by Pryor and Reed include the present in their works that feature slavery. In Pryor's assessment of America at the bicentennial and Reed's anachronistic style, I see a more explicit connection between the past and the present. As a result, the teleology this book lays out reveals comic rage as a dynamic form that became more frequent as African Americans began to explicitly confront white supremacist hegemony. Perhaps most important, *Furiously Funny* gives both voice and context to a form that previously existed on the margins of African American comic tradition. In recent decades comic rage has become significant as African American authors and artists have sought not merely to respond to stereotypes and oppression but to recast altogether the discourse on history, entertainment, literature, and nation.

Chapter Outline

Although this book views the changes and evolution of comic rage through the lens of various black literary explosions, it is important to emphasize that comic rage often works against the ideologies that are set by those literary movements. While these movements have all sought to challenge stereotypical representations of the role of African Americans in American life, they have consistently excluded humor as a primary literary mode of interrogating white supremacy. So, just as African Americans have undergone numerous name changes—from Colored to Negro to Black to African American—that often captured the African American life at various historical moments, the presence of comic rage is intimately connected, and often acts in opposition, to the politics, history, and cultural response engaged in by the mainstream of black activists and authors. While African American humor in literature is seen mostly through irony in the nineteenth century and satire in the early part of the twentieth century, we can observe variations in the manifestations of comic rage. Ellison's *Invisible Man*, for instance, remains firmly entrenched in the integrationist politics of the post–World War II period, but the humor that permeates the novel acts in direct contrast to the works of drama/tragedy of the Wright school, and its moments of comic rage are less aggressive than we eventually see in Reed, whose vision is counter to those artists at the height of the Black Arts movement.

My first chapter, then, builds on Schuyler's extended comic tone and examines how Ellison's *Invisible Man* enacted an unprecedented use of African American cultural tradition. In the wake of Wright's *Native Son*, the presence of comedy that was engendered by figures like Hughes was abandoned for an extended literary indictment of American racism. Ellison's novel contrasts with these works, not by eliminating rage, but by depicting the significance of African American cultural forms in expressing that rage constructively. Ellison's novel uses humor to critique the literature of the late nineteenth and early twentieth century from Twain to Wright while also depicting the use of African American cultural expressions in negotiating the growing racial tensions between World War II and the civil rights movement. *Invisible Man* is one of the most significant works in this book, not only because the myriad cultural expressions are the realization of the transference of the oral to the literary in African American literature, but because it balances humor and rage in a manner that makes the emergence of comic rage possible.

While Ellison's novel demonstrated that humor can succeed as a method of resistance, the development of comic rage was not limited to specific genres or to literature itself. Given how African American cultural tradition blurs the lines between its avenues of expression, chapter 2 examines the significance of African American comedic tradition through the changes in stand-up comedy during the 1950s and 1960s, when Dick Gregory emerged and was catapulted to fame. Gregory's comedy mirrors *Invisible Man* as a text where cultural elements within African America appeared in the mainstream as a challenge to racial stereotypes manifested through media representations and used to justify Jim Crow segregation. The groundwork for Gregory had been laid by comics like Redd Foxx and Jackie "Moms" Mabley, who differed from popular representations of African Americans in the early to middle twentieth century. Mabley, who utilized an immersion in African American cultural tradition to foster familiarity among her audiences, embodied a distinct African American female humor that we find in Hurston's work and that reverberates in the moments of comic rage in Fran Ross's novel *Oreo* (1974), Whoopi Goldberg's one-woman show *Live on Broadway* (1985), and Wanda Sykes's comedy special *I'ma Be Me* (2009). Gregory's act mixed the defiant confrontation of Foxx with the cultural familiarity of Mabley to become one of the most celebrated comics of his generation.

Gregory's inability to completely balance his comedy and rage demonstrates the necessity of aggressive elements of the African American comedic tradition to contain the militant rage that often emerges in response to white supremacist assault. The third chapter argues that the second half of the civil rights movement provided the necessary militancy from which comic rage could flourish. The Black Arts and Black Power movements are crucial sites in this study because, in addition to the shifts in African American literature that occurred during this time, the simultaneous transformation of various avenues of black cultural expression produced a collective resistance against white supremacy. As John and Dennis Williams note, "In the 1960s and early 1970s there

existed side by side black militancy, black piety, black academic rationalism, black political realism and black humor—and all were converging
on the system in flank and frontal assaults" (91). Works of comic rage
challenged the limiting ideological positions of black nationalism and
are often found on the chronological and critical outskirts of the period. Douglas Turner Ward's play *Day of Absence* does not possess the
type of militant revolt that the Black Power movement preferred. Its reverse minstrel show unmistakably reveals the centrality of race in the
construction of American identity that was a dominant part of black
nationalist philosophy. Aside from Ishmael Reed's personal influence on
Pryor, his *Flight to Canada* (1976) complicates the Uncle Tom/Nat Turner
dichotomy that many in the Black Arts movement embraced, even as the
neo-slave narrative reflects the movement's radical impulses. *Flight to
Canada* launched an assault on American myth and history that inevitably linked Schuyler and Ellison to a new generation of African American
artists.

In the fourth chapter I examine, in the decades that follow the civil
rights movement, the maturation of comic rage, buoyed by the emergence of a generation of African American artists born during that period, raised in integrated settings, and captured in Trey Ellis's "The New
Black Aesthetic." These artists favor parody as a mode to critique blacks
and whites alike and, in the process, expand African American literature
and art to embrace a complexity of black life, a continued challenge of
form, and a more varied tone. An important example is George C. Wolfe's
The Colored Museum (1986), which, like *Day of Absence* and many other
African American plays, takes direct aim at black-face minstrel shows
and stereotypical figures like Aunt Jemima. Comic rage in theater serves
as an important bridge between novels and stand-up comedy. African
American theater enacts the transference seen in novels into live performance and provides a unifying theme to the sometimes disparate
topics stand-up comedians cover in their acts. Just as *Day of Absence*'s
manifestation of abjection chooses the play format in order to initiate
a community breakdown because of the absence of the abjected race on
which it was dependent, *The Colored Museum* uses several vignettes to
examine the impact on the abjected, tracing the trauma suffered by African Americans in their attempts to negotiate racism. Wolfe's play seeks
the destruction of one-dimensional representations of African Americans in favor of an examination of the complexity and contradictions of

post-civil-rights African America. Reflecting comic rage's pervasiveness throughout literary genres and black popular culture, Paul Beatty's *The White Boy Shuffle* (1996) utilizes the rhetoric of hip-hop music in ridiculing the so-called progress of America, the void in African American leadership, and the African American athlete as multicultural messiah.

In the fifth chapter, I expand the impact of the New Black Aesthetic beyond literature and stand-up to include the presence of comic rage in film. In Robert Townsend's *Hollywood Shuffle* (1987) and Spike Lee's *Bamboozled* (2000), we witness an unvarnished interrogation of contemporary African Americans attempting to navigate a post-civil-rights America in which television and film have become primary sites in reinforcing racist stereotypes and notions of blackness. Townsend's character Bobby Taylor's desire to be an actor clashes with perceptions of the roles an African American actor can play. As Taylor wrestles with his responsibility to his community and his interest in celebrity, the movie openly castigates the simplistic expectations whites and blacks have of African Americans in film. Similarly in *Bamboozled*, the fake minstrel show that becomes a runaway success allows Lee to explore the television landscape of the 1990s, revealing the ways in which, despite their increased numbers, African American television shows rely on claims of authenticity (of "keeping it real") to cover simplistic depictions of black life. As writers, directors, and often actors in their films, Townsend and Lee exercise as much control as an author or a comic. Their ability to dictate the substance and tone of their work ensures the clear intent in the expression of rage that sits alongside its humor. Moving beyond satire, these works explode the traditional gestures of resolution by contending that no idealized vision of black life in film and television existed. In doing so, these works demonstrate the expanding presence of comic rage throughout black popular culture.

The sixth chapter solidifies the connection between Reed and Pryor—and between literature and stand-up—through its discussion of Pryor and comics who fulfill his legacy. For instance, Pryor's attempted film adaptation of Reed's novel *Yellow Back Radio Broke-Down* (1969) had a direct influence on the script for *Blazing Saddles* (1974), which Pryor cowrote with Mel Brooks. More important, Pryor's *Bicentennial Nigger* (1976), his "most political album" (148), was released the same year as Reed's *Flight to Canada* and similarly examines race and America at the bicentennial. One of the most immediate successors to Pryor was Whoopi Goldberg, whose *Live on Broadway* builds on Pryor's radical framework even as it pulls from the template that Moms Mabley constructed by directly confronting the oppression that sits at the intersection of race and gender. While many comics have attempted to succeed Pryor merely by replicating his act, chapter 6 argues that Chris Rock most effectively realizes Pryor's legacy of comic rage. Rock's willingness to openly criticize African Americans and whites fits within the tradition of works of comic rage. Rock's work, from *Bring the Pain* (1996) to *Never Scared* (2004), engages directly the historical moment of post-civil-rights America just as Pryor examined America at the moment of its bicentennial.

The key to comic rage, as I see it, is not simply the presence of rage or of humor. Being funny or angry is not enough. Comic rage is about the fusion of the two, when the voices of the disparate responses combine to exist at the same moment and in the same place beyond comedy's general purpose, which, in white America, has been entertainment. James Cone argues, "Anger and humor are like the left and right arm. They complement each other. Anger empowers the poor to declare their uncompromising opposition to oppression, and humor prevents them from being consumed by their fury" (309). Comic rage brings the "left and right arm" together to act as one against racist oppression. Like bell hooks, I see rage as potentially healing, possessing the ability to reverse white supremacist assault. As she suggests, "Confronting my rage, witnessing the way it moved me to grow and change, I understood intimately that it had the potential not only to destroy but to also to construct. Then and now I understand rage to be a necessary aspect of resistance struggle" (16). What separates these works is their refusal to succumb to the consumptive nature of rage. Following the "engagement with a full range of emotional responses to black struggle for self-determination" (19) that hooks sees as necessary, these works use humor as a way to avoid the possibility of despair and destruction. The works of comic rage in this book possess a militant rage that responds to white supremacist assaults and use humor to produce a psychic conversion whereby the African American perspective on race is centralized and oppressive national—and international—narratives are rejected.

(Re)Viewing Ellison's *Invisible Man*

Comedy, Rage, and Cultural Tradition
in an African American Classic

> But then as I listened to its taunting laughter and speculated as to
> what kind of individual would speak in such accents, I decided that
> it would be one who had been forged in the underground of Ameri-
> can experience and yet managed to emerge less angry than ironic.
> That he would be a blues-toned laugher-at-wounds who included
> himself in his indictment of the human condition. I liked the idea,
> and as I tried to visualize the speaker I came to relate him to those
> ongoing conflicts, tragic and comic, that had claimed my group's
> energies since the abandonment of the Reconstruction.
>
> **Ralph Ellison, introduction to 1982 reissue of *Invisible Man***

Scholars frequently point to Richard Wright's explosive novel *Native Son*
(1940) as the text that replaced the Harlem Renaissance's attempts to establish the humanity of African Americans with stinging indictments of
America's racist oppression. Coming on the heels of his 1937 essay "Blueprint for Negro Writing" and his well-regarded collection of short stories
Uncle Tom's Children (1938), Wright's novel demanded that its audience
view the external forces of white supremacy and poverty as the center of its protagonist's troubled life on the South Side of Chicago. That
protagonist, Bigger Thomas, represented for Wright several black men
that he knew throughout his southern childhood who openly defied the
status quo in states like Arkansas and Mississippi as well as thousands
of Biggers—black and white—made voiceless by a society rooted in racist oppression and class exploitation. Wright contended that writers of

the Harlem Renaissance had been too timid in their critiques of white racism because of their relationships with paternalistic white patrons. By contrast, Wright produced a parade of works that propelled his rage, and by extension the rage African Americans wanted to express, unapologetically to the forefront of readers' consciousness. There ensued a host of novels that followed Wright's pattern: a single African American character—usually male—responding to the social realities of racial and economic injustice, culminating in an act of violence against persons who, while not always the direct oppressors, were beneficiaries of and contributors to white supremacist rule. Protest literature—as many of these novels were deemed—provided African Americans with a site, particular in its clear and frank prose, through which their rage at white racism could be expressed. The protest novels' preoccupation with a violence that was the result of relentless oppression, however, left no room for the depiction of African American cultural traditions that could resist that oppression. Wright's belief in the declining significance of the church in black life certainly played a part, but just as important was his belief that stories involving black cultural traditions were often oversimplified and romanticized for the pleasure of whites, a charge he famously made about Zora Neale Hurston's best-known novel, *Their Eyes Were Watching God* (1937).

Yet even as the protest novel was becoming a fixture in the mainstream imagination and in publishing houses, it was being challenged, most directly by James Baldwin in "Everybody's Protest Novel" where he argued, "The failure of the protest novel lies in its rejection of life, the human being, the denial of his beauty, dread, power, in its insistence that it is his categorization alone which is real and which cannot be transcended" (23). In many of the novels of the "Wright school," the historical portrait of the angry, dangerous black male stereotype was reinforced by connecting the expression of rage with acts of violence. But in their embrace of violence to reflect the rage and despair, protest novels would often forgo any other responses that might make the case for racial equality. Outside the literary world, racial tensions were beginning to become more apparent as African American literature sought to reflect the dissatisfaction that many African Americans had begun overtly to express in the years prior to and after World War II.

The publication of *Invisible Man* in 1952 becomes significant, then, because of its incorporation of African American folk traditions as *part* of the numerous expressions of rage, particularly its use of the oral tradition of signifying.[1] In order to understand fully the targets of Ellison's signifying and rage, one must have "extensive knowledge," as Dickson-Carr suggests, of, among other things, "American history, especially the U.S. Declaration of Independence and Constitution, which are the defining documents in American political and cultural mythology" (29). As a post–World War II novel, however, Ellison's work captures the historical moment—in the tradition of Griggs and Chesnutt—whether it is the tensions caused by African American migration to the North, the contradictory existence of African American soldiers, or the growing, if divergent, black political consciousness. The moment in which the novel arrives requires, as Dickson-Carr points out, that the "reader of *Invisible Man* must be adept in African American history, from slavery through World War II, especially the arc of black intellectual and political activity from Booker T. Washington to W.E.B. Du Bois, Marcus Garvey, and Richard Wright" (29). Abandoning the noticeable absence of a distinct black folklore in Schuyler's *Black No More*, Ellison situates African American culture as a central element of the novel as he methodically dissects white supremacy through the obstacles his nameless protagonist faces. Surprisingly more violent than Richard Wright's celebrated novel, *Invisible Man* nevertheless reveals the myriad ways African Americans are oppressed and the numerous methods African Americans deployed in resisting that oppression.

In recent years, critics have begun to challenge more traditional perceptions by revealing the political arguments that Ellison articulated underneath his oft-celebrated literary accomplishments: symbolism, political neutrality, and irony. In particular, the 2004 collection *Ralph Ellison and the Raft of Hope* edited by Lucas E. Morel recognizes that *Invisible Man* sought to promote the most basic of democratic ideals through a single African American character's search for identity. The rewriting of the American novel into an African American adventure story cannot be overstated, for it allows us to trace the "lineage from Ellison" to the sustained emergence of comic rage, in the same way that, according to Kenneth Warren in *So Black and Blue: Ralph Ellison and the Occasion of Criticism* (2003), sees "some Black or neo-Black Aestheticians, who define themselves not through a broad identification with Western humanism but through their conviction that the full development of black American literature and culture requires the elaboration of norms and ideals from within the experience of black Americans" (16). My analysis of the novel continues in this tradition, especially *Invisible Man*'s contrasting of the unrelenting rage of the Wright school with African American humor. For example, Danielle Allen in "Ralph Ellison on the Tragi-Comedy of Citizenship," aptly asserts, "Laughter must somehow issue from anger and transform it; comedy teaches the forms of imagination that allow a metamorphosis in one's assessment of one's interests" (51). However, I seek to move further by discussing how humor, as well as other forms of African American cultural tradition, does not so much "transform" rage as provide constructive outlets for its expression.

The novel's examination of African American expressions parallels the bourgeoning African American sociopolitical ideology of the time, facilitating the progression from *Black No More* to the appearance of comic rage. This process, as I see it, is twofold. The first step involves Ellison's separation of rage from violence, which sets it apart from expressions of rage in the novels of the Wright school and differs significantly from mainstream perceptions that pathologize and trivialize African American rage. His novel is, to be sure, similar to other African American novels of the time in targeting its rage toward white supremacist oppression of African Americans. Unlike the works of Wright and his followers, however, *Invisible Man* delves into the capacity of African American cultural institutions and traditions to create spaces where African Americans can express and negotiate their rage. The second step prioritizes the use of humor as one of those cultural traditions by rejecting mainstream images of African American humor and replacing them with a mixture of irony, ridicule, and signifying. The expression of rage through humor, specifically through the use of African American vernacular tradition, made clear that the African American comic tradition that appears in other aspects of African American life could also be used as a way to counteract racist oppression. With its use of African American folk humor throughout, the novel was initially misinterpreted by critics, mainly because it was viewed through the lens of (white) American comic tradition or fears of how whites would respond to unrestrained implementation of African American humor. Although the presence of African American folk/street culture in the novel is now being recognized by critics, most fail to see its strategic humor as a mode of resistance and an expression of rage. This chapter, then, argues that *Invisible Man* is a—if not *the*—central text in the development of comic rage through its unprecedented infusion of African American cultural tradition, especially its deploying of comedy and rage, which demonstrates the possibilities for constructive resistance to and critical engagement in the effects of white supremacist assault.

The Wright Effect: The Birth of the African American Protest Novel

While there is debate on the exact dates of the Harlem Renaissance, it is reasonable to suggest that the literary shift away from that period began in 1937 with the appearance of Richard Wright's "Blueprint for Negro Writing," which strongly criticizes the Renaissance, asserting that "Negro writing in the past has been confined to humble novels, poems, and plays, prim and decorous ambassadors who went a-begging to white America" (45). Wright's critique of the literary scene was aimed at both the artist and the system that supported only a specific type of African American image: "Either [Negro writing] crept in through the kitchen in the form of jokes; or it was the fruits of that foul soil which was the result of a liaison between inferiority-complexed Negro 'geniuses' and burnt-out white Bohemians with money" (45). Here Wright contends that the paternalistic relationship between white patrons and black artists stunted the growth of African American literature and produced images of African Americans that either mimicked the values and ideals of the white bourgeoisie or, in their portrayal of working- and lower-class black life, presented variations on the blackface minstrel shows of the time. Wright's frustration that "Rarely was the best of [Negro] writing addressed to the Negro himself, his needs, his sufferings, his aspirations" (45) acted as a central tenet in his critique of the Harlem Renaissance. The onset of the Great Depression precipitated the end of the Renaissance as well as a thirst for works of social protest and determinism that reflected the impact of race and class in 1930s America. To that end, Wright's *Uncle Tom's Children*—especially the 1940 version—and his landmark *Native Son* are unabashedly concerned with the anguish, pain, and rage of its African American characters.

Although he advocated for portraits of African American life free from white influence, Wright remained concerned with the response of his white audience and challenged them to recognize that the characters they met were the creation of whites' continued support of a system of oppression and degradation. Encounters between blacks and whites, Wright's works contend, often end in unsettling violence as opposed to entertaining, comforting, or peaceful denouements. He established his concern with his white audience's response when he republished *Uncle Tom's Children*. To the four short stories originally published in 1938 he added a fifth story, "Bright and Morning Star," and a harrowing "auto-biographical sketch" of his young life in the South, called "The Ethics of Living Jim Crow." In his essay "How 'Bigger' Was Born" (1940) Wright re-calls, "When the reviews of [*Uncle Tom's Children*] began to appear, I real-ized that I had made an awfully naïve mistake. I found that I had written a book which even bankers' daughters could read and weep over and feel good about" (454). Obviously his white audience's easy dismissal of the book disturbed Wright, and the expanded edition in 1940 attempted to rectify the reception by altering the tone. Richard Yarborough explains, "Wright was reacting less to particular flaws in *Uncle Tom's Children* and more to mainstream American culture's capacity to defuse the potency of harsh critique through the very act of commercial consumption and subsequent emotional release" (xxvii). Much of the audience's response was due to the placement of "Fire and Cloud" as the last story. Building to a peaceful integrated march, that story ends on a note of triumphant idealism that did not reflect the actual state of race relations in the 1930s and 1940s. In actuality, the 1939 refusal to allow Marian Anderson to sing at Constitution Hall in Washington and the 1943 Detroit riots represent American racial unrest in the midst of World War II. The expressions of rage in *Uncle Tom's Children* would subsequently become lost in a wave of satisfying sentimentality.

By contrast, "Bright and Morning Star" chronicles the attempts of a black woman named Aunt Sue to protect her Communist son Johnny-Boy from a lynch mob incensed by his organizing of black and white sharecroppers. In this story Wright—who was a member of the Com-munist Party from 1933 to 1942—more explicitly embraces the strategies and ideologies of Communism as central to black progress. In "Fire and Cloud" the Reds are only one of the forces pulling at Reverend Taylor as he attempts to get the city government to provide relief for a black community near starvation in his Depression-era southern town. Taylor must navigate the whites' desire that he use his status as community leader to scuttle the idea of an interracial march being planned by the Reds, while also attempting to turn back the violence some members of the black community are planning, even as his job as pastor is being threatened from inside his own church. The beating of Taylor radicalizes him, and his embrace of the march galvanizes his congregation. The beating also produces empathy in the congregation and garners their support in part because of Taylor's support of nonviolence, but also because Taylor's reasons are not overtly Communist. In "Bright and Morning Star," however, the brutality that Johnny-Boy and Aunt Sue both face and mete out are as inexorable as the Marxist ideology they support. Along with the stories from "The Ethics of Living Jim Crow," many of which ended up in Wright's autobiographical *Black Boy* (1945), "Bright and Morning Star" makes evident Wright's desire to create a work that would provide no neat solutions or endings, particularly with regard to its expressions of rage. Not only did the changes to *Uncle Tom's Children* set the stage for the shocking and unsettling power of *Native Son*, but they provided a template that writers would return to consistently throughout the middle decades of the twentieth century.

The shadow that Wright and his works cast rendered African American writers' wrestling with Wright's legacy as a prelude to establishing their own, even when they had close connections to him. Baldwin forged an explicit father-son relationship with Wright, while Ellison was the best man at Wright's first wedding. Despite Baldwin's criticism of *Native Son*, echoes of both Wright and the novel permeate Baldwin's work from his posthumous appreciations in the essay "Alas, Poor Richard" to his novel *Another Country*.

Baldwin's belief that the protest literature served to reduce African Americans to a subhuman level was, to be sure, the result of a tendency toward thematic and geographical repetition on the part of the authors, which limited the view of African American life. Ann Petry in "The Novel as Social Criticism," while acknowledging the pitfalls of the "sociological novelists" reducing their characters, submits that part of the criticism of protest literature emerges from "the idea that art should exist for art's sake" (95). Overtly political novels' disqualification as "pure art" has been central in creating the art/propaganda dichotomy. Within this construction exists an inherent refutation of works that challenge the status quo or explicitly reject dominant ideologies and values. Petry recognizes that such an argument must conclude with the belief that "art (any and all art) is prostituted, bastardized, when it is used to serve some moral or political end for it then becomes propaganda" (95). African American literature, especially in the middle of the twentieth century, would be disproportionately affected by mainstream ideas about art because of the desire of many writers to reveal that America's idealistic rhetoric was not practiced when it came to providing equality for African Americans. The artists' willingness to document graphically the African American lives constantly under physical, emotional, and psychological attack only reinforced claims that works of the post-Wright period were less art than political doctrine. Petry responds to the art/propaganda construction by suggesting that novels are naturally political, reflecting the cultural ideologies that produce them: "The moment the novelist begins to show how society affected the lives of his characters, how they were formed and shaped by the sprawling inchoate world in which they lived, he is writing a novel of social criticism whether he calls it that or not" (95). Some of those novels, like William Attaway's *Blood on the Forge* (1941), Petry's own *The Street* (1946), and Chester Himes's *The Primitive* (1955), continued the tradition of social protest and naturalism by demonstrating the corrosive effect of white oppression. In doing so, these authors were able to pursue two significant projects: establishing that such rage did exist, and eliciting recognition that (a) such rage was not the result of black men being naturally angry but the result of white supremacist hegemony and (b) such rage, gone unchecked, would lead to violence against African Americans and, more important for the mainstream, against whites.

In Wright's novel, twenty-year-old Bigger Thomas, whose family needs money, contemplates robbing a white-owned store but instead takes a job as driver for the white Dalton family. Befriended by daughter Mary Dalton, Bigger attempts to help Mary sneak back into the Dalton house after a drunken outing with her boyfriend, but accidentally smothers her in his fear of being caught in her bedroom. The act of violence, a violence that Bigger sensed would emerge if he ever fully expressed his rage, awakens his consciousness and embodies the novel's broader attempt to indict American society at large for the inevitability of Bigger's flight, capture, and execution. The clarity of Bigger's rage alleviates African American hopelessness during a period when both humor and rage were either distorted or suppressed. The cultural institutions that historically sustained this particular group of African Americans erode into virtual meaninglessness in the novel. All the possible responses African Americans could employ—socially, politically, or economically—wilt under the onslaught of white supremacist oppression. The rage that Bigger feels takes on more importance and becomes a militant statement. Throughout the 1960s and 1970s, members of the Black Power and Black Arts movements exalted the killing of Mary as a revolutionary act that initiated Bigger's self-discovery and personhood. Yet Bigger's rage not only overwhelms him because of its suppression, but it cannot effectively be articulated, given the futility—if not outright absence—of the modes of resistance at his disposal.

This is most obvious in Bigger's rape and murder of his girlfriend Bessie. The killing of a black woman immediately complicates ideas of Black Nationalist pride and protest against white violence toward blacks. According to Jerry Bryant in *Victims and Heroes*, "by making the murders the seedbed out of which Bigger's sense of esteem and identity grows, by making Bigger less than attractive, Wright undercuts the view of *Native Son* as social protest" (199). I contend the novel stands as an example of the consumptive nature of rage when not allowed a constructive outlet. The manifestations of Bigger's rage—the killings of Mary and Bessie—remain partially acts of fear, but they soon expose the underlying element of rage that is an unmistakable part of his life. By becoming the vehicle through which the suppressed rage of African Americans can be fully articulated, Bigger serves his purpose as both literary figure and political symbol. Although Bigger embodies, in many respects, the "Bad Nigger" or the "angry black man," the novel refutes the idea that Bigger's actions are part of a genetic trait specific to African Americans, a stereotype very much alive in 1940 and one that still lingers in contemporary America. Instead the novel points directly to white racism as central to the second-class status and behavior that permeated African American life.

The rage that Bigger experiences mirrors that of African Americans during the early part of the twentieth century. Constructions of an angry and dangerous black male helped demonize African Americans' rage and devalue their challenges to racist policies and assaults. From the persecution of reviled African American boxer Jack Johnson at the beginning of the century to the Scottsboro Boys trials of the 1930s, African Americans were cast as a threat to the white race, justifying the suppression of African American rage through imprisonment, harassment, and murder. As a result, many African Americans found ways to hide their frustration, while the literature of the Renaissance attempted to portray an "acceptable" image of African American middle-class desire. *Native Son* set out to reverse perceptions and literary constructions. Bigger, as James Baldwin states in *Notes of a Native Son*, "forced his oppressors to see the fruit of that oppression: and he feels, when his family and his friends come to visit him in the death cell, that they should . . . be happy, *proud* that he has dared, through murder and now through his own imminent destruction, to redeem their anger and humiliation" (39). Wright's situating of the rage African Americans felt at their oppression in full view of white America significantly changed the course of African American literary tradition. Along with the publication of "Blueprint for Negro Writing," *Uncle Tom's Children*, and *Black Boy*, *Native Son* introduced a new era in African American literature, one that did not ignore the reality of rage but embraced it as an unavoidable part of African American life.

Ellison, for his part, initially saw *Native Son* as a novel that was part of a "movement toward a grasp of American reality"; reviewing the novel in "Recent Negro Fiction," Ellison, like Wright, criticizes the writing of the Harlem Renaissance for its absence of rage: "American Negro fiction of the 1920's was timid of theme, and for the most part technically backward. Usually it was apologetic in tone and narrowly confined to the expression of Negro middle-class ideals rather than those of the Negro working and agricultural masses" (11). By contrast, Ellison argues, "*Native Son*, examined against past Negro fiction, represents the take-off in a leap which promises to carry over a whole tradition, and marks the merging of the imaginative depiction of American Negro life into the broad stream of American literature" (17). The novel forgoes the middle- and upper-class portrayal of African Americans and concentrates instead on the underclass who are being directly affected by both racial and class discrimination.

Works from this post-Wright period differ from Wright's, nonetheless, in their connection between rage and violence. Bryant informs us, "Wright's action essentially begins with Bigger's murder of Mary. The consequences of the act of violence for Bigger, both positive and negative, make up the central issue of the narrative. The violence in *Blood on the Forge*, . . . *The Street*, *Knock on Any Door*, *The Primitive*, and other novels in their class comes, on the whole, near the end of the action" (223). Bryant believes that in these works the "central issue of the narrative is the unjust conditions that lead to that violence" (223), yet there is an important distinction to be made during this period. While Bigger Thomas's lack of options makes him unable to find other expressions for his rage beyond violence, characters in the novels that follow *Native Son*, while certainly viewing violence as an inevitable end in a racist America, see violence as the culmination of the systematic elimination of other, constructive avenues for the expression of rage. This becomes especially significant in *Invisible Man* when the educated, verbally gifted, and hardworking protagonist, having been stripped of any means to resist racist oppression, murders the Black Nationalist leader Ras the Destroyer during a riot. Thus, though Ellison's work engages a different project than other writers of his day, he is not separate from the argument of the time. Ellison's own comments lead him to a conclusion similar to Petry's with regard to the inherent politics of art. In his collection of essays and interviews *Shadow and Act* (1964) he contends:

> Now mind! I recognize no dichotomy between art and protest. Dostoevsky's *Notes from Underground* is, among other things, a protest against the limitations of nineteenth-century rationalism. . . . If social protest is antithetical to art, what then shall we make of Goya, Dickens and Twain? One hears a lot of complaints about the so-called "protest novel," especially when written by Negroes; but it seems to me that the critics could more accurately complain about their lack of craftsmanship and their provincialism. (169)

Ellison's argument about the inherent relationship between art and protest should cause us to recognize that *Invisible Man* cannot be seen as separate from the tradition and debate of the protest novel and the rage within that literature. Additionally, much of Ellison's "protest" is artistically conveyed through the use of humor, a mixture of parody, satire, and signifying that often coalesces into moments of comic rage. In doing the "crucial, if sometimes ephemeral, political work that novels do," which, according to Kenneth Warren, "is to transform noble and praiseworthy habits, beliefs, and actions into objects of scorn," *Invisible Man* demonstrates that a "novel's satiric, parodic, and irreverent portraits, even when making up only a small part of a book's aesthetic agenda, can still account for its most striking political and social effects" (25). That said, the key to the relationship between other novels of his era and Ellison's *Invisible Man* lies in realizing that while he provides a vision and tradition that is broader and deeper than his predecessors, he does not abandon the rage and protest that were at the core of the novels in the post-Wright era.

The rage in the post-Wright novels manifests itself through violence because ultimately it views violence as the only avenue available to African Americans. This, of course, ignores the inherent limitations, specifically the absence of cultural traditions African Americans employed in their attempts to channel their rage into more constructive arenas. Most of the Wright-school novels do not present extended examples of such cultural traditions but only, according to Baldwin, a "climate of anarchy and unmotivated and unapprehended disaster" (35). Baldwin also believes that the lone male figure, isolated within his own people, became "common to most Negro protest novels, which has led us all to believe that in Negro life there exists no tradition, no field of manners, no possibility of ritual or intercourse" (35–36). Baldwin's observation reveals the inability of naturalism to communicate accurately African American responses to racism. African American naturalism rendered its subjects incapable of escaping a violent end. In the novels' journey toward death or murder or both, naturalist fiction saw no means or consciousness that might in some way counteract the psychic effects of white supremacy. That "Wright could imagine Bigger, but Bigger could not possibly imagine Richard Wright" (114), as Ellison suggests in "The World and the Jug," results from the absence of any framework influential enough in his life that Bigger could conceive any response to racism other than the enactment of violence. Ellison vehemently rejected the limitations placed on Bigger's imagination by making the presence and expression of African American cultural traditions a centerpiece in all of his work. For instance, the tradition of African American sermons and the presence of jazz and blues in Ellison's novel act as means to negotiate the pain and rage, not only of and for the performer, but for the African American audience whose feelings they often simultaneously elicit, represent, and convey. Within these examples, elements of humor and rage are articulated in an attempt to transcend the effects of oppression and stave off the nihilism that could emerge. The combination of humor and rage in *Invisible Man* gains in importance through the rejection of naturalist constructions of African Americans as mere objects without the means to resist, transcend, or subvert oppression.

Given Petry's comments about the production of art, her novel *The Street* (1946) unsurprisingly comes closest to anticipating the achievement of *Invisible Man*'s fusion of art and protest. *The Street* tells the moving story of an African American woman, Lutie Johnson, attempting to raise her son in Harlem while facing racial and gender oppression, all while increasingly unable to funnel her rage at this oppression constructively. Similar to the Invisible Man in her education, talent, and hopefulness, Lutie collides head-on with the effects of white supremacist capitalist patriarchy, reducing her to a near desperation that ends in her murdering the hustler Boots Smith. Abandoning the unrelentingly solemn tone of the novels of Wright and Chester Himes, *The Street* creates a more complex rendering of the African American experience, particularly as regards African American women. Although Lutie's fate ultimately follows that of other protagonists in the fiction of the Wright school, there are clear signs of resistance rooted in African American cultural tradition. Lutie's use of her singing allows her to exercise agency that becomes part of her search to manifest her rage in constructive action. The presence of potential outlets for the expression of rage in the novel provides glimpses of other aspects of African American life, moments that include street humor, religious tradition, and urban folklore. In *The Street*, these elements act as possible responses to the struggles of race, class, and gender that she encounters.[2] *The Street* lays the groundwork for the exploration of African American cultural tradition in *Invisible Man*, which demonstrates how comedy and rage work separately from and in conjunction with one another to actively withstand racist assault.

Beyond the Rage of Wright: African American Rage in *Invisible Man*

The rage in Ellison's novel moves beyond the works of the Wright school through its extended inclusion of humor in much the same way that *Black No More*'s humor counteracted the sober treatments of race of the Harlem Renaissance. In addition, the novel's embrace of African American cultural tradition acts as a place where rage can be expressed aside from the violence that dominated the works of the Wright school. Ellison infuses *Invisible Man* with the varying, contradictory elements that make up the African American experience. Embodying the "double consciousness" that W.E.B. Du Bois made famous in his landmark book *The Souls of Black Folk* (1903), the novel balances the influence of white (T. S. Eliot and James Joyce) and black (blues, jazz, orality) cultures. It combines explicitly European and African traditions that manifest themselves in the body and culture of the people who emerged from the American institution of slavery and, of particular interest to Ellison, the failure of Reconstruction. Most important, Ellison's use of the folk tradition binds the novel's multiple interests. Like Langston Hughes and Zora Neale Hurston before him, Ellison infuses his work not with an exploration of African American bourgeois culture but with the rhythms and speech of the underclass often seen as the source of African American folklore.

The presence of humor and rage emerges out of the novel's use of African American folklore and alternately indicts and ridicules American myth and culture. *Invisible Man* thus achieves the goal for which Amiri Baraka in *Home: Social Essays* argues the African American writer should strive, specifically to "tap his legitimate cultural tradition," which Baraka believes occurs "by utilizing the entire spectrum of the American experience from the point of view of the emotional history of the black man in this country: as its victim and its chronicler" (111–12). The transference of oral culture to the written word in *Invisible Man* heavily contributes both to the racial critique fueled by the novel's rage and to the transcendent spirit that humor provides. More important to the development of comic rage, the signifying the novel utilizes allows the characters to reject violence as a response while expressing a clear anger at the gulf between American philosophy and practice.

African American rage actually emerges not as the result of a singular incident—although often ignited by singular incidents—but from the continued oppression of African Americans that spans generations. Therefore, in *Invisible Man* the rage expressed by the protagonist-narrator, while certainly the result of white supremacist assault, cannot be separated from the revelation of his grandfather's rage. The grandfather's deathbed words haunt the family: "Live with your head in the lion's mouth. I want you to overcome 'em with yeses, undermine 'em with grins, agree 'em to death and destruction, let 'em swoller you till they vomit or bust wide open" (13–14). The narrator, often compared to his grandfather during his childhood, feels those final words haunt him in particular. A closer look at the grandfather's rage reveals his rejection of violence for more subversive forms of resistance, even as he refers to himself as a traitor: "all my born days, a spy in the enemy's country ever since I give up my gun back in the Reconstruction" (13). His expression of rage surprises his family, and the memory of how "he had spoken of his meekness as a dangerous activity" (14) confuses the narrator. The grandfather's rejection of violence forces the narrator to discover other ways to channel his rage. Throughout the novel the narrator's attempts to express rage without the use of violence drive his search for identity. He responds by simultaneously trying to embrace white mainstream culture and values while seeking to destroy them. He tells us, "Whenever things went well for me I remembered my grandfather and felt guilty and uncomfortable. It was as though I was carrying out his advice in spite of myself" (14). He struggles with his grandfather's wishes, and his ensuing inability to negotiate the rage he tries to suppress causes tension within him. As he attempts to suppress his rage, he only delays its expressions, which appear at the apex of each episode and indirectly spur him to the next chapter of his life.

In "Ralph Ellison's *Invisible Man*" Marcus Klein posits that for the narrator "his grandfather's riddle defines his every gambit," which leads him "to wish his way out of the curse, and the curse composes his being, his actions, and his purpose. He comes to each adventure saying Yes and he learns, or in every adventure but the last he almost learns, at the same to say No" (79). The narrator's inability to escape his grandfather's words contributes to the increasing frustration he feels. His blind acceptance and idealism eventually lead to his expression of rage at a society that continues to be revealed as cunning, as his grandfather warned. We find an important example when the grandfather's curse and the rage the narrator suppresses collide during his fight with Lucius Brockway before the paint factory explodes. The protagonist, already frustrated because of his treatment by the union members upstairs, attempts to remain calm even as Brockway threatens to kill him. He remembers in his mind, "You were trained to accept the foolishness of such old men as this, even when you thought them clowns and fools," and yet he is unable to control himself because "this was too much . . . [Brockway] was not grandfather or uncle or father, nor preacher or teacher" (171). From this statement it becomes clear that the narrator's fear of articulating his rage emerges from his attempts to suppress the rage of his grandfather, even though that rage has been, symbolically at least, passed to the narrator. The intensity with which he fights Brockway reflects his attempts to free himself from his grandfather's influence, as if killing Brockway would be a metaphorical killing of his grandfather and his legacy.

The narrator's fear of expressing his rage represents the larger misrepresentation of African American rage as pathological rather than an inherent response to oppression. For example, Jerry Bryant in *"Born in a Mighty Bad Land"* informs us, "Ellison writes in a time when the Stagolees and the John Hardys would more probably be sent to Harlem's Lafargue Psychiatric Clinic than be memorialized in songs sung by itinerant guitarists and work gangs, when rage is a psychiatric problem rather than a motive for the violent defense of a man's reputation" (72). This historical equating of African American rage with psychiatric dysfunction characterizes the larger attempt to suppress expressions of rage. Usually through the promotion of the image of the "angry black man," mainstream society considers African American rage a condition that should be cured, avoided, or repressed. However, I believe, as bell hooks does, that we must begin to see African American rage "as something other than sickness, to see it as a potentially healthy, potentially healing response to oppression and exploitation" (12). African American rage continues to be connected with violence as its only possible manifestation. This representation ignores other modes of resistance that rage initiates, which makes Ellison's novel a significant departure from contemporaneous novels. Though Stephen B. Bennett and William W. Nichols in "Violence in Afro-American Fiction" point out that *Invisible Man* contains "the kind of apocalyptic rage commonly associated with contemporary black militants," which "has been part of the imaginations of the best black writers in America for some time" (175), the novel uses a number of different tactics to manifest such rage. *Invisible Man* differs from many of those earlier novels not in the absence of rage but in the construction of African Americans as subjects actively creating moments and places where rage can be funneled into a passionate response.[3]

Wright's status as the standard of African American letters, perhaps exacerbated by Ellison's personal relationship to him, rendered Ellison's challenge to the formula that *Native Son* inspired crucial to the African American literary tradition generally and to expressions of comic rage specifically. Addressing Irving Howe's indictment of him in "Black Boys and Native Sons," Ellison in "The World and the Jug" responds, "It is not for me to judge Wright's courage, but I must ask just why it was possible for me to write as I write 'only' because Wright released his anger? Can't I be allowed to release my own? What does Howe know of my acquaintance with violence, or the shape of my courage or the intensity of my anger?" (115). Here Ellison distinguishes between multiple expressions of rage and castigates Howe for assuming that black rage must be expressed monolithically according to his (and Wright's) standards. Even while Ellison does not dismiss violence as a mode of expressing rage, he ultimately rejects it because of his belief in other avenues of expression and resistance. *Invisible Man*, then, revises ideas about the ways in which rage can be expressed. Critical thinking about *Invisible Man* suggests that Ellison's rejection of violence simultaneously discounts the rage that resulted in violent acts. Additionally, the labeling of *Invisible Man* as an "apolitical" work separate from the overt protest of the novels of the Wright school misleads critics to argue that the humor in the novel does not serve as a critique of oppression. In the novel, however, Ellison's political project clearly and unmistakably articulates a rage against the physical and psychic wounds caused by racial subjugation.

We find an example of critical misinterpretation of the rage in *Invisible Man* when Jerry Bryant sees the narrator's refusal to kill the anonymous white man in the prologue as contradictory. Writing in *Victims and Heroes*, Bryant recognizes Ellison's preference for irony over violence: "It is not simply the Invisible Man's pulling back at the last minute that differentiates him from the killers of the Wright group. It is his pervasive sense of ironic comedy. Such an ironist can never give in fully to his 'frenzy' or feel a sense of grievance so powerfully as to commit murder to redress it" (225). Bryant cannot reconcile the narrator's reference to himself as a "coward" because he did not kill the white man: "the narration seems to be saying that what makes him a coward at the end of his prologue makes him free at the end of his memoir. By this logic, to be free is to be a coward. And to be a coward is to be afraid to use violence" (227). Such a misunderstanding exemplifies the larger misrepresentation of African American rage. By examining Bryant's belief that the narrator's actions are contradictory, we can see how African American rage goes beyond mainstream perceptions that contribute stereotypical images.

First, Bryant makes a telling distinction between *Invisible Man*'s characters and those of the Wright school: "Where Bigger Thomas, Lutie Johnson, and Jesse Robinson *feel* and react emotionally *in extremis*, Ellison's narrator *thinks*" (227). Like Shakespeare's Hamlet, Ellison's protagonist constantly vacillates, dissecting every action and circumstance almost to a fault, only to realize that he is more naïve than he thought. Bryant suggests that he "reflects, mediates, and philosophizes. He calls himself a 'thinker-tinker,' one who plays with theories and words. The result is a narrative voice that is ironic and detached, addicted to inconclusiveness and contradiction" (227). Casting the narrator as the source from which the novel's indecision develops, Bryant fails to recognize that larger forces produced him, and that with the narrator's "ironic and detached" stance, Ellison departs consciously from the Wright school's naturalistic impulses that relegate its characters to sociological objects incapable of undermining or transcending the forces that have caused their oppression. The violence that occurs in those novels seems inherent in African Americans because they lack any other avenue for expression. In *Invisible Man* the narrator's rage develops in conjunction with his ability to reason his way around the forces that oppress him. He actively seeks alternative means of expressing dissatisfaction. His decision not to kill the anonymous white man, then, should not be read as linking freedom to cowardice. Instead the narrator frees himself from the expectations of protest novels through his ability to express rage in a way that eschews violence. Similarly, viewing himself as a "coward" acts as an ironic commentary on the limitations of black naturalist fiction, much as *Notes from the Underground*, in Ellison's view quoted above, acted as "a protest against the limitations of nineteenth-century rationalism." The novel enacts its protest through the protagonist's continual recourse to his skills as an orator to express his rage.

Lutie Johnson loses her career as a singer, and Bigger Thomas never seriously pursues his desire to fly planes. Ellison's narrator, by contrast, invariably finds himself in situations where his oratorical skills result in his advancement. He thus avoids considering violence as a primary strategy of resistance, despite the inevitable emergence of violent encounters. The novel clears up Bryant's "attempt to find coherence in the attitude toward violence" by using the protagonist's rhetorical skill as a critical outlet that separates his rage from acts of violence. He rejects violence because he believes that it will ultimately be destructive. He therefore feels that he is a coward not because he thinks violence is the answer but because he is forced to simultaneously suppress the corresponding rage. He fails, as a result, to heed the advice of his grandfather and successfully funnel his rage through subversive action instead of violent revolt. By the time the narrator almost kills the anonymous white man, he mistakenly sees the rage that he feels as inseparable from the violence that he almost enacts. Ellison's rejection of naturalism begins in the prologue's refusal to kill the anonymous white man and remains consistent throughout the novel. Unlike Bigger with his sense of dread at the violence inside him, unlike characters of the Wright school for whom violence becomes an inevitability, Ellison's narrator shows no predisposition to violence as a response to racism. Nevertheless, as in those other works, we discover how methodically all of the outlets have been stripped away from the narrator. Even though the beating of the white man mirrors the novels of the Wright school in its presentation of violence as the only recourse with which characters are left, the narrator's restraint signals the possibility of outlets of expression that cannot be erased. Throughout the novel, Ellison presents numerous moments where the expression of rage occurs without violence. In particular, the narrator's rhetorical skill embraces African American oral culture while consistently articulating anger at the external forces that surround his community. More important, the narrator's oratory fuels the novel's use of humor as a crucial element in critiquing white supremacy while avoiding the consumptive rage of other works of its period.

The novel highlights the narrator's rhetoric in the first chapter when he attempts to give, at a celebration of young African American students, the Booker T. Washington "Atlanta Compromise" speech that had been so successful at his high school graduation. The accommodating speech, contrasting with young Richard's refusal to change his graduation speech in Richard Wright's *Black Boy*, acts as the narrator's first step in following his grandfather's advice. He appears before the most powerful whites of the town, who force the narrator and other young African American boys to engage in a "battle royal." Before this free-for-all prizefight, the boys are obliged to watch the performance of a white exotic dancer with an American flag painted on her body. The boys, while potentially aroused, know the danger in viewing the body of a white woman in front of white men. The protection of the white female body from hypersexualized black men was a central tenet of white southern culture. The painting of the American flag painted on the idealized white female body exposes the interconnectedness of race, sex, and violence in America's construction of racial identity.

After the battle royal the soundly beaten narrator, with blood in his mouth, attempts to give his speech. The image counters Booker T. Washington's belief that social and political conciliation would lead to an eventual acceptance of African Americans. Here myth and idealism are met, violently, with the reality of America's racial history. The hecklers' interruptions of the narrator's speech discourage him from further use of this mode of resistance, and he abandons oratory, even though its importance becomes apparent to the reader, during his abridged college career and, eventually, his membership in the Communist stand-in Brotherhood in New York. He does not deploy his skills again, in fact, until he witnesses an elderly couple being evicted from their home. In using this ability, he comes to see that his rage, as bell hooks would say, "has the potential not only to destroy but also to construct" (16). The fear that he felt at the presence of his rage begins to dissipate, the result of his ability to channel that rage toward a constructive purpose. Hooks realizes, as the narrator eventually does, that "Rage can act as a catalyst inspiring courageous action" (16). The speech he gives when he witnesses the older couple being evicted and a riot brewing demonstrates the power of rage in leading to action. Without the recovery of his oratory, the narrator seems destined to follow in the violent, self-destructive footsteps of the Wright school protagonists. In finding his voice, he at once staves off the possibility of rage consuming him and provides necessary rhetoric for the couple, and the Harlem community more generally, that effectively responds to oppression.[4] A parallel process happens with comic rage, in that it provides African American audiences with the opportunity to enunciate their dissatisfaction.

The narrator's rage sits just below the surface and seems to emerge only at moments of clear injustice. The sight of the elderly couple being thrown out of their home evokes a response that disturbs him: "I looked at the old people, feeling my eyes burn, my throat tighten," forcing him to turn away, "feeling myself being drawn to the old couple by a warm, dark, rising whirlpool of emotion which I feared. I was wary of what the sight of them crying there on the sidewalk was making me begin to feel" (205). He acts because, as he says, "I knew that they were about to attack the man and I was both afraid and angry, repelled and fascinated. I both wanted it and feared the consequences, was outraged and angered at what I saw and yet surged with fear" (208). His rage eventually forces him to act, to openly resist the white supremacy that surrounds him, even though he is unaware of what he will do. The narrator effectively articulates the rage that has been building since he was expelled from school through this oratorical ability, which catches the attention of the Brotherhood. Through his partnership with them, his rage develops most fully. His rise within the organization provides—for a time—an outlet for his rage. Yet his popularity breeds jealousy in the Brotherhood.

In a nod to both Wright's and Ellison's eventual rejection of the Communist Party, the Brotherhood's white privilege and restrictive policies exploit and marginalize both the narrator and another black member, the very gifted and popular Tod Clifton. While the narrator gets reassigned to address "the woman question"—about which he has very little to say—Clifton, who has been an example to him on how to funnel his rage in constructive directions, disappears, essentially dropping out of history. Clifton's absence erodes the potential for the narrator's rhetoric to effect the change he wants. His speech at the funeral of the slain Tod Clifton continues as a mode of resistance, this time against the Brotherhood itself. It is only after this option has been taken away, by his expulsion from the Brotherhood, that violence actually becomes a legitimate possibility and, inevitably, erupts. Through this realization we can begin to separate rage and violence, a move that resists the dominant culture's misrepresentation of African American rage.

Ellison avoids misrepresentations of black rage by presenting moments of rage and violence not only for their literary significance in the story but as part of the real and lasting pain brought on by the continued oppression of African Americans. The pain of being treated like second-class citizens leads to violence in the novel that moves beyond the merely symbolic. Expressed through surrealism by Ellison, violence occurs in oppressed communities once other avenues of resistance fail. For example, Jerry Bryant connects violence to the boomerang that stands as a metaphor throughout the novel, suggesting that "the narrator is moved along by an equivalent of this boomerang, some violent situation that boosts him to the next phase of his education" (231). Bryant correctly points out, "Violence is thus part of the *atmosphere* of [Invisible Man's] journey to self-discovery," as well as the novel's use of violence to expose "the sham of the authorized view, the safe and logical group" (231). However, he fails to recognize violence as the culmination of the absence of inclusive, democratic organizations that would provide an outlet for collective and constructive expressions of rage and acts of resistance. Although the narrator's intent remains to fulfill the grandfather's subversion of white supremacy, violence as an expression of rage inevitably occurs in the novel. Even though each "material change that violence brings about is an expression of a psychological one," the acts themselves serve as part of the continued repression of the narrator's possibilities, each time leaving him more physically and mentally bruised than before. The acts, "the battle royal, the riot at the Golden Day, the explosion of the boilers in the paint factory, the shock therapy at the paint factory hospital, the fracas at the eviction scene, the murder of Tod Clifton by the policeman" (231–32), must be seen as a whole, part of a larger cycle of oppression pervading African American life. As the episodic structure coalesces around the increasingly assertive irony, the acts of violence become, underneath Ellison's magnificently descriptive scenes, darker, more horrifying, and virtually uncontrollable. The narrator's rage fuels the scenes that begin to more quickly critique the byproducts of white supremacist oppression and accelerates the clash between himself and the external forces that stifle his expressions of selfhood. The separation between rage and violence disintegrates as the continued oppression and the inadequacy of the surrounding opportunities combine to turn violence into the de facto manifestation of rage.

Instead of violence being cast as synonymous with African American rage, as Bryant's work implies, the narrator's dwindling choices render violence as the only available expression of rage, save insanity or suicide. While the narrator has given proof throughout the novel of his ability to critique the inconsistencies of the society around him, the systematic elimination of his options—the end of his education, his unemployment after the explosion at Liberty Paints, his exile from the Brotherhood—parallels his relationship and rivalry with the Ras the Exhorter, symbol of black nationalism and chief perpetuator of African American rage that manifests itself in violent defiance and militant action. Ras acts as a frequent antagonist to the narrator in part because of their clear ideological differences, but also because of the persuasiveness of his message among the same underclass blacks that the narrator and the Brotherhood seek to recruit. Also, unlike the narrator's attempts to suppress his rage by embracing a more accommodationist stance, Ras embraces his rage and constructs a counter-representation that celebrates blackness and black life. Yet the novel shows his counter-representations to be as simplistic as the stereotypes against which he rails. Additionally, the transformation of his name from Ras the Exhorter to Ras the Destroyer at the end of the novel signals the clear link he makes between rage and violence, a link the narrator opposes. While Ellison's novel resembles those of the Wright school in the presence of violence in its climactic scene, the narrator's journey contains a sense of hopefulness and deflection as opposed to the nihilism that characterizes other novels of that period. Instead of becoming a sociological object, the narrator, despite his naïveté, consistently asserts the agency that makes him a fully realized character.

The creation of Ras himself reveals an important element about the construction of the novel and the source material for Ras. Ellison confirms this in an interview in *Shadow and Act*:

INTERVIEWERS: Isn't Ras based on Marcus Garvey?

ELLISON: No. In 1950 my wife and I were staying at a vacation spot where we met some white liberals who thought the best way to be friendly was to tell us what it was like to be Negro. I got mad at hearing this from people who otherwise seemed very intelligent. I had already sketched Ras but the passion of his statement came out after I went upstairs that night feeling that we needed to have this thing out once and for all and get it done with; then we could go on living like people and individuals. No conscious reference to Garvey is intended. (181)

Even if we are to believe Ellison's denial of an intended similarity of Ras to Garvey, or of the narrator's college and its founder to the Tuskegee Institute and Booker T. Washington, we must consider the consistent rendering of images of specific ideologies and traditions in African American culture. The fact that Ellison does not intentionally construct Ras to reflect Garvey suggests the similarity in how African American ideas of nationalist rage get articulated. The rage that Ras espouses emerges from Ellison's own anger at being stereotyped by what Garvey might call "crocodiles as friends." Ellison's comments also recall his response to Irving Howe's belief that black rage can only be expressed in the way that Richard Wright imagines it. The novel contrasts the rage of the Narrator with that of Ras, casting the latter's as too consumptive and violent as opposed to the irony and surrealism that characterizes the narrator's expressions. While Ellison may not intend any resemblance of Ras to Marcus Garvey, the similarity to Garvey—and eventually Malcolm X— reflects a larger similarity that we see in the appearance of nationalist figures in African American literature and life as well as their distinct expression of black rage.

Although we see Ras initially as a figure of separatism and violence, he negotiates his rage much more effectively than either the narrator or Clifton. Danielle Allen writes, "In *Invisible Man* Harlem has its one fury, Ras, a Caribbean-born political activist who preaches revenge on his street corner" (51), but I see that fury as more multifaceted than Allen allows. Although the eviction scene makes clear the rage of the African American community in Harlem—not to mention the rage that is underneath the narrator throughout the novel—Ras's full engagement with the underclass remains unquestioned. His community loves him, not simply because of his overt defiance and calls for violence, but because he embodies the full range of African American cultural responses to oppression. For instance, Ras captures the essence of the double-voiced nature and multidimensionality of black vernacular and folk culture. In the novel, as the narrator listens to a group of men who tell the story of Ras, we witness the narrator's ambivalence: "I lay in a cramp, wanting to laugh and yet knowing that Ras was not funny, or not only funny, but dangerous as well, wrong but justified, crazy and yet coldly sane. . . . Why did they make it seem funny, *only* funny?" (426). Gayl Jones, in *Liberating Voices: Oral Tradition in African American Literature,* sees Ras's story as "the nature of the riddle-joke at the edge of danger, the comic and serious jammed into the same space" (147). The narrator does not realize that the men do not see Ras's story as solely funny, but instead respond to his rage with an understanding laughter that reflects the rage they themselves possess. Their laughter becomes one of connection, not only with Ras, but with their own attempts and desires for resistance. The presence of Ras also reveals the power of orality in spurring others into action, a key expression that the narrator abandons after his expulsion from the Brotherhood. The narrator's loss of oratory as an outlet to express his rage forecasts the increasing dissatisfaction of the African American community. As figures like the narrator and Tod Clifton find themselves marginalized and exploited by the Brotherhood, their ability to articulate the collective dissatisfaction of the African American community erodes and, with the death of Clifton and the expulsion of the narrator, dissipates. Thus the climax of *Invisible Man* depicts the collective rage of the voiceless: the riot. The transformation of Ras from Exhorter, which denotes the use of orality as a weapon to express rage, to Destroyer mirrors that of a community that has lost its means of overtly resisting racist assault. The only option, then, is destructive action, resulting in the riot and the murder of Ras by the narrator.

Forced underground and unable to use oration as an avenue to express his rage or effect change because of his isolation, the narrator turns to the written word. Writing serves the same purpose for him that oration

played in the past. Here again, we see a movement away from naturalism, which has, at least in African American literature, promoted the
destruction of the protagonists, either by their murdering of someone
or by their own death. Even though some characters achieve a certain
consciousness of the forces that surround them, those revelations come
too late to prevent their eventual demise. In *Native Son*, for example, Bigger's ability to express himself other than through violence comes only
as he stands in prison with the knowledge that he will die. By contrast,
in *Invisible Man*, not only does the narrator survive the riot—where
previous works of the period might have ended—the awakening of his
consciousness signals an opportunity for him to resist oppressive forces
proactively once he emerges from the underground. The narrator, consistent with the uncertainty that characterizes him throughout the novel,
believes he has failed as a result of his writing: "The very act of trying
to put it all down has confused me and negated some of the anger and
some of the bitterness" (437). I contend, however, that the act of writing
channels his rage into a constructive enunciation of the overwhelming
frustration that led him to self-destructive action. Telling his story pairs
the rage he expresses with other emotions necessary for "the possibility
of action" (437). The narrator's desire to leave the underground arrives
because of his fully realized selfhood, a selfhood rooted in constructive
expressions of rage in concert with other tools of expression present in
the prologue. Bryant argues, "The laughter into which he explodes in the
midst of murder is a sign that his consciousness is too acute for him to
expect success from violence" (225). The narrator's writing, then, balances that rage with other elements to form a nexus of resistance.[5]

Bryant correctly recognizes that "*Invisible Man* introduces us immediately to an act of violence. It is an act, moreover, that resembles the
familiar concluding encounter in the novels of the school of Wright, in
which the African American protagonist is pushed by racist conditions
beyond his or her rational control" (224). With the prologue of the novel
presenting what is chronologically its end, the story centralizes oral culture and nonlinear concepts of time while also rejecting the typical ending of the protest novels. By placing that ending, of black violence heaped
upon whites, at the beginning of the book, Ellison literally and symbolically moves beyond the tradition of social realism popularized by Wright,
challenging the reader to go further in probing other manifestations of

rage. Ellison seems to be demanding that readers ask, "Where do we go from here?"

Breaking New Ground: Humor and Cultural Tradition in *Invisible Man*

Ellison provides the answer through the major distinction between *Invisible Man* and other novels of the period: the use of humor. In "The World and the Jug" Ellison notes, "In *Native Son*, Wright began with the ideological proposition that what whites think of the Negro's reality is more important than what Negroes themselves know it to be" (114). In particular, Darryl Dickson-Carr notes Wright's role in the devaluing of humor in the novels in the late 1930s and 1940s, suggesting that "his attack upon literary depictions of black life that did not fit the politics of his seminal essay 'Blueprint for Negro Writing' did not leave much place for satire and its rhetoric in the future of African American authorship" (86). To be sure, moments of humor appear in novels of the 1940s and 1950s, but they are not a primary concern. Alongside the appearance of African American cultural traditions that often buffer the external forces and byproducts that assault the bodies and psyches of African Americans, the midcentury novels could be criticized for their lack of humor before anything else. Their outstanding emotion, rage, builds unceasingly throughout the novels and rarely encounters anything to accompany it, save anguish.

Also in his review of *Native Son*, Ellison points out the lack of work that embraces African American folk/street experience during the Harlem Renaissance: "Except for the work of Langston Hughes, [the Renaissance] ignored the existence of Negro folklore and perceived no connection between its efforts and the symbols and images of Negro folk forms" (12). *Invisible Man* attempts to fill the absence of those folk forms, as Ellison embeds his use of humor in African American folklore and rejects the traditional concern of whether or not "white folk got it" in favor of the exploration of the distinctive African American cultural tradition from which the narrator's voice pulls. The novel's myriad uses of humor impact its presentation of black folk culture, which meant that the novel was not always celebrated or understood. John Killens, in his 1952 review, argued that the book subscribed to the worst stereotypes of

African Americans: "A million Negro veterans who fought against fascism in World War II are rewarded with a maddening chapter [of] crazy vets running hogwild in a down home tavern. The Negro ministry is depicted by an Ellison character who is a Harlem pastor and at the same time a pimp and a numbers racketeer. / The Negro people need Ralph Ellison's *Invisible Man* like we need a hole in the head or a stab in the back. / It is a vicious distortion of Negro life" (7). Killens's "crazy vets" references the Golden Day chapter, when the narrator takes the white northern philanthropist Mr. Norton to get a drink after hearing the story of Jim Trueblood, an African American man the African Americans in the area despise. The focus on the Trueblood story, a tale of incest filled with symbolism about race, desire, and performance, often ignores Ellison's critique of the hypocrisy of discriminating against African American veterans who fought to maintain a democracy in which they could not participate, as well as the doctor who encourages the narrator to resist oppression subversively. To be sure, Kenneth Warren argues that Norton represents a "white paternalism" that Ellison critiques, but more important, "What Ellison illustrates by confronting Norton with Trueblood and the denizens of the Golden Day is not only the inability of [a white rational and benevolent] grid to predict and account for the people that Norton meets, but also the irrationality and pathology that motivates Norton's philanthropic relationship to black populations" (38–39). Many of the images of African Americans could initially make whites wince and blacks like Killens irate, given the history of blackface minstrel shows in America. Yet we can easily see many of the seemingly stereotypical black characters as complex renderings who hint at Ellison's use of comic rage. Throughout the novel Ellison's depiction of the same characters that Killens lambastes often launches critical broadsides at white Western constructions of race, democracy, and liberalism. For instance, just as the novel uses the Trueblood story to expose Norton as a white liberal who views African Americans as primitive children for whom he must care, when the narrator moves to New York the novel uses the contrast with Ras to eventually expose the charismatic Brother Jack as a manipulator of African Americans in Harlem. The presentation of the African American underclass, then, often becomes an avenue to express comic rage at whites.

Robert O'Meally, in his introduction to the 1988 collection *New Essays on "Invisible Man,"* informs us that Killens was not the only critic to miss the critique that Ellison hid in his humor, if they saw the humor at all: "*The Yale Review*'s James Yaffe, for example, extols *Invisible Man*'s 'tightly effective' 'brooding, bitter tone' and its 'passages of great sociological interest'" (11). O'Meally believes many white critics missed the humor initially because of its deep roots in African American culture, suggesting "some jokes in the book derived from Afro-American vernacular experience, from folklore and stage shows that had not, at least by the fifties, 'crossed the tracks' from black to white America" (11). The text creates an insider/outsider relationship in which only those readers familiar with the tradition of black folklore understand its references. The novel centralizes the lives of lower-class African Americans and implicitly demands that those unfamiliar with their cultural traditions work to understand the perspectives of the insiders, a demand that fundamentally challenges their privilege. The novel celebrates a distinct African American cultural experience that includes subtle (and not so subtle) jabs at white supremacy.

The authors of the Wright school failed to realize that comedy, like rage, plays an integral part in African American culture's attempts to resist racist oppression. Ellison's recognition of this results in the injection of humor into his novel at almost every turn. Dickson-Carr argues that both Ellison and Hughes—in his Jesse B. Semple stories—"distance themselves from the explicit protest of Wright's naturalistic fiction, choosing instead to use the folk, whether northern or southern, as signs of infinite possibilities" (89). A major factor in their critique of "America's failure to live up to its promised social contract in the racial arena" was their use of "a distinct sense of irony and satire that is exceedingly difficult to find in protest/social document fiction" (89). Not only does humor sit as an important part of Ellison's overall use of African American cultural tradition and history in general, his use of comedy connects various aspects of those traditions to each other, from black vernacular to tricksters and ultimately to rage. In this chapter I especially explore humor's role in critiquing white supremacy and hypocrisy. The rage that lies underneath the instances of comedy is articulated orally, especially through the use of signifying. In viewing the humor that runs throughout the novel, one must not solely compare it to the American comic tradition, which, like the philosophy *l'art pour l'art*, rejects the use of art to critique.

Many attempts to discuss the humor in the novel have based it solely on the American comic experience, an approach that engenders misinterpretation of certain moments and themes in the novel. In 1960 Earl H. Rovit went so far as to argue in "Ralph Ellison and the American Comic Tradition" that the race of Ellison and his protagonist "both is and is not important. From the severe standpoint of art the racial fact is negligible, although there are doubtless areas of meaning and influence in *Invisible Man* which sociological examination might fruitfully develop. From the viewpoint of cultural history, however, the racial fact is enormously provocative" (158). This becomes especially evident when one considers the figure of the trickster.[6] Perhaps this contributes to Ellison's claim in "Change the Joke and Slip the Yoke" that although he "knew the trickster Ulysses just as early as I knew the wily rabbit of Negro American lore," in his mind "I could easily imagine myself a pint-sized Ulysses but hardly a rabbit, no matter how human and resourceful or Negro" (58). While Ulysses might provide the literary influence for Ellison's use of the trickster, his deployment of humor throughout the novel generally finds its roots in a folk/street humor that critiques instead of merely entertaining. More likely, then, Ellison recognized the African American experience as a dual existence, so that his protagonist was both Western and black, searching for an identity within that paradigm. Amiri Baraka identifies this existence when he argues in *Home* that the "cultural memory of Africa informs the Negro's life in America, but it is impossible to separate it from its American transformation" (111). Traditionally, American ideas of comedy, especially as it refers to African American performance and mainstream perception of it, have involved the absence of sociopolitical critique. Therefore, Ellison's conception of art's ability "to transcend" has led many to cast the protagonist as an Everyman figure who can represent universal (i.e., white) themes, journeys, and truths.[7] Here we see the next stage in the process of co-optation of African American art. The first stage, which we saw enacted during the Harlem Renaissance, was the labeling of black art forms "primitive" or "raw" in order to foist white mainstream values and ideas onto those forms. The next, then, devalues the importance of distinct African, if not African American, characteristics in the creation of that art form. This allows for mainstream culture to claim the form as its own, to call it "universal," and—perhaps most important—to avoid the idea of acknowledging the influence of blackness.

O'Meally argues that the images of the novel were intended to expose the negative legacy of racist traditions so they can be appropriately
confronted: "Tod's dancing Sambo dolls, symbolizing his manipulation
by the Brotherhood and prefiguring his suicide, and the stereotypically
wide-smiling, blackfaced penny bank at Mary's—both crass images raise
the question of the social function of ethnic stereotypes and humor"
(12). In addition, the novel plays, as does Schuyler's novel, on the black
male/white female taboo. Unlike in Schuyler's novel, however, the black
man rejects the white female, inverting the stereotypical construction of
white female purity and uncontrollable black male sexuality. The narrator
becomes the object of infatuation for Sybil, a sex-crazed member of the
Brotherhood. He attempts to elicit information from her and, when she
passes out after failing to seduce him, he writes her a message—SYBIL,
YOU WERE RAPED BY SANTA CLAUS. SURPRISE (395)—that ridicules her exoticizing of black men and the history of fear and fascination evoked by
sex between black men and white women. Underneath Ellison's humor
lies the larger project of the mask blacks put on to cope with and resist
white supremacy. He notes in "Change the Joke and Slip the Yoke" that
"the Negro's masking is motivated not so much by fear as by a profound
rejection of the image created to usurp his identity. Sometimes it is for
the sheer joy of the joke; sometimes to challenge those who presume,
across the psychological distance created by race manners, to know his
identity" (55). Instead of promoting the idea of blackface as a legitimate
representation of African Americans, the novel challenges these images
by attempting to destroy them from the inside. Here we can see echoes
of the African American blackface entertainer Bert Williams, who sought
to reverse stereotypes with his portrayal of more complex representations than his white counterparts.

Moving further, *Invisible Man* follows comic rage's impulse not just
to critique one side of the color line. The novel contains a number of
moments that ridicule or challenge African Americans, particularly African American leaders. The novel questions their motivations in much
the same way it questions whites.' In particular, the novel uses implicit
references to W.E.B. Du Bois's popularizing of his Talented Tenth philosophy. Contrasting Booker T. Washington's focus on industrial education for millions of former slaves, Du Bois believed that the responsibility of leading the race rested with its most talented members and that

they should be especially nurtured in roles of leadership. Embracing an African American exceptionalism, the notion of a talented tenth conveniently aligned with a small but important black bourgeoisie who found themselves caught between a white world that frequently denied them and a black world from which they were too often disconnected. Warren notes, for instance, "Although black elites have been sincere in their desire to 'uplift' the race, the most visible measure of their success has not been the triumph of so-called bourgeois values among the nonprofessional laboring classes but rather the substitution of black professionals, managers, and intellectuals for their white counterparts within those institutions charged with administering to the needs of black populations" (27). Many of these figures, under the guise of racial uplift, not only reinforce the color line but secure a socially and economically beneficial standing for themselves. Despite the narrator's use of Washington's speech after the battle royal, many expect him to become a leader of his people in the tradition of the Talented Tenth. However, the expectations that surround the narrator's rise to prominence connect to a respectability politics rooted in class distinctions. When discussing the rage that appears when African Americans call for equality, bell hooks sees a clear class distinction. She argues that "affluent blacks are rarely linking their rage to any progressive challenge and critique of white supremacy rooted in solidarity with the black masses" (29). In the place of such a challenge, hooks believes middle- and upper-class African Americans substitute a "narcissistic rage," one that is "not interested in fundamentally challenging and changing white supremacist capitalist patriarchy. They simply want equal access to privilege within the existing structure" (29).

When the narrator attends college, we see the most obvious example of the black elite's complex relationship to its own rage, racial politics, and its place within the black community: Dr. Bledsoe, president of the college. Although Bledsoe wisely employs the "mask" that many African Americans have historically used in presenting a more "acceptable" image to whites, his ultimate goal is the maintenance of his power and the fulfillment of his greed. Both are threatened by the narrator when he takes the white philanthropist Mr. Norton to hear the Trueblood story and then to the Golden Day. For this, Dr. Bledsoe essentially expels the narrator and provides him with letters that, unbeknownst to the narrator, initially prevent him from getting a job in New York. The novel continues a parody of the ideology of Booker T. Washington that began with the protagonist's speech after the battle royal. In "*Invisible Man* and *Juneteenth*: Ralph Ellison's Literary Pursuit of Racial Justice" Thomas S. Engeman informs us, "The sterile Tuskegee-like college *appears* a model of Booker T. Washington's benevolent ideal of progress through education, although it proves only an empire of illusion and tyranny. The college corrupts students by demanding they accept segregation, and their own inferiority, enabling their oppressor, President Bledsoe, to become wealthy and honored" (95). Although *Invisible Man* does not view such leaders with the outright malevolence that *Black No More* does, save Dr. Bledsoe, the novel uses African American cultural expressions to explore how the black elite hampers the progress of other members of the African American community through the construction of narrow, exclusive ideals of blackness. The presence of African American folklore, in response, presented through characters like the ever elusive, rebellious Peter Wheatstraw and B. P. Rinehart, infuses the narrator's journey with scenes that reflect the complexity of African American culture and force the audience to question both white and black attempts to "solve" the race problem. So, according to Warren, "The stinging portraits of Mr. Norton and Brother Jack seemed to augur well for the assault on white paternalism," while the novel simultaneously examines the black elite, "who presumed to speak on behalf of the race from within the race, and who could claim on the basis of their identities to know whereof they spoke" (40). Thus we see Dr. Bledsoe manipulating his African American students for personal benefit or Mary Rambo encouraging the narrator to adopt a DuBoisian Talented Tenth philosophy. Through folklore, comic rage appears throughout the novel to examine the impact of the intersections of race, class, and power. Ellison's use of African American humor in his critique demonstrates its ability in helping transcend and deflect pain, uncontrolled rage, and fear.

Ellison imbues the novel with a humor that sits within the larger framework of African American folklore, whether it is the critique of racism through members of the "progressive" Brotherhood who believe the narrator "should be a little blacker" (230) or the inherent white supremacist rhetoric in the slogan at Liberty Paints where the narrator works: "If It's Optic White, It's the Right White" (165). Ellison informs us in "The Art of Fiction" that "there is the old saying amongst Negroes: If you're black, stay back; if you're brown, stick around; if you're white, you're right. . . . In my book this sort of thing was merged with the meanings which blackness and light have long had in Western mythology: evil and goodness, ignorance and knowledge, and so on" (173). Yet, too often critics choose to examine Ellison's humor against the (white) American comic tradition, instead of pursuing a more detailed recognition of the African influences throughout the novel. Ellison himself in "Change the Joke" has argued, "I use folklore in my work not because I am a Negro, but because writers like Eliot and Joyce made me conscious of the literary value of my folk inheritance" (58). Many, however, misinterpret this statement. Instead of more closely examining stereotypical notions of African American humor or the novel's impact on the use of African American humor-as-critique, many have judged the novel according to the expectations of mainstream American humor. Perhaps, then, it is more accurate to suggest that critics see humor in *Invisible Man* as a blackface version of the larger institution of modern comedy.

Understanding the elements that characterize the African American comic tradition begins with recognizing African American humor's traditional place outside the mainstream. As Mel Watkins explains, "The most conspicuous characteristic of African American humor is its insistent impious thrust. Never fully accepted by mainstream society, most blacks never subscribed to the popular American notion that, essentially, humor was only a playful diversion or innocuous entertainment, one that only occasionally referred to pertinent real-life situations" (476). African American humor's deployment for the daily encounters with hegemonic oppression provides a template from which a number of other responses and themes can be explored. So, while traditional ideas of humor might be manifested in lighthearted treatments of relationships in a romantic comedy, African American comedy might examine the ways in which humor negotiates the real and lasting pain and tension in those same relationships.[8] The targets of African American humor are often historical and contemporaneous situations and forces that have an effect on race in America in order to navigate the pain, rage, joy, and complexity of African American life.

The second step, then, in viewing *Invisible Man* outside the American comic tradition is the recognition of the origin of many of the references in the novel. For example, Watkins notes that many of the figures and traditions in African American culture were "firmly based in the West African tradition of storytelling—one in which fables and tall tales provided entertainment but were also used for moral instruction and protest" (72). The numerous manifestations of black oral tradition remain the most common elements of African American culture that can be traced to an African source in the novel. Figures like Brer Rabbit, who often pops up in the novel, and the Signifying Monkey, which I will discuss later, introduce us to animal tales that have permeated African American folklore, most of them originating from multiple African sources. These figures are clearly manifested in characters throughout the novel. The narrator, for instance, can be seen as Brer Rabbit himself. From the pervasive theme "Keep This Nigger-Boy Running" that forces the narrator from episode to episode and into the presence of his Brotherhood recruiter/adversary Jack the Bear—the bear being the frequent opponent of the rabbit—the narrator comes to epitomize the rabbit in African American folklore, constantly attempting to outsmart, or outrun, his stronger opponents. Apparently Ellison's claim that he was unable to view himself as the "wily rabbit of Negro American lore" does not translate to an inability to view his characters in such a manner. Writing of Zora Neale Huston's collection *Mules and Men*, Watkins argues that her "vivid documentation of the combative nature of much black verbal wordplay illuminates one of the central components of African-American humor—signifying, ranking, or (currently) *dissin'*. Intricately connected to that popular strain of humorous expression is a maxim that simply warns, 'If you grinnin', you in em'" (453). Thus we can review the narrator's grandfather's final words as an indicator that his uses of humor and orality have historically worked together as a mode of subversive resistance. His call to "live with your head in the lion's mouth" and "overcome 'em with yeses" and "undermine 'em with grins" encourages the narrator to employ African American orality as a weapon, one that acts not just as entertainment but as confrontation.

The narrator's relation to the rabbit becomes most apparent after the explosion at Liberty Paints when, still shaky after the blast, he finds himself at a factory hospital being questioned. As the questions—"What is your name?" "Who are you?"—hover unanswered, the narrator's thoughts reveal their deeper importance in the novel. Eventually, when the odd question "Who was Buckeye the Rabbit?" is asked, the narrator's response seems an affirmation: "I laughed, deep, deep inside me, giddy with the delight of self-discovery and the desire to hide it. Somehow *I* was Buckeye the Rabbit . . . or had been, when as children we danced and sang barefoot in the dusty streets" (183–84). Here the narrator identifies with the figure of the rabbit, while connecting him with the African American tradition of "playing the dozens." In this same scene at the hospital, the novel comments on the portrayal of Brer Rabbit, who was used in the late nineteenth century through Joel Chandler Harris's stories to construct images of peaceful, inferior African Americans after Reconstruction. At one point the narrator is asked, "Boy, who was Brer Rabbit?" to which he thinks, "He was your mother's back-door man" (184). In addition to being quite funny, the combination of references in this exchange—the racial history of Brer Rabbit, the fear of black male sexuality, and the disrespect inherent in the term "boy"—coalesces to reject the treatment and questioning the narrator receives. The rabbit reflects the novel's broader use of African American folk tradition throughout as a mode of resistance. The primary mechanism for such defiance is orality, which goes beyond the narrator's first-person telling. In the novel, the dialogue and the comments become critical because of the rhythmic, linguistic, and tonal characteristics that are significant in depicting African American vernacular and folk culture.

The other central animal figure in *Invisible Man* is the Signifying Monkey. Just as the figure of Brer Rabbit in African American folklore can be traced to the African hare, the Signifying Monkey too emerges from an African source. In Henry Louis Gates's preeminent work, *The Signifying Monkey*, he points out, "If Esu-Elegbara stands as the central figure of the Ifa [a Yoruba culture] system of interpretation, then his Afro-American relative, the Signifying Monkey, stands as the rhetorical principle in Afro-American vernacular discourse" (44). Gates argues that a relationship between the two arises from "their functional equivalency as figures of rhetorical strategies and of interpretation" (53). Appearing most famously in the African American "toasts" that document his constant antagonizing of the lion, the Signifying Monkey provides a template from which we can view various uses of African American oral traditions. Esu and the Signifying Monkey guide and symbolize the tone, substance, and rhythm of their communities. Gates states, "If Esu is the figure of writing in Ifa, the Signifying Monkey is the figure of a black rhetoric in the Afro-American speech community. He exists to embody the figures of speech characteristic to the black vernacular" (53). The tradition of signifying in particular becomes the most important of these modes. Gates believes, "Signifyin(g) epitomizes all of the rhetorical play in the black vernacular. Its self-consciously open rhetorical status, then, functions as a kind of writing, wherein rhetoric is the writing of speech, of oral discourse" (53). In explaining signifying, I hope to demonstrate its vital role in the expression of comic rage.

The text of *Invisible Man* itself generally represents the Signifying Monkey through its articulation of comedy and rage, manifesting itself in the storytelling, folk tales, and in-jokes that create an insider/outsider relationship with the reader. Beyond the black/white dichotomy on which previous works have focused, we see "the *trinary* forces of the Monkey, the Lion, and the Elephant" (55) that Gates reminds us are important. Historically, in the African American toasts, the monkey's signifying leads to the beating of the lion at the hands of the elephant, who stands as a superior opponent to the lion and a crucial weapon that the monkey deploys to defeat him. Similarly, Gates views the text of *Invisible Man* as the signifier, which allows us to see it as the monkey leading the symbolic Lion (white supremacist oppression) into the path of Elephant, represented in Ellison's novel by the spirit of the American Dream as found in the Declaration of Independence and the Constitution. The acts of rebellion by characters in the novel expose the inherent contradictions of white supremacy in a country that claims freedom for all. Like the "rhetorical genius" monkey who "is intent on demystifying the Lion's self-imposed status as King of the Jungle" (56), according to Gates, many of the characters challenge racist assumptions fostered by white supremacy, necessitating their expulsion. Therefore, the novel's adoption of black vernacular tradition, particularly signifying, ridicules racist oppression and conveys the novel's rage through a humorous critique that can only be fully recognized by those familiar with African American folklore.

While there are numerous moments within *Invisible Man* where the text signifies on white supremacy's effect on whites and blacks—certainly too many to point out here—it also signifies on literature as a larger form. Ellison makes his project clear when he argues in "The World and the Jug" "that protest is an element of all art, though it does not necessarily take the form of speaking for a political or social program. It might appear in a novel as a technical assault against the styles which have gone before, or as a protest against the human condition" (137). Just as the content of the novel ridicules and "assaults" racist oppression in the United States, the text of the novel deals with previous styles in African American works. This resembles the monkey's "poetry" which, according to Gates, stands in "opposition to the apparent transparency of speech" by calling "attention to itself as an extended linguistic sign, one composed of various forms of the signifiers peculiar to the black vernacular" (53). *Invisible Man*, for example, could be considered an "extended linguistic sign" on *Native Son* and novels of the Wright school. Gates believes that "Ellison relates to Wright as the Signifying Monkey relates to the Signified Lion. He parodies Wright, as a mode of critical Signification" (121). Ellison's relationship to Wright, to be sure, would not look like a literary historical line based solely on skin color. In fact, Ellison's belief in the use of folklore, though derived from his white ancestors, makes the influences of African American folk culture an important part of my examination of his work. Gates suggests that although Ellison's claim that "he simply stepped around Wright" should be considered legitimate, Ellison also "played the dozens on Wright's texts as he swerved past him" (121). Given his not refuting the influence of white authors on his work, I contend that the relationship between Ellison and Wright, as well as other African American writers and figures, sits much closer than Ellison might admit. At the very least, other writers and figures are so ingrained in the fabric of African American culture and life that Ellison inadvertently conjured them as he embraced the folk tradition.

Continuing with the text as signifier, black oral expression in the novel deploys signifying as one of many techniques in its portrait of black life. Gayl Jones posits, "*Invisible Man* is a multistructure of oral traditional forms—jazz and jazz solos, blues, oral storytelling, sermon, oratory, ballad" (150). The African American sermonic tradition instilled in the novel has served as a major element in oral expression and performance in African American life. The sermon in the prologue offers instances of the cadence, call-and-response, and signifying that are frequent throughout the novel.

"Brothers and sisters, my text this morning is the 'Blackness of Blackness.'"

And the congregation of voices answered: "That blackness is most black, brother, most black . . ."

"In the beginning . . ."

"At the very start," they cried.

" . . . there was blackness . . ."

"Preach it . . ."

" . . . and the sun . . ."

"The sun, Lawd . . ."

" . . . was bloody red . . ." (7–8)

Gates argues that the sermon "Signifies upon Melville's passage in *Moby-Dick* on 'the blackness of darkness' and on the sign of blackness, as represented by the algorithm *signified/signifier*" (236). Beyond Melville, Ellison sets his sights on the idea of blackness in the white imagination. "The trope of blackness in Western discourse has signified absence at least since Plato," writes Gates, and Ellison and Ishmael Reed both "critique the received idea of blackness as a negative essence, as a natural, transcendent signified; but implicit in such a critique is an equally thorough critique of blackness as a presence, which is merely another transcendent signified" (236–37). While Ellison's intent eschews the idea of blackness as superior to whiteness in the way a black nationalist might interpret the sermon, he does seek to erase the idea of blackness as empty and dangerous and, indeed, invisible. Blackness for Ellison, and by extension "black" culture, possesses distinct characteristics that must be recognized as significant, even as it coexists with whiteness.

Beginning with the sermon in the prologue, through to the exploration of the narrator's own talents as an orator, the novel constructs an African American community where aspects of sermonizing operate at will. In *The Craft of Ralph Ellison* (1980), Robert G. O'Meally writes, "Though no other sermons per se exist in the novel, in several instances characters employ the styles of black preachers. Homer A. Barbee clasps his hands and chants in sermonic style. [The protagonist's] improvised speech on the steps of the dispossessed old couple's apartment house rings with the spirited repetitions of the sermon" (98). The manifestation of orality shifts smoothly from place to place, depending on the environment. Figures as diverse as the well-respected Barbee, Ras (as the Exhorter), and the elusive Rinehart belie one-dimensional portraits of black oral culture, reinforcing Ellison's deployment of black sermonic tradition as a central component in the narrator's journey of self-discovery and in the novel more generally. For example, O'Meally points out, "As he walks the streets in Harlem, the Invisible Man's southern politeness and meekness gradually dissolve into the dozens and signifying" (100). The flexibility of black vernacular allows the novel to move from sermon to signifying with ease and familiarity, while maintaining the integrity of the oral tradition. It also provides a number of different verbal modes by which its users can communicate with each other and resist racist assaults by inverting the power dynamic. Even within individual modes there remains the possibility to shift meaning and use. Like O'Meally, I see the sermon in the prologue as defining blackness through "the black form in which the question is posed" (98). That question—What does blackness mean?—gets answered, then, through the sermon itself, filled as it is with numerous aspects of black vernacular tradition.[9] The seamless transition makes the possibility of comic relief and serious critique more likely here than in other vernacular forms. Humor in the novel serves a triple purpose, in that it fuses its entertainment of readers, criticism of racist assault and white supremacist hegemony, and revelation of African American cultural tradition's ability to express rage constructively.

Music, Comedy, and Rage

This chapter views instances in *Invisible Man* where rage and humor have been expressed separately as well as together. Yet no full understanding of the simultaneous existence of comedy and rage in the novel can be achieved without examining the importance of music to the novel's construction and its expression. One must first acknowledge that the novel consistently refers to jazz and blues legends, an unsurprising fact given Ellison's training as a musician at Tuskegee. Peetie Wheatstraw was the recording name for blues guitarist William Bunch in the 1930s, and the name of the character Rinehart recalls a lyric from blues singer Jimmy Rushing, a friend of Ellison's. Perhaps a more telling connection comes when the novel, in continuing the theme of a narrator "kept running," adopts another mantra to describe the narrator's story: "They Picked Poor Robin Clean." This particular phrase arises from the 1930s old Blue Devils Orchestra. In "On Bird, Bird-Watching, and Jazz," Ellison informs us that this tune "was a jazz community joke, musically an extended 'signifying riff' or melodic naming of a recurring human situation, and was played to satirize some betrayal of faith or loss of love observed from the bandstand" (231). Ellison reveals an important juxtaposition when he says, "Poor robin was picked again and again, and his pluckers were ever unnamed and mysterious. Yet the tune was inevitably productive of laughter even when we ourselves were its object" (231). The sight of the band making light of a potentially tragic situation highlights the realization that all might be subject to the same fate, one that echoes in the final words of Ellison's novel: "Who knows but that, on the lower frequencies, I speak for you?" (581). Ellison's extension of the "poor robin" metaphor, then, is a jazz technique that comments on the human search for identity.

Gates acknowledges that the orchestra's act is a "parody" that "is twofold, involving a formal parody of the melody of 'They Picked Poor Robin' as well as a ritual naming, and therefore a troping, of an action 'observed from the bandstand'" (105). The "signifying riff" that Ellison refers to in jazz reverberates similarly throughout the novel. Ellison has defined signifying as "rhetorical understatements," and his use of it includes parody, satire, and troping. Gates argues, "The riff is a central component of jazz improvisation and Signifyin(g) and serves as an especially appropriate synonym for troping and for revision" (105). Consequently, black musical art forms that use rhetorical strategies rooted in African American oral tradition, like jazz and blues, heavily inform the narrator's journey and story. The narrator—and by extension the black community in *Invisible Man*—gets repeatedly betrayed. The betrayals progressively unfold in an expectedly humorous manner that helps manage the anticipated sadness and anger embodied in the tradition of the blues.

The blues successfully captures the essence of comedy and rage that is significant to both the novel and the development of comic rage. Rage emerges out of the tragic stories of oppression that are often expressed in blues songs. The use of humor in the novel tempers the concomitant rage, an approach that casts rage as a critical aspect in challenging oppression, but one that cannot be sustained constructively without other emotional responses. We can view the importance of the narrator's acceptance of the full range of his human emotions at the end of the novel. O'Meally suggests, "By the time [the Invisible Man] sits down to write his memoir, he has gained something of the ironical perspective of the blues. He has learned, too, from the blues of the wisdom of his forefathers, the humor, bitterness, love, disappointment, and the will to endure" (93). Humor, then, not only provides an alternative to the rage in the novel but contributes to Ellison's vision of representing the complexity of humanity. As he states in "Blues People," "The blues speak to us simultaneously of the tragic and the comic aspects of the human condition and they express a profound sense of life shared by many Negro

Americans precisely because their lives have combined these modes" (256). The blues serves to address the frustration with white supremacy through complexity and negotiation the way Wright and his contemporaries did through the use of violence. In *Invisible Man*, while the rhythm of the writing and the stories of the characters are driven by jazz and black vernacular culture, the core of the novel is a reflection of the blues. Tragedy and comedy, laughter and rage may coexist in a scene, a moment, or a character. The novel exemplifies a musical form articulated in writing. Whether in the novel as a whole, or in scenes that signify on previous works, or in the verbal performances of its characters, the blues infuses *Invisible Man* with moments of African American humor that seek to negotiate the pain and rage felt toward white supremacy.

Nowhere does the combination of comedy and rage reveal itself more effectively than through the figure of Tod Clifton. His presence acts as a gateway to the final development of the protagonist. The Brotherhood's manipulation becomes most apparent to the narrator through the person of Clifton. Searching for self-identity just as the narrator does, Clifton reveals his ambivalence when the two men initially confront Ras. Ras recognizes the conflict in both men and attempts to recruit them. As Ras seizes on Clifton's conflicted self, the narrator notices that "Clifton looked at Ras with a tight, fascinated expression, pulling way from me," while Ras uses Clifton's racial consciousness to awaken his rage: "What they do to you, black mahn? Give you them stinking women?" (281). Clifton's attempt to attack Ras immediately after this statement exposes him, sparking his eventual disappearance and separation from the Brotherhood.

The novel makes clear that Clifton respects Ras, particularly his connection to his own rage and his use of that rage to promote a pride in his blackness. Clifton confirms this to the narrator: "'But it's on the inside that Ras is strong,' Clifton said. 'On the inside he's dangerous'" (285). Clifton, on the other hand, cannot negotiate his rage, and the Brotherhood's manipulation of that rage only intensifies his frustration. Surprisingly, Clifton possesses more potential than any of the other characters to reconcile the rage within him. The novel depicts him as popular, handsome, intelligent, and fearless. Yet he displays consistent doubts and a crisis of identity from the damage white society has done to him. As his only response, he "plunges outside of history" and, in an unnervingly comic, tragic, and infuriating scene, reappears selling Sambo dolls. In an altercation with the police, he is gunned down. Michael Cooke points out in *Afro-American Literature in the Twentieth Century* that Clifton's defiance of the police makes it "clear that he has not simply come apart and sunk into cheap lewdness and greed" (100). Cooke sees Clifton's acts as rebellious, believing that through him "Ellison condenses the slow social movement from signifying to rebellion" (100). The narrator witnesses the entire scene. This strengthens his own search for identity and rekindles his rage, which manifests itself in the speech he gives at Clifton's funeral in opposition to the Brotherhood's instructions and leaves him without a vehicle to express his frustration. Clifton's self-degradation exemplifies the destructive effect rage has on the self. In this sense, Clifton can be accurately compared to another figure whose self-destruction allowed for a misrepresentation of black rage: jazz great Charlie "Bird" Parker.

Parker, known as much for his controversial persona as for his genius as a musician, represents a more confrontational type of African American artist, anticipating politically outspoken athletes like Jim Brown, Muhammad Ali, and Bill Russell. To counter the more accommodating and perpetually happy images of other African American artists, specifically Louis Armstrong, Parker purposely adopted a radically different performative and political approach that mirrored the literary postures of Richard Wright and, eventually, LeRoi Jones. When Parker, and later Miles Davis and Charlie Mingus, shift away from the previous generation's problematic representations, Ellison in "On Bird" recognizes the purpose: "The thrust toward respectability exhibited by the Negro jazzmen of Parker's generation drew much of its immediate fire from their understandable rejection of the traditional entertainer's role—a heritage from the minstrel tradition—exemplified by such an outstanding creative musician as Louis Armstrong" (225). Although the denunciation of what Armstrong represented would lead to "musicians employing a calculated surliness and rudeness," Ellison notes that the result was "a comic reversal" in which "the white audience expects the rudeness as part of the entertainment" (225). For Parker in particular, comedy, rage, and race are particularly salient. Parker's inability to negotiate his rage—whether as a musician or as a person—resembles Clifton's in that the result was the pathologizing of black rage by the mainstream. Clifton would be reduced to the figure of black criminal that must be "policed" by the white power structure. Parker, as Ellison describes it, would become "a sacrificial figure whose struggles against personal chaos, onstage and off, served as entertainment for a ravenous, sensation-starved, culturally disoriented public which had but the slightest notion of its real significance" (227). The white audience attributed Parker's rage to a new wave of African American expression, one that was, in their minds, embedded within African Americans instead of a reaction against minstrelsy and contemporaneous racism. In Clifton's case, the police officers who see him only as a threat in need of policing and the Brotherhood who manipulate him for their own ends combine to reduce him to a criminal and traitor.

Like Clifton, Parker constantly wrestled against being reduced to mere entertainment for white consumption. Ellison states, "No jazzman, not even Miles Davis, struggled harder to escape the entertainer's role than Charlie Parker. The pathos of his life lies in the ironic reversal through which [he struggles to escape what in Armstrong is basically a *make-believe* role of clown" (226–27). Ellison convincingly argues that the musicians of Armstrong's generation, even Dizzy Gillespie during Parker's time, wore their "clown" personas as masks that belied their intelligence and dignity. As a result, they did not become, as Parker and Clifton did, unable to separate the offstage reality from the stage persona. Ellison's fascination with Parker comes through in his description of the artist's musical style: "For all its velocity, brilliance and imagination there is in it a great deal of loneliness, self-deprecation and self-pity" (230). Yet Ellison relates Parker's faults to pathos instead of rage, in much the same way Clifton's death is robbed of its political significance by all but the Invisible Man.

The inability of Clifton and Parker to express their rage effectively results in their self-destruction, Clifton because he cannot find an appropriate avenue for its expression and Parker because he refuses to construct a stage persona that would allow him to negotiate his rage more usefully. Parker, as Amiri Baraka might see it, allowed racist assaults onstage and off to limit his expression of rage to what could be heard through his music, and its consumptiveness bled out in his persona. In the climactic scene of Jones/Baraka's award-winning *Dutchman* (1964), the black male character Clay reveals through Charlie Parker that African American musical expression has been a significant outlet for African American expressions of rage, even when it has been interpreted as genius by white America:

Charlie Parker? Charlie Parker. All the hip white boys scream for Bird. And Bird saying, "Up your ass, feeble-minded ofay! Up your ass." And they sit there talking about the tortured genius of Charlie Parker. Bird would've played not a note of music if he just walked up to East Sixty-Seventh Street and killed the first ten white people he saw. Not a note! (35)

In *Dutchman* Baraka acknowledges that the repression of rage—and the subsequent adoption of white supremacist values—is a foolish, even suicidal, quest. Danielle Allen points out that "anger can rarely make people visible to one another, for it derives from specificity of experience and particularized views of how the world should be" (51). Other expressive forms become necessary to convey the dissatisfaction and engage in constructive debate and provide effective resistance. "Pure anger," Allen recognizes, "may be a motivation to speak," as was often the case for the narrator, "but it cannot determine the form that rhetoric takes if speech is to undo invisibility and facilitate democratic representation" (51). We can identify figures, however, that provide Parker and Clifton with templates for negotiating their rage. For Parker, specific examples were Armstrong and Gillespie. For Clifton, we can see the narrator's grandfather, the doctor at the Golden Day, and Brother Tarp. While Clifton may not know all of these particular men, they represent an African American cultural tradition that created ways for members of its community "to deflect racial provocation and to master and contain pain" (111), as Ellison states. In *Killing Rage*, bell hooks argues that the rage African Americans feel toward "white supremacist aggression . . . is not pathological. It is an appropriate response to injustice. However, if not processed constructively, it can lead to pathological behavior—but so can any rage, irrespective of the cause that serves as a catalyst" (26). African American humor, then, stands as an effective mode of expressing rage without subscribing to stereotypical ideas about African Americans, their humor, and their artists.

Clearly Ellison's major project endures as the freedom to act as individuals and avoid being forced to conform to certain expectations as members of specific groups. The narrator exposes the inherent hypocrisies in the rhetoric of America's democratic and pluralistic ideals that starkly contrast with America's racist practices against African

Americans. Ellison's desire for the achievement of true American democracy does not question whether the intent of the Declaration of Independence and the Constitution was ever full equality. After all, Alfred L. Brophy suggests that Ellison's "conception is not that the Constitution changes, but that we can return to that original covenant. Here, of course, he may be engaging in his own creation myth!" (133). Ellison's optimistic view of the ideals of the Constitution reflects comic rage for his generation, one deeply connected to the integrationist, nonviolent segment of the civil rights movement. As important, the emergence of comic rage in literature would be mirrored by a similar appearance in African American comic tradition, also largely influenced by the sociopolitical climate and ideology from the late 1940s through the early 1960s. One figure who reflects this shift toward a more confrontational black rage in both the comic tradition and African American political life is the comic/activist Dick Gregory. Gregory represents, in his standup and his activism, the same balance between comedy and rage that Ellison achieves in his literature.

2

Dick Gregory, Moms Mabley, and Redd Foxx

Bridging the Gap between Comedy, Rage, and Race

First of all, it is obvious that black humor as a whole did not tend
to reaffirm the outside world's opinion of blacks. On the contrary, no other mechanism in Afro-American expressive culture
was more effective than humor in exposing the absurdity of the
American racial system and in releasing pent-up black aggression
toward it.

Lawrence W. Levine, *Black Culture and Black Consciousness*

Comedy is friendly relations.

Dick Gregory, *Nigger*

Comic rage emerges from a nexus containing African American cultural
tradition that employs uncensored elements of African American humor
as an avenue for the expression of militant rage. Although *Invisible Man*
clearly signaled the possibility of success in such a nexus, other areas in
African America had a direct effect on realizing the potential of comic
rage. The sources of cultural tradition from which Ellison produced the
novel's humor existed from slavery until the 1940s. Yet by the time Ellison's novel appeared, the tone of the humor and rage he deployed had
begun to undergo a significant change. The aggressive strains of humor
that appear in *Invisible Man* became popularized, as dissatisfaction with
Jim Crow segregation led to the birth of the civil rights movement. Historically, the African American comedic tradition thrived beneath the
radar of white mainstream culture. Ellison's novel introduced white
America to black folk humor as an important avenue for negotiating rage

and resisting racist oppression. Similarly, African American comedic tradition in the mid-twentieth century reconfigured stereotypical notions
of humor derived from the blackface minstrel show tradition, primarily
through stand-up comedy.

John Limon's *Stand-up Comedy in Theory, or, Abjection in America*,
which I discussed in my introduction, is particularly pertinent here because the concept of abjection in his work provides a vital link between
stand-up and literature. Operating from the premise that the majority
of nationally known comics in 1960 were heterosexual Jewish men, Limon's exploration of comics like Lenny Bruce, Richard Pryor, and El-
len DeGeneres expands his theory of abjection and discusses its manifestation through the evolution of stand-up in America. Limon makes
clear that Bruce's significant impact on Pryor rests on the outrage that
often became the focal point for the critical study of Bruce's act. Pryor
separates himself by understanding that, as Limon puts it, "To get the
joke . . . is not to join Bruce in his wallowing; it is to revel in the transformative power of joke work" (23). Pryor, and by extension comic rage,
seeks to make his (white) audience understand the nature of his rage,
not so that they might be absolved, but so that their core perceptions
about race and identity will be challenged. Therefore, while some African
American artists use traditional structures of joke work and literature in
order to effectively convey comic rage, the works in this study challenge
those forms in order to maintain the focus on a critique and breakdown
of white supremacist oppression and its byproducts. These advances did
not take place in a vacuum, and comic rage's eventual "challenging [of]
its master" (Kristeva 2) and re-visioning of those structures run virtually
parallel to each other and to the changes in the mid-to-late twentieth
century.

By the early 1950s and into the 1960s, the shift away from the prewar
comedy styles popularized by Eddie Cantor and by Abbott and Costello
was well under way. Mort Sahl critiqued politics in ways that can still
be seen today, Lenny Bruce seemed to challenge the system at every
conceivable turn, and Phyllis Diller attempted to become a one-woman
feminist movement. Meanwhile, African Americans had begun to make
breakthroughs in mainstream America. While many of these figures, like
Jackie Robinson and Nat King Cole, pulled heavily from elements specific to African American culture, they were often forced to adjust certain aspects of those traditions in order to appeal to white audiences.

Similarly, an unprecedented shift in the humor that infuses *Invisible Man* was being played out in the small network of African American night-clubs in segregated sections of rural and urban population centers.

Though African American comedic tradition, like rage, permeated various black cultural expressions before World War II, the realm of stand-up comedy provided the best opportunity for direct, uncensored confrontation of white audiences. In radio, film, and theater, the exploration of African American culture regularly produced distortion. As live performance, stand-up comedy was infinitely more difficult for others to edit, and thus was the perfect complement to literature in the development of comic rage.

Redd Foxx and Moms Mabley were two of the more famous performers on the black comedy network, also known as the Chitlin' Circuit. Both used vulgarity and frequent sexual references, or "blue humor," which limited their exposure; however, their embrace of key tenets of African American comedic tradition would form the foundation of the expression of comic rage. Previously, the only mainstream forms of African American humor confirmed stereotypes of African Americans as buffoonish caricatures. Immersed in African American folk humor, both Mabley and Foxx adopted its tradition of moving from subversion to reversal to confrontation. As Mabley challenged the portrayal of African American women as asexual mammy figures, Foxx pioneered the fusion of humor and rage by introducing the figure of the Comic Bad Nigger into the fabric of African American folk/street culture. Both, however, would remain virtually unknown in the white mainstream until the success of one of their direct comic descendents, Richard Claxton "Dick" Gregory. Eliminating most, if not all, of the sexually explicit language that limited Foxx and Mabley, Gregory still pulled from African American humor's ability to negotiate, as well as confront, issues of race, an inherent aspect of Foxx's and Mabley's acts.

Gregory's crossover fame, which began virtually overnight with a 1961 appearance at the predominantly white Playboy Club, helped create a space in the public sphere where issues of race could be engaged. As with the sit-ins and marches of the first half of the civil rights movement, it became necessary for comics to make their challenges to racism in front of mass white audiences in ways that would not alienate them. Because of Gregory's own involvement in the civil rights movement, especially his relationship with Martin Luther King, he and his routine acted as the perfect vehicles to express the frustrations of African Americans. Through the efforts of Gregory, many comics who utilized unrestricted forms of African American humor, like Mabley and Foxx, were able to achieve mainstream success. Gregory's style of comedy owed its groundbreaking mainstream success to the directness of his racial humor, which pushed the limits of traditional stand-up. His efforts forecast extended works of comic rage that act as abjections because his mixture of humor and rage becomes, in Julia Kristeva's words, "what disturbs identity, system, order. What does not respect border, positions, rules" (4). Although Kristeva frames her discussion of abjection in terms of the criminal or the traitor, this chapter and project view abjection through the lens of the abjected race, African Americans, who are consistently expelled as part of the construction of (white) American identity, yet return and establish their own radical vision that challenges those constructions. Like the transcendent power of the blues that Ellison celebrated, the monster that initiated Gregory's breakthrough created a space where a more transcendent and resistant response to racism could be embraced, one where the combination of humor and militant rage was deployed for all to see. Yet in the end Gregory would abandon stand-up comedy to become a full-time activist and speaker. The militancy and ultimately the restrictiveness of the Black Arts and Black Power movements made the traditional Western structures of art insufficient to fully express rage at much of the racial turmoil of the latter years of the 1960s. Gregory's ability to balance his humor with his rage allows us to chronicle the evolution of comic rage both within and, eventually, outside of Western forms and criteria. We can see his success as a necessary step, one that mirrored the critical and crossover success of Ralph Ellison's *Invisible Man*. Against the backdrop of the late 1950s and early 1960s and the clear cultural influence of Foxx and Mabley, this chapter examines the impact of Dick Gregory, particularly through his 1964 autobiography *Nigger*, on African American political and cultural life through his attempts to balance African American rage and comedy to reverse historical and still pervasive notions of race in America.

Sexy Mama and the Comic Bad Nigger: Moms Mabley and Redd Foxx

About the woman born Loretta Mary Aiken in 1894 and known primarily as Jackie "Moms" Mabley, we know less than about her contemporary male counterparts, although she continues to be remembered by them as the standard by which African American female comics are judged, and many African American male and female comics today list her as an important influence. Prior to Elsie A. Williams's impressive 1995 book *The Humor of Jackie Moms Mabley*, little work was done on her. Lawrence W. Levine's section "Black Laughter" in his 1977 *Black Culture and Black Consciousness* provided one of the few extended considerations of Mabley's role in the African American comedic tradition. Most information about her focused either on the longevity of her career or on her unique position as a woman in a predominantly male field. This is understandable, considering that Mabley was performing in nightclubs as early as the 1920s and as late as the 1970s—and that women in stand-up comedy have remained extremely rare. Although African American women do maintain important places in the African American comic tradition, before Whoopi Goldberg's one-woman show *Live on Broadway* opened at the Lyceum Theater in 1985, virtually no African American women were best known as comediennes. Pearl Bailey and Della Reese, both of whom spoke fondly of Mabley as an influence on them, were known more for their musical, stage, and screen talents than for their humor. Goldberg's 2013 HBO special *Whoopi Goldberg Presents Moms Mabley* not only helped to expand the breadth and depth of material on Mabley but also fortified the link between Mabley and Goldberg in much the same way critics see Alice Walker drawing a literary maternal link to Zora Neale Hurston.

Recent works have examined the folk humor employed by a number of African American women, whether through the novels of Hurston or in folk sayings. Although African American comedic tradition, particularly stand-up, has been dominated by men, there exists a vibrant and influential female humor in African American expressive culture, not only in folk sayings but throughout black female literature, most recently collected in Daryl Cumber Dance's *Honey, Hush!: An Anthology of African American Women's Humor* (1998). While the breadth of African American female humor has yet to be captured in a full-length work comparable to *Invisible Man*, humor remains significant as part of the larger formation of African American female communities in resisting white supremacist patriarchy. Dance, in her introduction to the collection, reveals the "ba-ad woman" as known for her "verbal dexterity" and points out: "One of the distinctive marks of the black woman's verbal power is her *sassiness*. Both in her speech and her behavior, the sassy female is impudent, saucy, vigorous, lively, smart, and stylish" (2). Mabley embodied a black female tradition that moved beyond traditional (white) female humor while subverting patriarchal assumptions by white and black men. Williams argues, for instance, that Mabley's insistence "I don't do no domestic" was a refusal to perform the "duties expected of housekeepers or maids, to which so many black women were confined" (71). Mabley's move away from casting herself in the domestic space, in her real life as well as her humor, contrasts with stereotypical notions of African American female work and traditional female subject matter. Williams posits that the "context of her response, however, is most applicable to the kind of comic routines she performed. Unlike several of her white counterparts, such as Phyllis Diller, Erma Bombeck, Betty MacDonald, and Jean Kerr, Mabley generally excluded focusing on domestic duties as sources of humor" (71). The difference between Mabley's act and those of her white female contemporaries reflects the gulf between white female critiques of patriarchy and black female critiques of the intersections of race and gender.

Appearing regularly at the Apollo Theater for much of her career, Mabley, according to Watkins, "foreshadowed the shift to direct social commentary and standup comic techniques that would define humor by the late fifties" (393). The length of Mabley's career and her role as a comedienne deserve more study, to be sure, particularly her significance to African American comic tradition. Like Foxx, Mabley was notorious for her use of blue humor in her acts. Both comics also drew from the underground tradition of African American humor that frequently confronted racist oppression and helped both the performer and the audience to negotiate their rage at that oppression. Also, like the other acts, Mabley was funny and entertaining. As a performer influenced by vaudeville, Mabley sang, danced, and told jokes. The variety of her act speaks to the depth of her talent. It comes as no surprise, then, that she balanced the entertaining and the openly political with ease. While her jokes about younger and older men drew consistent and extended laughter, they also clearly challenged historical notions of gender dynamics, particularly

African American female sexuality, acting as abjections to male rhetoric that objectifies the female body and marginalizes women generally and African American women especially. Mabley, in contrast to Foxx, constructed an act that was primarily a celebration of African American vernacular culture and collective resistance. Much of her popularity with African American audiences arose from her reflection of a distinct and recognizable African American cultural tradition.

While Foxx's use of folk humor emerged mostly from the spontaneity and aggressiveness of his verbal performances, Mabley's more relaxed persona encouraged an inclusive communal experience. Mabley's popularity stemmed in large part from an almost total immersion in African American folk tradition. Her wit and material emerged from an experience that most in all-black audiences connected to. Levine suggests, for example, that "the familiarity of Moms Mabley's humor consisted not in its material—the bulk of which was original and topical—but in its style and intent. Her jokes were her own, but the contours of her humor were so traditional that it was probably indistinguishable from folk humor to her audiences" (364). Instead of a constant confrontation with her audience, Mabley acted as an encouraging voice that made the audience feel safe and celebrate their cultural solidarity. Affectionately referring to her audience as her "children," she pursued a different tactic from Foxx's verbal assaults. Specifically, Mabley established an atmosphere that directly connected to the lived experiences of her black audience. As Levine notes, "Recognition was the focal point of Moms Mabley's humor. Many of her jokes were familiar" (363). Mabley fostered the impression that she was dispensing homespun mother wit. This began with the clothes she wore for her act, clothes that differed markedly from her own more stylish outfits. "From the twenties onward," Williams writes, "Mabley began to develop the Granny persona and started to wear the floppy hat, the multicolored house dress, oversized bedroom shoes, and to refer to herself constantly as Moms" (48). Offstage she often wore men's clothes, and many of her friends claimed that she was a lesbian. For Mabley, then, the intersections of race, gender, and sexuality might not inform the representation of her humor, but they certainly impacted its style and substance. She rooted her humor in conversations that mature working-class African American women would have among themselves.

Mabley's methods, in acting as a bridge between minstrel tradition and the middle of the century, often took her act in directions that her peers did not conceive or could not execute. Williams notes that "Mabley's humor might be an old maid or a widow, yet she is aggressive enough to direct and control her own sexual needs" (82). Her most popular routines, usually involving her desire for younger men and her derision of older ones, are proof of this. In one show, she commented that one man she met was "old as water and twice as weak!"[1] Her expressions of desire for young men signified on historical male desire for younger women to reinvigorate them or to resolve their midlife crises. Playing on the assumptions embedded in the more acceptable pairing of older men and younger women, Mabley challenged the role of the passive female object that was often part of male comic routines. Williams posits, "Mabley's humor attacking the old man exacts the justified retribution for sexism in traditional American culture. Moreover, her frank discussions on male impotence provide sexual catharsis for women and invite females to celebrate their sexuality, to be at home sexually in their own bodies and to cast off male domination" (82). Even today, comedy continues to be a primarily male space, and much of the material centers on discussions of women through a patriarchal lens. While female comics invert these assumptions in their acts, they maintain the dichotomy of male subject and female object. Mabley's act becomes groundbreaking because it mirrors the abject in toppling both racism and sexism. African American women are an especially marginalized group, and often they have been forced to respond solely to race and only in the manner forged by African American women. In challenging stereotypes both of race and of gender, Mabley's work moves beyond the "object" that reinforces white supremacist capitalist patriarchy. Like other works of comic rage, Mabley's act cannot, in Kristevan terms, "seem to agree with the [object's] rules of the game. And yet from its place of banishment, the abject does not cease challenging its master" (2). Works of comic rage are "banished" because they resist easy categorization, particularly in popular literary responses to stereotypes of African Americans. Those literary responses—passing novels and protest fiction, for example—take on a tragic tone that maintains power dynamics even as they seek to reveal the destructive results of those dynamics. As an African American woman, Mabley becomes doubly important, not simply because of her historical significance but because her brand of comedy often challenges the dynamics of gender as well as race. In her own act Mabley addresses these myths, both through her refusal to be silent on important social issues and through her frequent jokes drawing attention to her sexual desires. Audiences know, for example, that underlying Mabley's distaste for old men is their inability to please her aesthetically and sexually. Thus she makes her sexuality central to the audience's view of her, resisting the erasure of herself as a sexual being that most white audience members would attempt.

By engaging with material previously associated with men, Mabley redefines mainstream perceptions about female humor. Yet she remains part of a larger African American female tradition that fearlessly engages themes beyond the domestic sphere. Usually involving attempts to turn racial and sexual stereotypes on their heads, African American female humor moved from daily mother wit to sexual ridicule to racial critique even as it maintained black folk tradition's ability to act as a buffer against the threat of pain, isolation, and death. Sometimes the humor counteracts painful stories by creating a female community, as in Hurston's *Their Eyes Were Watching God* (1937), Ntozake Shange's *for colored girls who have considered suicide/when the rainbow is enuf* (1977), and Alice Walker's *The Color Purple* (1983). In other cases it attacks racial and/or sexual myths. One instance of the latter is the old folk tale quoted by Dance in which a widow's minister asks her, "How in the world is you gon' be havin' a baby and yo' husband been dead more dan a year!" The punch line: "'He might be dead,' she retorted, 'but I ain't'" (377). Mabley uses a similar joke in her routine, substituting the husband's one year with twenty and making the age of the mother's child fifteen. The joke plays on expectations of female versus male behavior. The overt implication is that the woman cannot control her sexual desires, but the tone of Mabley's act casts the minister's expectation that she not fulfill those desires as ludicrous. Mabley's humor, then, becomes part of a larger tradition of African American female comedic experience, one with which her audiences on the Chitlin' Circuit—particularly her female audience—were likely to be familiar. Playing on the image of the kindly grandmother who seems at the center of the folk elements in black comedic tradition, she nonetheless rejects the image of the black mammy who dedicates herself to the service of a white family's needs. In its place Mabley fosters a style featuring the sensibilities and experiences of predominantly black audiences, making them feel part of a communal experience and a collective resistance. Dick Gregory would eventually tailor the warmth Mabley exuded for use in front of his white audiences during the height of his popularity, even as he openly challenged racist narratives that reinforced white supremacist oppression.

Similarly, Mabley's performances represented a communal rejection of the devaluing of African American culture by the white mainstream. Such rejection was demonstrated by a refusal to accept the images that were prevalent during the early and mid-twentieth century, images that related solely to the promotion of white superiority. Alongside the vicious distortion of African Americans portrayed in *Birth of a Nation*, African Americans were only able to play comic fools to white heroes, such as Stepin Fetchit, or parental figures who helped whites achieve *their* potential. Save in the films of Oscar Micheaux, African Americans found themselves at the mercy of mainstream representation in film, on the stage, or in the media. Usually, as in the case of minstrel shows, these portrayals did not involve the lives of African Americans beyond the white presence. What Mabley's humor sought to do was to subvert destructive perceptions of African Americans specifically and, perhaps more important, of African American culture in general. Because of its familiarity to the audience, Mabley's humor safely and constructively engaged issues of race. Where most challenges in public spaces are forced to adopt the majority culture's language and cultural ideals in order to make the case for equality and legitimacy, African American humor reconfigures racial power dynamics and hierarchies to centralize African American vernacular performance and cultural experience in attacking destructive portraits of blackness. Mabley's act signified on traditional ideas of humor and images of African Americans in the content of the act. It also, like *Invisible Man*, signified on previous conceptions of African American humor demonstrated in the blackface minstrel show or in nostalgic literary representations of the antebellum South. Mabley's performances worked as an effective counternarrative in which both performer and audience contributed in the retelling of the African American experience in America, not only from an African American perspective but in a language that could alternately heal and critique, entertain and challenge. Mabley, then, can be seen as one of the most representative figures of the historical traditions and myriad possibilities in African American comedic tradition.

Mabley's friendly tone, however, does not diminish the rage that she expressed in her humor. Through her act we can view a form of overt collective resistance. Mabley did not seek to establish a traditional comic/

audience relationship in which a distinct line between comedian and the audience is rarely crossed. Given the call-and-response nature of African American vernacular experience, such a relationship would seem unlikely. Mabley sought to go beyond mere entertainment. Her acts were equal parts celebration, cultural sharing, and elderly advice. Mabley's routines rested on the presentation of what Williams describes as "homespun folk imagery, colloquial sayings, stories, and jokes commonly known by the African American community—a body of lore which points to the perpetuation of a cultural tradition from the 'woman of words' to the community and, equally, from the community to the 'woman of words'" (78). This symbiotic relationship between performer and audience affirms the effectiveness of African American cultural tradition in transcending, and at times resisting, the forces and products of oppression.

Mabley's commentary about racial politics frequently inverted the power dynamic through her constant references to President Lyndon Johnson as "boy" or her claims that Mrs. Eisenhower referred to her as "Mrs. Mabley," both inversions of the linguistic elements of the racial power dynamics that African Americans encounter in their daily interactions with whites. Mabley demonstrated an awareness that went beyond domestic concerns, and within these particular themes we can begin to see her plainspoken grandmother persona as an opportunity to launch commonsense critiques of stereotypical images of African American womanhood. The clearest manifestation of the fusion of comedy and resistance in Mabley's act came in her subversion of popular images of African American women. Mabley's especial target was the mammy figure, an image of African American women that dominated movies and popular culture for decades. The asexuality of the character became central in casting the mammy figure, as celebrated a construction as the Stepin Fetchit/Uncle Tom figure had been in representing the loyal, subservient African American male. Although usually sassy and stern, mammies ultimately served as trusted and irreplaceable confidantes, informants, and mother figures to whites. Implanted in the contemporary imagination by Hattie McDaniel's historic, Oscar-winning portrayal of Mammy in the 1939 movie *Gone with the Wind*, the mammy figure remains, according to some recent critics, a key image in white American perceptions of African American women.

Mabley deliberately separated herself from the mammy figure that many audiences, particularly white, would have associated with her. Yet she maintained a connection to the "subject" of the Mammy figure even as she continued to threaten it, appropriating the figure in her friendliness if not in her dress. The dress, often a casual housedress, clearly signaled her unwillingness to clean for someone else. The stage became her house, where she held court and bowed to no one else's rules. Often the process of establishing the stage as hers began with her opening words: "No *damn* MAMMY, *Moms* / I don't know nothing / 'bout no log cabin; I ain't never seen / No log cabin . . . Split level in the suburbs, *Baby!*" The emphatic rejection of the label "Mammy" immediately proclaimed Mabley's awareness of historical constructions of female blackness, and her intention to openly defy them through her act. In a similar routine, Mabley signified on another popular manifestation of the Mammy character. Sidling onstage, she would demand of the lighting crew, "Make me look like Lena Horne—*not Beulah, LENA!*" Williams highlights the dichotomy revealed through this comment: "Mabley's allusions evoke the two dominant female entertainment stereotypes: the tragic mulatto and the mammy" (99). In casting African American women as asexual mammy figures, tragic mulattas, or sexually exotic, one of the major omissions was life outside the white gaze or presence. There existed no predominantly African American world where the internal lives of mammy characters were explored in depth. The limited representations left no room for the complexity or diversity of characters, which might subvert hegemonic ideas of African American inferiority. Although the comment fails to provide an interrogation of the dichotomous viewing of African American women and beauty, my interest lies in Mabley's appropriation of the mammy figure in order to expel the figure from mainstream constructions of African American womanhood.

Williams points out that "Beulah—the comic domestic—played by Hattie McDaniel, Ethel Waters and Louise Beavers—suggests the Aunt Jemima mammy figure who was essentially the loyal servant and nurturer catering to and serving the needs of whites and having few physical or emotional needs herself" (99). Though it started as a radio show, the thirty-minute comedy become so popular that it was eventually aired on television from 1950 to 1953. McDaniel was the first African American woman to play the role, after two white actors—one woman and one man—initially portrayed Beulah during the radio show. The casting of McDaniel, Waters, and Beavers, African American women who were acclaimed for their movie roles as mammies, represented a clear desire to transfer the specific construction of the mammy figure from film to television. Although, as Donald Bogle notes in *Primetime Blues: African Americans on Network Television*, "Both radio and television attempted to present Beulah within some semblance of an African American cultural context," ultimately "Beulah's purpose in life was maintaining order and decorum for those she willingly served" (22–23). Mabley's rejection of the mammy figure popularized in *Gone with the Wind* and maintained by *Beulah* exposes the intersection of race and gender, not simply limited to issues of beauty, but to issues of sexuality and cultural recognition as well. For instance, Mabley's frequent references to her sexual activities can be seen as a direct response to Beulah's relationship to her boyfriend Bill Jackson. As Bogle informs us, "Beulah and Bill's relationship was a safe comic romance (not a vibrant adult coupling that might make us believe Beulah's got a sexuality after all) that was unfulfilling (and perhaps unconsummated) for Beulah" (22). Similarly, Mabley centralized African American cultural experience in her routines, an important distinction from the mammy's primary role as caregiver of whites and adopter of white middle-class values and ideals.

So, while her initial appearance played toward the part of the traditional mammy figure, her overall routine acted as a form of subversion, much like Bert Williams's performances in blackface. Both performers elicited sympathy and explored a complexity that traditional (white) blackface performers ignored. Mabley not only arose out of the same minstrel show tradition, but she also engaged in the African American cultural tradition of masking, like Bert Williams and Louis Armstrong, in order to confront mainstream perceptions of blackness. African American audiences recognized the need for masking and the humanity, rage, and awareness behind it. The recognition between Mabley and her audience, fostered by the audience's own acts of masking in front of whites, strengthened the communal connection Mabley encouraged. Both artist and audience understood the use of the mask not only as a tool of survival but also as a site from which critiques could be launched against the racist constructions on which the mask was based. Levine argues that for Mabley the "humor of exposure and absurdity" was a style that "figured prominently in her repertory" (365). Mabley integrated her specific comic critiques into the form of the minstrel show, particularly the stand-up routines and the music. In one routine, Mabley would announce that she was attempting to perform an opera. After she and her pianist Luther engaged in a play of black folk speech versus standard English, Elsie Williams relates, "Luther would shift to what he thought Moms wanted—ostentatious and intricate piano chords. Moms would immediately interrupt Luther, to signify on him, making him the comic butt, a role which early on had been reserved for the female in the male-dominated profession" (120–21). At this point Mabley began her song against the backdrop of recognizable popular tunes. The content, however, was altered to comment on issues such as "ghetto life, segregation, and racism" (121). One such routine found Mabley signifying on James Meredith's integration of the University of Mississippi. Relaying her defiance of the white South with comic verve, Mabley resembled the Signifying Monkey of African American folklore as her verbal bravado neutralized her physical disadvantage: "[The Klan] don't scare me with their bomb threats / I'll say what I wanna say! / And ain't a damn thing they can do about it / 'Cause I ain't going down there no way!" (121). Switching smoothly between tunes, Mabley at one moment would bemoan "School days, school days / [Mississippi Governor] Barnett said, 'To hell with-the-congressional-rule days!" and soon after hilariously proclaims, "So, take me out to the ball game (to the campus) / And if we don't win it's a shame. / But with our trust in the Lord / And the National Guard / We'll get in just the same" (121–22). Though some critics viewed her humor as confirmation of the stereotypical images of African Americans, her jokes maintained a definite confrontation of racial stereotypes and oppression.

For instance, in one of her acts during the 1960s, Mabley informed her audience, "You know the first thing I would do if I was President? I would give a c-e-r-t-a-i-n Southern Governor a job as Ambassador to the Congo and let him go crazy looking for a men's restroom with WHITE on it" (119). Although not referring specifically to any one southern governor, this joke conjures up images of infamous segregationist governors Ross Barnett of Mississippi and George Wallace of Alabama, with Mabley pointing out the ludicrous and degrading practice of segregation by conveying the hilarious image of powerful racist whites rendered helpless when their worst nightmare—being surrounded by African Americans not subservient to them—gets fully realized. Mabley used the minstrel show mask to her advantage and, unlike jazz musician Charlie Parker and Tod Clifton in Invisible Man, prevented her rage from overwhelming her through the use of various forms of resistance, whether in the open rejection of the mammy figure, the initiation of African American collective resistance, or the method of "exposure and absurdity" in her humor.

Mabley's persona would resonate loudest in the style of Dick Gregory, as he did not so much confront his audience as invite them into his comic universe. Operating in a tone of inclusion at the moment of sociopolitical change, Gregory removed the mask that Mabley and others subverted without losing the ability to ridicule the racist assumptions that continued to plague the country. Gregory's unmasking revealed another important comic influence, one whose fearless confrontation of white racism transformed one of the most notorious figures in American and African American imagination—namely, the Bad Nigger—into an uncensored viewing of race and discrimination in America.

In *The Autobiography of Malcolm X* (1965), as Malcolm recalls his days as Malcolm Little, he tells us that the nickname Detroit Red was given to him as a way to distinguish between the three red-haired, conked, Midwestern African American men known as Red in Harlem at that time. While one, named St. Louis Red, was part of the criminal underworld that Malcolm was involved in before his conversion to Islam, the other, known as Chicago Red, became friends with Malcolm at a speakeasy where the two worked. Malcolm states, "Chicago Red was the funniest dishwasher on this earth. Now he's making his living being funny as a nationally known stage and nightclub comedian. I don't see any reason why old Chicago Red would mind me telling that he is Redd Foxx" (99). As referenced in the introduction, Malcolm's autobiography may not qualify as a work of comic rage, but Malcolm himself stands as a crucial figure here. More specifically, he remains, more than forty years after his death, the most recognizable purveyor of African American rage in late twentieth-century America. As Cornel West writes in *Race Matters*, "Malcolm X articulated black rage in a manner unprecedented in American history. His style of communicating this rage bespoke a boiling urgency and an audacious sincerity" (95). Malcolm's militant rage permeates this book as the veritable engine that drives comic rage. According to West, Malcolm's rage emerged from his love of African Americans resulting in a psychic conversion that Malcolm saw as a significant mode of resistance: "Malcolm X's notion of psychic conversion holds that black people must no longer view themselves through white lenses. He claims black people will never value themselves as long as they subscribe to a standard of valuation that devalues them" (96). West rejects the contention that

Malcolm's rage was an inherently violent or destructive response, even though it did not reject violence as a legitimate option for an oppressed people. Malcolm avoided allowing his rage to consume his rhetoric and his life by employing other, life-affirming responses. Like Pryor's use of humor to prevent his domestic troubles, drug use, and near-death experience from destroying him, Malcolm used humor to augment the rage he directed at racism. Malcolm's characterization of Foxx is how many African Americans viewed him long before Foxx's success on television or with predominantly white audiences. Called the King of the Party Records because of the huge popularity of his notoriously dirty albums at parties, Foxx continues to be considered the best comic of his generation and, in relation to this study, stands as the linchpin that connects comic rage in the early part of the twentieth century to the present.

Beginning with the 1955 release of his first LP, *Laff of the Party*, Foxx would release dozens of comedy records, eventually selling 20 million copies and making him a household name within the African American community. Malcolm's description of Foxx suggests that his ability to make people laugh was not limited to the stage, confirming Della Reese's comment that Foxx was "God's pure humor."[2] The spontaneous feel of his stage act, which often involved pacing, confrontational comments to the audience, and constant drinking and cigarette smoking, differed greatly from Gregory's more structured routines. Gregory, in his introduction to Dempsey J. Travis's *The Life and Times of Redd Foxx*, says, "Foxx was really the king of comedy and timing. He had one of the fastest comedic minds on the planet. I was good at what I did but mine was planned and premeditated" (viii). By the time he encountered Malcolm at Jimmy's Chicken Shack on Seventh Avenue in Harlem, the man born with the name John Elroy Sanford in 1922 had dropped out of high school, moved to New York with friends to make an attempt at music, and tried his hand several times at professional comedy. Though most recognize Foxx from the highly successful sitcom *Sanford and Son* (1972–77), his contribution to African American comedy can be traced to his days in the 1940s and 1950s on the Chitlin' Circuit. Many younger comics, among them Timmie Rogers and George Kirby, were beginning to bring a new type of African American image into the mainstream. Foxx refused to abandon his specific style to fit their mold. This may account for his inability, like Mabley's, to achieve mainstream success until late in the 1960s—a lingering sore subject for Foxx, who had watched for years as his white peers were acclaimed as geniuses of their form. Perhaps this explains why Foxx's more direct style, which included raunchy material and overt challenges to racism, would come closer to the embodiment of the Bad Nigger of African American folklore.

Other African American comics, to be sure, drew on the folk humor that was the backbone of African American humor. Most, however, attempted to adjust their routines' more controversial elements to appeal to whites. Yet we can draw clear lines from the celebrated, groundbreaking work of Lenny Bruce to Foxx's aggressive style and uncensored use of critical elements of African American comic tradition. Considering whether Bruce's act is "pure urban squalor," John Limon argues that in achieving abjection, Bruce "does not annihilate the abandoned repulsiveness of the city" but "commutes it on behalf of a commuting society," namely suburbanites, which "demands to be outraged in order not to be outraged" (23). The audience's response creates a paradox in which the comically expressed aggression gets rejected in favor of attempts by whites, "for the sake of lawns and laundered cash, to leave behind profanity and, in the process, also the sacred" (23). Thus, while Limon understandably celebrates "the transformative power of joke work" in African American stand-up, especially Pryor's ability to make the horrors and tragedies of his life hilarious, the dismissal of rage negates the joke. For the comics discussed here, joke work articulates rage for an audience often forced into silence in front of the larger society. Before Pryor, however, the comic articulation of rage had been developing in the mainstream for at least a decade.

Foxx himself recognizes Bruce as significant to his own opportunities as a stand-up. In *The Redd Foxx Encyclopedia of Black Humor*, Foxx points out that Bruce "was honest. He said things that were not conventional to say. But they needed to be said and Lenny was the first to say them. He was crucified for telling the truth. He was a great influence on me" (235). Watkins argues that Bruce's style, identical to "the street wit of the black musicians and night people with whom he associated," demonstrated "a profane contempt that was both alien and frightening to mainstream America" (485). In his relationship to African American comedy, Bruce can recall Elvis Presley's adoption of African American R&B and gospel styles in his recordings and musical performances. However, unlike Presley, Bruce should not be seen as a simple imitator of an African American style or as a pawn in attempts to put a white face on an African American art form. Bruce's more direct commentary on white middle-class values alone would seem to place him in the same tradition as African American humor. Watkins believes, for instance, that unlike "blackface minstrels, whose corked-up appearance and vernacular speech often disguised an essentially non-black or anti-black spirit, Bruce, in some of his material, conveyed a comic *attitude* reflecting prominent aspects of genuine black American humor" (485). Bruce's whiteness made it possible to bring previously underground characteristics of African American humor to white mainstream audiences who did not see African American comics without fearing racial backlash. Watkins credits Bruce as a pioneer because in using "the satiric profanity of the toasts created by black hipsters, hustlers, and pimps, he unveiled the blasphemous, often obscene perceptions of African-American humor at its least assimilated levels" (486). Despite his early death in 1966, the same year the term "stand-up" was coined, Bruce's attempts to bring elements of African American comic tradition to the mainstream should not be downplayed, as he made possible their eventual display in front of white audiences.

Considering the impact Bruce would have on Foxx, we can see in Foxx's act the same defiance in attitude and style coupled with the centrality of uncensored African American folk/street humor that Bruce attempted. Where Bruce's use of this humor was radically different from his white counterparts', Foxx's act—despite being in the same vein of African American comedic tradition—ran counter to the impulse of African American comics in the 1960s who were attempting to appeal to white audiences. In fact, Foxx's maintenance of a very specific African American persona separates him from other artists of his time. As Watkins says, "Unlike the other comedians who broke into the mainstream comedy during the sixties, Foxx delivered his humor in an unmistakably black voice," and his "relentlessly aggressive stage image" communicated "a pride and belligerence that was associated with more militant factions of the African-American community" (516). In the image they projected onstage, many of the newer comics reflected the nonviolent, integrationist philosophy represented by figures like King and organizations like the Student Nonviolent Coordinating Committee (SNCC) that dominated the late 1950s and early 1960s. The comics' forays into racial issues in front of integrated audiences sought to reverse the previous stereotypes of African Americans without alienating the white middle class, to whose privilege they wished to gain access. Foxx rejected this more ingratiating style—which did not involve "Tomming," as Gregory would point out—for an unflinching ridicule of racial stereotypes that resembled Malcolm X's blunt, fearless challenges to his white audiences. Watkins goes further, arguing that "Foxx conjured up visions of insolence and independence more reminiscent of black folklore's Bad Nigger. Of the sixties comics, only Gregory challenged in a similar manner, but since his defiance was intellectual, it triggered a cerebral response" (516). Though Gregory's alteration of certain aspects of folk humor was necessary to make its presentation in the white mainstream possible, we cannot ignore the importance of the figure of the Bad Nigger that Foxx embodied, which underlay Gregory's ability to be (as Gerald Nachman quotes him describing himself) "an intelligent black man standin' flatfooted" in front of white audiences "tellin' 'em about their business" (485). The Bad Nigger, into whom Foxx inserted a distinct black comic voice, remains one of the most controversial characters in the white and black imagination.

In *"Born in a Mighty Bad Land": The Violent Man in African American Folklore and Fiction*, Jerry Bryant writes that the Bad Nigger, also referred to as the bad man, "was the white man's worst dream: the slave or (after Emancipation) the laborer who refused to knuckle under. . . . He was the out-of-control black man, the surly slacker, the belligerent troublemaker, and occasionally the killer of whites" (2). Unlike the trickster figures the rabbit and monkey, there exists no masking between the bad man and his target. The bad man's defiance of mainstream values and laws is not for the purpose of humor or subversion. He focuses on, as Levine suggests, "vanquishing [his] adversaries without hesitation and without remorse" (408). Emerging from the "Postbellum black songs" that "are studded with boasting, threats, and the language of violence," tales of the bad men were often based on the exploits of real figures such as John Hardy and Railroad Bill. Their encounters with whites, in which the bad men continually elude capture and leave dead bodies in their wake, resulted in the "moral hard man" being viewed with pride by African Americans because his fearlessness reflected their own militant rage at white oppressive power. Beyond the ballads, toasts, and stories that involve the bad man, there exist more specific and current manifestations of the Bad Nigger. In the early twentieth century, the most notorious was Jack Johnson, the first black heavyweight champion. Johnson infuriated whites not only with his dominance in the ring but with his open defiance and flamboyance outside it.[3] Of particular significance was his relationships with white women. His three wives and numerous mistresses were white, a direct flouting of the sexual taboos Schuyler and Ellison later ridiculed in their novels. The same fearlessness would appear in Foxx's act. If Mabley took on the persona of a mammy figure in order to subvert popular thinking about African American women and sexuality, Foxx became the Bad Nigger to lend authenticity to his comic claims and boasts.

The Bad Nigger has been barely able, if ever, to contain his dissatisfaction with racism, and he has often resorted to violence to express his rage. The bad man, Bryant suggests, "may be the product of a suppressed collective rage, his violence a displacement of his anger from the white oppressor to the less dangerous targets of other blacks. But he is seldom formulated in those terms" (6). This seems due to the bad man's general refusal, or inability, to employ other forms of resistance beyond violence. Surrounded by hegemonic constructions that devalue blackness, he also contends with limited forms of resistance, which makes self-destruction more likely. Bryant sees the Bad Nigger as "unconcerned with white presence," and "therefore an unusual window upon the inner life of the unlettered African American community" (6). Despite the intimate relationship between the Bad Nigger and the underclass African American community that produced him, there remains an uneasiness about the unpredictability of his actions. Although elements of heroism surface in the bad man's confrontational lifestyle, he was not necessarily heroic. Levine points out that "whatever needs the bad men filled . . . , black folk refused to romantically embellish or sentimentalize them. Missing entirely from black lore was the Robin Hood figure so familiar in the folklore of other Americans and other cultures" (415). Although a number of literary representations of the bad man have attempted to construct a more overt political purpose to his actions, his violence against African Americans inevitably reveals the more characteristic apolitical, amoral violence that the bad man enacts. So while Bigger Thomas's murder of Mary in Native Son can initially be seen as a nationalist blow against a corrupt white system, the murder of Bessie complicates such a strict nationalist reading.

The reluctance of African Americans to cast the bad man as a revolutionary figure lies in the realization that some Bad Nigger figures— as opposed to the "moral hard men" Levine discusses—enact violence and terror upon those in their own community. In works of comic rage, then, the violence that the Bad Nigger executes transforms into rhetorical attacks and structural re-visioning. For example, a comic might level his/her ridiculing gaze on some African American behavior or revel in the verbal destruction of hecklers.[4] Unlike literary representations of the Bad Nigger which, according to Bryant, "make him a man who has mastered the violent methods of the conventional 'bad nigger' but who has graduated to bourgeois self-control and renounced violence for the rewards that middle class conformity gives him" (7), the humor of Foxx seeks no such suppression or co-optation. Instead, Foxx's routine funnels the rage the Bad Nigger typically expresses into verbal assaults and overt rhetorical defiance of the white mainstream's cultural norms. Here the Comic Bad Nigger distinguishes himself from other performers, and comic rage emerges in his act as a result. His primary mode of attack, humor, inherently neutralizes violence without dismissing the militant rage at the core of the desired violence. The Comic Bad Nigger thus remains connected to the tradition of the Bad Nigger who, as Levine states, "express[es] the profound anger festering and smoldering among the oppressed—anger that we have seen expressed in myriad ways in black lore; anger that could suddenly burst forth" (418), while avoiding traditional connections between black rage and violence. Verbal assaults replace physical ones, forcing the white audience to recognize its role in the oppression of African Americans.

The frustration seen in his act demonstrates Foxx's less militant solutions to racism. Like the Bad Nigger, Foxx displays a disdain for any mode of resistance other than direct confrontation. For example, in his *Encyclopedia of Black Humor*, Foxx comments on the strategy of nonviolent marching in the civil rights movement: "Ain't no way I'm gonna let a cracker go upside my head with a stick and I do nothin' but hum 'We Shall Overcome.' I'm going to cut him" (239). Foxx views the marchers' refusal to fight back as an act of submission, which he cannot conceive, much less accept. His response, in his own mind at least, registers simply: stab the police, regardless of the consequences. As a Comic Bad Nigger, however, Foxx does not enact the violence that he threatens, although his portrayal implies that he might if threatened. Instead he uses humor to point out what he sees as the absurdity in not responding violently. For him, an inherent contradiction exists in police officers attacking marchers advocating for their civil rights. The point echoes Malcolm X's contention that violence against police brutality or white assault should not be considered violence but self-defense. The humor emerges from Foxx's directness, which hints at a truth that African American audience members recognize in themselves: the inherent and reasonable desire to defend themselves, despite the strategic rationale behind nonviolence. Again, however, such comments made Foxx a less desirable comic in front of mainstream white audiences, which might react negatively to his threats of violence.

Regardless, Watkins reports, for instance, that there eventually arose "more belligerent black folk heroes on the horizon who would bring a new, disdainfully satiric dimension to African-American humor" (463). The addition of the Bad Nigger attitude to African American humor would introduce a more direct challenge and harsher critique of white racism.[5] Foxx's material reflected the four distinguishing characteristics of the Bad Nigger as set forth by William H. Wiggins Jr.: "(1) an utter disregard for death and danger, (2) a great concentration on sexual virility, (3) a great extravagance in buying cars, clothes, etc., and (4) an insatiable love of having a good time" (54). In much of Foxx's act, race went unmentioned, giving way to frequent comments on women and sex, parties and sex, money and sex. Appearing onstage in flashy suits and jewelry, Foxx drank and smoked and waxed philosophical on any number of issues. Often in his shows he would unleash a litany of toasts, all involving some sexual act. A typical sequence recorded in Watkins's compendium *African American Humor* begins with "What's better than a tiger in your tank? Lipstick on your dipstick," then switches to "Toast. What's the difference between a Peeping Tom and a pickpocket? A pickpocket snatches watches!" (207). Toasts—rhymed narratives over a beat, proclaiming the exploits of either another character or the speaker—have been a hallmark of African American vernacular expression. In his routine, Foxx would synthesize his toasts into a rhythm that fit the dynamics of stand-up comedy, while the routine stayed purely sexual, privileging the exploits of his subject alongside daily concerns of the toilet, crime, and the gas tank.

Foxx's humor, like the figure of the Bad Nigger, never concerned itself so much with racial politics as with establishing a clearly aggressive tone. In relating a story involving President Lyndon Johnson and the first African American mayor, Carl B. Stokes of Cleveland, Foxx couched it within the black/white sexual taboo: When Johnson asks Stokes about the size of his penis, Stokes says, "Well, just before I have sex I always beat it on the bedpost four times." Johnson goes home and attempts this, whereupon Foxx delivers the punch line: "Lady Bird woke up and said, 'Is that you Carl?'" (210). One wonders how much of the Bad Nigger he summoned onstage was the result of years filled with frequent disappointments and the mainstream's failure to recognize his talent. Foxx's years in virtual obscurity seem also directly related to his specific style. Yet Foxx seemed to find in comedy a way to channel his rage into a constructive act that forced an interrogation of racial stereotypes and pushed the comic edge. Advice from friends and others to abandon his use of vulgarity and sexually explicit jokes would be disregarded, not because of his inability to succeed at it—as the hilarity of *Sanford and Son* attests—but out of a repudiation of convention and censorship.

Many have criticized *Sanford and Son* for Foxx's unflattering role as the lazy, irascible junkman father. The character of Fred Sanford, a name that Foxx got from his deceased biological brother, was often considered a negative role model and a borderline stereotype. This assessment certainly has merit, given how many white audiences overlook the show's racial critique and blindly accept the show as simple broad comedy. *Sanford and Son*, though, reflects Foxx's influential and politically charged humor. In Joe X. Price's *Redd Foxx, B.S. (Before Sanford)*, the chapter "The Real Sanford" by Foxx himself states, "I believe in fighting prejudice in my own way. I have faith in the power of humor. With it you can fight bigotry, hate, anything at all. I like to think that after people have heard my act, they may go out with a better attitude" (106). Discussing the Redd Foxx Club that he opened and eventually partnered with Bill Cosby, Foxx revealed that "one thing I didn't like that [Cosby] did was to take down all my pictures of show biz people off the walls and put up militant sayings and militant pictures. Nobody on the wall was smiling. When I saw it, it affected me so bad I had them all down again" (118). Aside from showing a side of Cosby that contrasts with his popular color-blind image, this comment demonstrates that for Foxx, like the importance for Ellison of producing good art, politics never took precedence over the technique of humor.

In his *Encyclopedia of Black Humor*, Foxx advised younger comics, "You've got to learn your craft, and comedy takes craftsmanship. The more you work at it, the better you will be at it" (236). It is perhaps because of this that Foxx's transition from Comic Bad Nigger to lovable television character should not be surprising. His shift to a more main-stream-friendly form of comedy was due to his versatility. Nevertheless, Foxx's comedy, because of its rootedness in African American folk/street humor, contained inherent observations on race. These observations were highlighted by Foxx's antagonistic tone. Aside from critics' failure to mention the importance of a show that featured a black-owned business, the understudied presence of the African American folk humor pervasive throughout the show, virtually unseen in television history, is particularly vexing. Among the most important elements was "the dozens" frequently engaged in between Foxx and comedienne Lawanda Page, who played his sister-in-law. Page also represented Foxx's larger de-sire to help African American comics gain exposure to mainstream audi-ences. Many comics that Foxx knew from his days on the Chitlin' Circuit made appearances on the show, including series regulars Page and Slappy White, who had formed a comedy duo with Foxx early in their careers.

Sanford and Son, then, can be seen as a bridge between the Chitlin' Circuit and the white mainstream, a space, not unlike *The Flip Wilson Show* (1970–74), where more uncensored types of African American folk humor could be expressed. Foxx's eventual departure from the show, due to salary demands and creative differences, and creation of the variety show *The Redd Foxx Comedy Hour* (1977–78) can be read as attempts by Foxx to inject more folk humor—as well as more risqué material—into mainstream television. More likely, he wished to capitalize on the suc-cess of Flip Wilson's variety show. Wilson, whom Foxx had catapulted into the mainstream by mentioning him on Johnny Carson's show in 1965, had become a comic superstar by the 1970s. Similar to *The Richard Pryor Show* (1977), Foxx's sketch comedy provided him with the best op-portunity to re-create the popularity of his stand-up routines. Pryor's show, which lasted only four episodes, suffered from the same battles with the network censors and the same low ratings that forced Foxx's show to end. While the quotient of sexuality and vulgarity was the most cited reason for the poor ratings and censorship clashes, I continue to believe that Foxx's attempt to deploy more aggressive aspects of African American humor was a major reason behind the failure of his show. His role as the beloved Fred Sanford turned out to be too ingrained in the minds of television audiences, many of whom dismissed the folk wit and social criticism that the show contained. Foxx never fully achieved the desired balance between uncensored black folk humor and mainstream success, which, to my mind, demonstrates the importance of the freedom of stand-up comedy in the development of comic rage. Yet in viewing his pre-*Sanford* comedy we can see the necessary move away from the minstrel tradition toward the more aggressive critique of racism that would infuse the comedy of Dick Gregory and dominate the comic rage that characterized Richard Pryor.

On Monsters: The Comedy and Rage of Dick Gregory

The humor that Foxx and Mabley drew on was usually tailored for the predominantly African American clubs where they performed for most of their careers. Their challenging of destructive stereotypes in front of African American audiences created a moment for healing and solidarity, but it did little to reverse those images in the white mainstream imagination. Because of the vulgarity and uncensored racial humor of these shows, Foxx and Mabley were not allowed to perform in white clubs or gain mainstream exposure for decades. Mabley and Foxx achieved mainstream success only after the presentation of African American racial critiques had been successful in front of white audiences, most famously through the efforts of Dick Gregory.

Gregory arose, to be sure, out of a period in American comic history that made his presence more possible. The fascination with various forms of humor has produced volumes of work, yet the genre of stand-up comedy remains severely understudied. This is partly because the term "stand-up" was not coined until 1966, although the genre existed decades before, and its phenomenal rise in American popular culture made it one of the most important cultural expressions of the latter portion of the twentieth century.

Gregory's emergence as a figure who challenged racial stereotypes, especially against the backdrop of the bourgeoning civil rights movement, should not come as much of a surprise. "Like Bruce and Sahl," writes Nachman in *Seriously Funny*, "he used his comic tools to build a playing field much larger than comedy" (481). But since he was the lone African American voice explicitly addressing race in front of white audiences, his journey was very different from those of his white peers who were not seen as the only representative of their group. The role of the African American entertainer-as-representative became especially significant during the 1950s and 1960s. As racial tensions increased, Watkins argues, many whites had to directly confront "their personal convictions about race and equality. . . . Since African-American entertainers were among the most visible representatives of the black community, for many Americans they assumed a disproportionately significant role in this process" (499). The presence of comedy, in contrast to music and sports, provided an extended consideration of race that diverged signficantly from the violent, tragic images that confronted Americans on television. In addition, comedy framed the discussion of race in terms that left audiences with a sense of hope rather than despair. "Many mainstream Americans," Watkins suggests, "shaken by blacks' intensifying push for equal rights, were primed for a satirical African-American voice that mirrored the moral and ethical candor displayed by such Civil Rights leaders as Martin Luther King, Jr." (500). Gregory's appearance, as well as the shift in African American comedic tradition, seems directly connected to the social, political, and historical moment. That moment involved a direct challenge to the second-class status of African Americans in the United States. As in all the chapters here, we see the scope, tone, and maintenance of moments of comic rage emerge from the continual shifts in African American political ideology and thinking.

As Nachman describes it, "Dick Gregory's arrival as the first major breakthrough black comedian seemed a logical step in the racial revolt of the fifties and sixties—a case of being not just in the right place at the right time, but, more crucially, of being the right man for the job" (482). Just as it was critical that baseball be integrated by Jackie Robinson rather than other Negro League players, it was critical that Gregory became the voice that white audiences would turn to in search of education couched comically. Although his white comic counterparts seemed to burst onto the scene from a comic universe unknown, the subjects that Gregory would engage had been around for decades and were being covered by other artists at the moment that Gregory got his break.

Born in St. Louis in 1932, Gregory was a poor child in a family on welfare. In his 1964 autobiography Nigger with Robert Lipsyte, Gregory traces his use of comedy back to his boyhood days attempting to avoid ridicule: "I got picked on a lot around the neighborhood; skinniest kid on the block, the poorest, the one without a Daddy. I guess that's when I first began to learn about humor, the power of a joke" (40). Recognizing that the teasing would never stop, Gregory surmised, "if I made the jokes they'd laugh *with* me instead of *at* me. I'd get the kids off my back, on my side" (41). Achieving his goal with relative ease, Gregory eventually turned the jokes on his tormentors, engaging in classic "dozens" confrontations. Here we can see the beginnings of the deflection that would come to characterize his humor in front of white audiences. These confrontations were Gregory's initial experiences with the use of African American humor. The first section of the autobiography, "Not Poor, Just Broke," chronicles his frustration with the absence of his father's and his efforts to negotiate, through sports and humor, the stark reality of his early life in St. Louis. In Gregory's portrait of welfare, what was then called "relief," he informs the reader that his mother secretly worked in addition to receiving aid. Gregory argues that "the system didn't want her to get off relief, the way it kept sending social workers around to be sure Momma wasn't trying to make things better" (28). Thus the formation of Gregory's comic critique evolved from the intersection of race and class he endured. While he employed a distinctly African American style in his humor, his desire to comment on the "world situation" had its roots in the early days and experiences in poverty-stricken St. Louis and foreshadows his eventual use of militant aspects of African American comedic tradition.

Nevertheless, humor serves a number of purposes in Gregory's autobiography. He artfully mixes memoir and "mainstream" wit, with stories about how his time in the army led to his first experiences as a stand-up and humorous adventures that find him taking a girlfriend and her family to the drive-in movie, buying Scotch, and getting gas with only five dollars. In the book Gregory consistently returns to humor—whether getting a job, meeting his wife, or becoming famous—in order to advance professionally and negate the moments of nihilism and anger that threaten to consume him. An important moment comes when, after the death of his mother, Gregory admits, "I went back to school numb and I stayed that way for most of the next four years, through the rest of that year at school, through two years in the Army, through the last year at college. It wasn't a sleepy numbness; it was a cold, hard, bitter numbness" (87). Throughout the period, Gregory's numbness does not spill over into violent action, though it does teeter on the brink of self-destruction. Gregory's humor consistently intervenes, which often makes his feelings of apathy and dissatisfaction difficult to recognize. Gregory's colonel once muses aloud that Gregory is "either a great comedian or a goddamned malingerer" (91). Gregory, of course, becomes the former, anchoring the book with a tone that balances the stories he tells against the backdrop of the Great Depression, World War II, and the civil rights movement. What permeates the autobiography, however, and lingers behind much of his success is his rage, what he labels "the monster."

Referred to at various points in *Nigger*, the "monster" acts as the driving force in his evolution from poor St. Louis child to star athlete to superstar comedian and activist. Gregory describes his days as a track star: "I'd stand up real slow, and feel this thing start to take me over, this monster that started at my toes like hot water flowing upward through a cold body. By the time I got down the [stadium] steps I'd be on fire" (56). Slipping in and out of him throughout the track meet, the monster resembles an uncontrolled competitive fire. It had, however, once been as much a source of fear as of strength. Gregory confesses, "I'd wake up screaming sometimes myself, my legs cramped and twisted under me," so that his mother would ask, "What is it, Richard, inside of you makes you go out there? I'm really afraid for you, Richard" (58). The elements that he eventually incorporated into his routine—like signifying, playing on the audience's prejudices, and infusing the work with his underlying dissatisfaction—began with his battles on the streets of St. Louis.

Gregory drew awareness of the need to change his act for a white audience from the experiences of other African American comics. He recounts: "I went downtown that Monday night to a white club and watched Nipsey [Russell] work that audience of white night-club owners. It was the same routine he had killed the customers with at Roberts, but that night Nipsey just sat up there and died. He couldn't get the same response he got at Roberts" (131). Gregory concluded that the whites in the audience at the Roberts Show Club, an African American nightspot on Chicago's South Side, had been laughing out of overwhelming white anxiety instead of amusement. Gregory thereupon constructed a stage act tailored to white clubs, where audiences were less likely to laugh at the overt racial humor that succeeded in places like the Roberts. Part of that construction involved the discussion of subjects other than race. Gregory observed: "I've got to go up there as an individual first, a Negro second. I've got to be a colored funny man, not a funny colored man" (132). This, he reasoned, would forge a connection with audiences who may have dreaded jokes that were specific to African American culture and experience. From there, Gregory could broach the subject of race. As he put it, "I've got to make jokes about myself, before I can make jokes about them and their society—that way, they can't hate me" (132). Gregory refused to rely on denigrating white American society in the way the writers of the Wright school were accused of doing. Nor was Gregory's use of humor solely an avenue for the expression of his rage or an attempt to capitalize on his white audience's embarrassment about their privilege. In crafting his stage persona to succeed at white clubs, Gregory purposely emulated Mabley's more welcoming attitude. Perhaps because of his singular ability to find topical jokes that appealed to both black and white audiences, Gregory rocketed to the mainstream success it would take Foxx and Mabley decades to achieve. Paralleling the selection of Jackie Robinson to integrate Major League Baseball, Gregory's success resulted from equal parts sociopolitical moment, personal temperament, and luck.

Gregory, like Ellison, achieved success through the employment of African American folk culture. He often grounded his jokes in folk sayings that were well known to African Americans and translated them to the routines in front his predominantly white audiences. We can highlight the link between African American literature and black stand-up particularly through the rhetorical, specifically the transference of African American vernacular tradition into previously European forms. In literature, black oral tradition manifests itself through the needed flexibility of language that demonstrates an understanding and internalizing of American values and ideals while also providing a form of resistance understood by other African Americans. In an America attempting to establish a distinct national literature, African American vernacular tradition appears both to reflect democratic ideals and to express skepticism because of the country's racist practices. To effectively achieve transference, of course, means moving beyond telling white stories with only physically black characters speaking in artificially black voices. Such a process includes the exploration of a diverse, complex African American folk culture and tradition. In stand-up such a process seems more direct. Language stays fluid in stand-up, with changes depending on the success of the act or the relationship with the audience. Stand-up's immediacy with the audience allows comics to adjust their jokes and timing to fit the rhythm of specific performances. They have an opportunity to employ two of the most basic concepts of African American oral tradition, namely improvisation and call-and-response. While such concepts appear in both the style and content of literature, the immediacy of stand-up comes closer to the essence of African American comedic tradition. Here the transition may be easier, needing only to subscribe to the formula of the stand-up genre: setup, joke, punch line. I say easier, not because I believe stand-up comedy to be simpler than writing literature, but because prose and drama must meet a separate set of expectations in order to be considered effective. As Limon states, "Stand-up comedy does not require plot, closure, or point. Jokes may be as short as ingenuity allows, and there need not be anything *but* jokes. Constant, unanimous laughter is the limit case" (13). While this separates stand-up from other forms of humor, it can act as an ideal space for comic rage because it does not always seek a clear solution or direct its audience to a role approved by hegemonic order.

In one routine Gregory suggests that football is the perfect sport for African Americans because "it's the only sport where a black man can chase a white man and 40,000 people stand up and cheer."[6] Beneath the laughter that follows, made possible by the pleasantness of Gregory's delivery, lies the grim history of racial violence that has permeated the country's history, usually involving white violence on black bodies. Gregory removes the proverbial mask that African Americans have often worn in front of whites to turn thoughts of racial violence on their head. He situates football as a space where African Americans can express their rage in ways that are not only constructive for their psyche but forms of entertainment and celebration for whites. This last part, of course, emerges as doubly important because Gregory here transforms a potentially volatile subject into an acceptable mainstream joke. The use of a sports reference highlights the historical importance of sports, comedy, literature, and music as among the few spaces where African Americans have been celebrated for their excellence. Subsequently they have served as platforms where criticisms of racism gain legitimacy. The fame achieved by figures like Robinson, basketball champion Bill Russell, football giant Jim Brown, tennis stars Arthur Ashe and Althea Gibson, and boxers Floyd Patterson and Muhammad Ali provided a status whereby they reached a larger audience about ongoing racial inequality. Unlike many contemporary African American athletes, such as Michael Jordan and Tiger Woods, who attempt to remain politically and racially silent in order to maximize their marketing appeal, African American athletes in the first two decades after World War II acted as representative figures for their communities who commented on racial discrimination in sports or in society at large. Aside from his role in baseball, Robinson also participated in the civil rights movement, speaking and marching at various nonviolent demonstrations. Ali's refusal to be inducted into the military was based on his membership in the Nation of Islam and his belief that American racism was more a threat to his life than anything going on in Vietnam. Gregory's own fame provided a similar opportunity to speak on issues of race and racism. Gregory's football joke was also important because it could be used in front of both black and white audiences, even as it had different meanings for the two. African Americans were more likely to respond to the recognition of their own desire for physical confrontation and the role of football in negotiating that historical frustration. Whites, already made comfortable by Gregory's well-practiced act, came to view the joke as a friendly satiric jab without fully understanding or interrogating its deeper meaning.

"Some critics said that white audiences laughed to neutralize their guilt," says Nachman, "but something else was at work: Gregory was helping to defuse black-white anger by getting whites to laugh at his racial jokes" (494). This particular accomplishment sounds easier than its actual execution. We must consider that previous racial humor, at least in white America, primarily reinforced white hegemonic constructions of blackness as buffoonish, illiterate, and inferior. They rarely, if ever, challenged those notions. As Julia Kristeva points out, "The time of abjection is double: a time of oblivion and thunder, of veiled infinity and the moment when revelation bursts forth" (9). Thus, even as Gregory delivered insightful and furious critiques on American racism, he would construct it in a way that allowed important realizations to take place in white America. His strategy recalls the construction of African American images at the midpoint of the twentieth century, if not before. Figures like Robinson and King stressed their humanity as well as their race, in order to make connections with liberal and moderate whites who might be uncomfortable dealing solely with race.

The nonviolent, inclusive strategy employed by figures such as Gregory, King, and Robinson drew heavily on the influence of an important and powerful segment in the African American community: the black middle and upper class. Many well-known African Americans attempted to embody a middle-class ethic and aesthetic in the public space that reflected the growing population of African Americans who abhorred images of lazy, shiftless Negroes permeating mainstream culture.

Middle- and upper-class African Americans rejected such images in an attempt to connect to white bourgeois ideology. This, many hoped, would promote the case for equality—as well as individual benefits for a select few. While E. Franklin Frazier's seminal study *Black Bourgeoisie* (1957) excoriated the African American middle and upper class for living in a world of "make-believe," this segment of African America continued to dominate the formation of political ideology, especially the promotion of integration. However, the efforts of the African American bourgeoisie were often ineffective before the civil rights movement because their expression of what bell hooks calls "narcissistic rage" (28) did not connect to African American cultural traditions that could mobilize the African American masses. Gregory's work differed from Frazier's description and became a conduit through which comic rage could flow, as the substance of Gregory's act explicitly pulled from African American folk/street humor that successfully articulated rage at racism, even as the construction of his image and initial political ideology resembled the African American bourgeoisie from Frazier's analysis.

Much of Gregory's rage emerged from the fear of poverty, of the world from which he drew the tone and consciousness of his routines. Upon first glance, such a fear resembles the underlying fear of many of the black elite. Yet Gregory's seems to extend beyond the actual economic status. Building off his mother's expectations for her children to escape an underclass lifestyle, Gregory's narrative contains an unprecedented work ethic that finds him "hustling" selling newspapers, excelling as a track star, and struggling to perform and run his own comedy club. Gregory forecasts his own relationship to perceptions of class-based values and behaviors by revealing his mother's performance for social workers: "My Momma would have to stand there and make like she was too lazy to keep her own house clean. She could never let on that she spent all day cleaning another woman's house for two dollars and carfare" (28). The echoes of such class performances reverberate throughout the book, and throughout the civil rights movement itself.

Gregory's discomfort with any moment that resembles his days on relief is obvious. After losing a job one October, he writes, "January came and I was still out of work, and there was something about unemployment compensation that began to remind me of relief: The way they make you stand in line, the way they narrowed their eyes when they asked questions" (100). The performance extends to both sides of the class line, as Gregory discovers when he gets a regular stand-up job at a small nightclub. He explains that, to the audiences, "You're those people's biggest entertainer, the biggest one they know, probably the biggest they will ever know. The stars on the top have created such an atmosphere of glamour that even the entertainers on the bottom can step in and get respect" (107). According to Gregory, then, "That's why you have to knock yourself out to dress well and act right and keep yourself up. You can never say: Look here, I'm just a small-time entertainer and my suits don't have to be pressed or my act too sharp or my manner right" (107). In Gregory's mind, "the system" forces a specific type of class performance from its poorest members, perpetuating a dichotomy that casts the middle and upper classes as morally superior and the lower classes as deceitful and lazy when they do not "act right" by subscribing to the middle class's values and ideologies. Thus we can see his middle-class presentations as a strategic appropriation that connects him to the middle-class mainstream that whites and blacks saw as "universal." His initial embrace comes from his attempts to avoid the poverty that plagued his childhood. Yet Gregory's performance presents an irony in its use of the folk/street culture that many of the black bourgeoisie stringently avoided. Gregory's balancing of the two worlds eventually reverses stereotypes of African American comedy.

Previous representations of African American humor contrasted with, and often trumped, the actual individuals who played the roles. Although both Hattie McDaniel and Lincoln Theodore Monroe Perry (Stepin Fetchit) were starkly different from the characters they played onscreen, they could not fully separate themselves from those representations in the popular imagination. Foxx notes in Price's *Redd Foxx B.S.*, "It used to be the average white person's concept of black comedy was two guys in plaid suits, shuffling out with a broom and doing an act in blackface. A stand-up comic couldn't find a job" (107). A more contemporaneous example is *Amos 'n' Andy*, which aired on radio from 1928 to 1955 and on television from 1951 to 1953, and which drew both wrath and praise from the African American community. Its collection of characters became some of the most recognizable presentations of African Americans in the first half of the twentieth century. Theirs was a world of scheming, bragging, and loitering, with never a hint of negotiation, defiance, or subversion of white supremacist hegemony. For whites, the show acted as a continuation of the minstrel show tradition modernized for a radio and television audience. Like *Beulah*, *Amos 'n' Andy* was initially performed by whites and seemed to confirm historical perceptions of African Americans.

Despite criticism of its negative stereotyping, *Amos 'n' Andy*, like *Sanford and Son*, was popular among many in the African American community, although for a very different reason than for the show's white audience. Donald Bogle offers the same rationale for its appeal that he gives for the community's embrace of *Sanford*. It was "the pleasure the African American audience still experienced (at this time in history) at again seeing African American performers relating to one another, establishing a semblance of a Black community and an approximation of Black life and culture" (191). Where the two shows differed was in *Sanford and Son*'s clear dissatisfaction with racist oppression, as opposed to the blissful ignorance of *Amos 'n' Andy*. As Bogle states, the characters in *Sanford* "were so quick to voice their anger about the system's inequities and its racism that viewers seldom criticized them for trafficking in some of the same distorted tomfoolery as *Amos 'n' Andy*" (38). Although it was promoted as a show that provided moments of African American folk humor, *Amos*—perhaps because of its initial conception in the white imagination—never embraced the racial consciousness inherent in African American humor. In order to avoid resembling the popular image of African Americans during the time, Gregory and others began to merge the public image and the private self. Although African American cultural traditions like black vernacular and comedic performance were important factors in the acts of the new comics, their presentation of those traditions differed greatly from stereotypical mainstream representations of African American humor. Gregory constantly performed in conservative suits, as did comic peers Nipsey Russell, George Kirby, and Timmie Rogers, in total contrast to Mabley's house dress or Foxx's flashier style. In addition, black comics were armed with the ability to address white audiences directly, which had previously been considered too aggressive. The critiques in which the comics engaged, then, could not be easily dismissed or forgiven. The younger generation of black comics confronted white audiences with material that criticized whites or social inequalities that whites approved. While whites sought to maintain the hegemony that made African Americans the sufferers of abjection, Gregory's comedy sought to break down the assumptions on which race in America is based and, using African Americans as the abjected race, continue to force the audience into moments of "revelation."

Watkins notes, however, that Gregory's limited experience on the Chitlin' Circuit allowed him to effectively abandon such stereotypical presentations of African American humor as "a passively slumped shoulder while delivering a punch line, an overly exaggerated widening of the eyes, or an apprehensive glance in search of approval from non-black crowds." As with the presentation of African American humor that Russell and Rogers had made inherent in their acts, Gregory's lack of actual stage time in predominantly African American clubs helped him, leaving him "practically untutored in the evasive, indirect humor of the black stage" (501). With a style that engendered trust in his audience, Gregory successfully articulated dissatisfaction with racism and white America without backlash. Watkins argues that Gregory's "monologues mirrored the bitingly satiric perceptions of the most alienated segment of black America but, because they were delivered deftly and without rancor, were not perceived as obloquy" (498). Also, even as comics like Russell and Rogers combined a well-groomed appearance with standard English speech, Gregory believed that his imperfect English was part of the reason that white audiences liked him. Though this might seem like an instance where stereotypical images come into play, Gregory's use of African American English afforded him the opportunity to embrace African American oral traditions. The flexibility African American English provided would become critical in the racialized portion of his act in negotiating the pitfalls of performing in front of an all-white audience.

The economic and racial politics of his presence in a club constantly surfaced throughout the beginnings of Gregory's career, made more difficult by his attempts to avoid what he terms "bitterness." Like pioneering African American artists and authors before him, Gregory would be faced with the dilemma of balancing tone and style with his rage against racism. As with Ellison, Gregory used the tradition of signifying in successfully appealing to larger audiences while articulating dissatisfaction with racist oppression. Purposely removing routines about sex, for fear it would make him the Bad Nigger that Foxx was often cast as, he was increasingly concerned that "some day, somewhere, I'd be in a white club and somebody would get up and call me a nigger" (133). He recognized the economic risk his presence might create: "The customers are going to

tie in that uncomfortable feeling with that club—even after I'm gone—
and the club owner know this. He would rather keep me out of his club
than take a chance on losing customers" (133). When eventually a heckler
did call him a nigger, Gregory, who had been running through options
with his wife, was ready: "The audience froze and I wheeled around without batting an eye. 'You hear what that guy just called me? Roy Rogers'
horse. He called me Trigger!'" (134). By referring to a horse, Gregory's response made the heckler seem absurd. In addition, it connected Gregory
with the audience through their shared knowledge of the well-known and
well-loved Rogers, whose likeability the audience extended to Gregory.

Standing before another white audience and confronting a problem
of a different sort, Gregory again turned to folk tradition to handle the
situation. Upon hearing a drunk white female refer to him as "handsome," Gregory recognized the danger, literally, in a verbal misstep. "Every white man in the place froze. That's the sex angle, thrown right in
your face, and the whole room hates you for it" (135). Gregory called out
to her, "Take another drink. You'll think you're Negro. Then you'll run up
here and kiss me and we'll both have to leave town in a hurry" (135). Here
Gregory subverts the stereotypical relationship of the African American male predator and the white female victim. In this setting the white
female possesses power over Gregory, like the lion over the signifying
monkey, because of Gregory's race. He can neither eagerly approach nor
rudely humiliate her, so he uses her arrogance and privilege against her.
Instead of responding to her flirtatiously or sexually, he casts himself as
the prey, one completely aware of the consequences of any acknowledg-
ment of attraction or distaste for the woman. According to Gregory, his
tactic "busted it. The room came all the way down again, and you could
hear the relief in that explosion of laughter. If there was any hate left in
that room, it was for that girl" (135). Gregory again connected with the
audience without offending them, increasing his likeability. By demonstrating an acute knowledge of the sexual taboos of the time for the audience's sake, he deftly regained control of the show. Nachman suggests,
"Gregory walked a fine and dangerous line between ingratiating and jiving, persuasive and aggressive, sympathetic and servile" (494). Gregory
embodied the black vernacular tradition of verbal ambiguity and wordplay that we see in the works of Johnson, Hughes, Hurston, and Ellison.
In addition, he moved beyond the historical usage of African American

comedy, in which humor could serve as an act of psychic healing and cultural sharing, as with Moms Mabley, to engage in a racial analysis that would be recognizable and acceptable to white audiences. Perhaps most important, Gregory used laughter to lessen the racial tensions that had emerged during the 1960s, making white audiences much more likely to trust him when he finally decided to navigate the racial terrain in his act.

"By the mid-sixties," Watkins informs us, "as he became more involved in the Civil Rights movement, Gregory's humor became more caustic and bitter" and eventually his "political activism forced him to cancel concerts and club dates and, gradually, comedy became a secondary enterprise" (503). In the course of this seemingly more aggressive change, Gregory reversed many of the rules that he had previously established. One difference came in the insertion of the more uncensored jokes he had previously rejected. For example, in a joke involving an African American man new to his suburban neighborhood, Gregory recounts that while cutting his lawn the man gets asked by a white neighbor: "What do you get for doing yardwork?" To which the African American man answers: "I get to sleep with the lady of the house. You need any help?" (132). Here Gregory clearly plays on the black male/white female sexual taboo, even as he comments on the white suburbanite's assumption that the man is working for someone white. Gregory, like Mabley, brings the issue of sexuality to the fore in an attempt to force the audience to view him, and African Americans, according to their expressions of full humanity. Yet this represents a clear departure from the Gregory of the early 1960s. In *Nigger* he had warned, "Stay away from sex, that's the big pitfall. If you use blue material only, you slip back into being that Negro stereotype comic. If you mix blue and topical satire that white customer, all hung up with the Negro sex mystique, is going to get uncomfortable" (132–33). According to Gregory's earlier belief, the lawnmower joke's signifying on racial stereotyping would be lost because of the audience's focus on the reference to a possible sexual relationship with the white suburbanite's wife. Some may view this as the inherent shortcoming of comedy to adequately address social ills; however, Gregory's eventual move away from the stage emerged out of the incompatibility of the persona and style he had constructed and the more critical material he attempted to use. Gregory's insertion of black street humor into his routines for his white audiences resulted in a comedy that produced important tensions alongside African American comedic tradition. Many African American comics were familiar with a more confrontational style. In dealing with hecklers, for instance, Watkins notes that Gregory's retorts to white audiences paled in comparison to "Timmie Rogers's 'Shut up, fool!' or Richard Pryor's ultimate equalizer, 'What about yo' momma?'" (496). While such tactics would seem inconceivable in front of white audiences, they often defined the tone and style that a comedian could use in front of all-black audiences. Moreover, any attempt at delivering more abrasive jokes would be rejected by audiences seeking a more lovable figure. Gregory's solution, according to Watkins, "was, again, diversion: deflect the hostility and potential insult, make a joke of it" (496), and this would come to characterize his act, making more direct confrontation—of hecklers or of racial subject matters—less acceptable.

Eventually, however, the "bitterness" that Gregory had been able to deflect toward pioneering forays into race relations began to spill over into his act. He cites the beginning of his transformation at a moment in Jackson, Mississippi, in 1962 when he heard about an old man whose wife died while he was in jail for leading a voter registration drive. Having heard too about the efforts of Clyde Kennard and James Meredith to integrate Mississippi colleges, Gregory states that his time in the South had initiated an important shift. "For the first time, I was involved. There was a battle going on, there was a war shaping up, and somehow writing checks and giving speeches didn't seem enough" (159). His participation in demonstrations and marches would lead to the cancellation of performance dates, often because of imprisonment. Also, Gregory eventually lost his belief in the effectiveness of comedy, as white audiences seemed to accept his racial jokes as part of the *authentic* African American comic experience. Much like the whites who, Ellison believed, celebrated Charlie Parker's rudeness and hostility as part of a legitimate jazz experience, white audiences would come to see attending Gregory's show as a chic political act—similar to claiming to have marched with King—one that proved their open-mindedness and exempted them from interrogating their own complicity in perpetuating white supremacy. That Gregory's mode of discussion of such issues was less confrontational than his peers' only made him more desirable.

The radicalizing of Gregory's thinking and humor reveals the problematic negotiation of race, class, and rage that many African Americans faced in the early years of the civil rights movement. Also, the change in Gregory's act reveals the difficult balance in producing extended works of comic rage. Gregory began to lose his balance when his increasingly explicit rage could not be effectively contained within the traditional structure of stand-up comedy. As the civil rights movement took on a more militant tone, the (white) middle-class audiences to whom Gregory appealed soured on his political shift and comic recalibration. Gregory found himself rejecting even moderate or ambiguous reactions, such as when he was told that he had to "know" he would not fight back during peaceful demonstrations. The comedy used by artists of the early civil rights movement became insufficient to express comic rage because they embedded their humor with mainstream, accommodating ideas of black resistance. Redd Foxx's impact on Dick Gregory, despite his relegation to the Chitlin' Circuit, remains important because the confrontation in his act reflected the militancy found in the rhetoric of Malcolm X and Richard Pryor. Gregory's success, then, maintained the fearlessness of Foxx's routines and led directly to the evolution of sustained expressions of comic rage.

Gregory's recognition of his audience's response informed his frustration with his comedy's role in his life and its ability to effect change for others. "Making people laugh failed to fulfill Gregory," says Nachman. "The world, he decided, needed to hear more candor, a harsher, more urgent message. Eventually the preacher in him edged out the performer in a friendly takeover" (482). In the late 1960s Gregory ceased to temper his rage, manifesting it in the more aggressive elements of African American humor he had not incorporated before. Viewing himself as an African American before an entertainer, he saw comedy as incapable of facilitating change. By 1967, according to Watkins, he would begin referring to himself as a "social commentator who used humor to interpret the needs and wants of Negroes to the white community, rather than as a comedian who happens to deal in topical social material" (503). Converting to activism virtually full time, Gregory would run for mayor of Chicago in 1966 and for president of the United States in 1968. His personal redefinition demonstrates the role humor can play in seriously engaging issues of race. He recognized that the expression of comedy alone would be ineffective in convincing white audiences to act against the pervasiveness of racism. In relinquishing his role as a comic, however, Gregory seemed to be suggesting that African American humor in a traditional comedic structure was unable—in the mainstream at least—to make an unfettered and successful examination of white supremacy.

The rage that Gregory expressed in his activism feels palpable throughout *Nigger*, though audiences easily dismissed it because of Gregory's deflection. Toward the end of the book Gregory points out: "A scared Negro is one thing. A mad Negro is something else. I had always gone down South scared. But in September [1963], when I went down to Selma, Alabama, Whitey had a mad Negro on his hands" (200). Angered by the infamous Birmingham church bombing that took the lives of four young African American girls, Gregory reveals more explicitly his attempt to integrate militant rage into his comedy: "I was mad. I told that audience how surprised I was to see a dumb Southern cop who knew how to write. The crowd was nervous. They had never heard such talk in front of a white man before" (200). Though Gregory's boldness conjures memories of Foxx's comic Bad Nigger attitude, the mixed audience's nervousness highlights the rarity of such comically expressed rage in nonblack spaces, as well as the expectations of Gregory himself. Using barely hidden vitriol as he comments that the only thing a southern white man "has to be able to identify with is a drinking fountain, a toilet, and the right to call me a nigger" (201), Gregory moves the audience's mood from shock and concern to audacity and enjoyment. Gregory recalls with pride, "And they were cheering now, and screaming and laughing and the white cops up front looked pale. The crowd wasn't afraid of them" (201). In front of predominantly white audiences, however, Gregory's more militant act would not have the same effect. Coupled with a growing disdain for stand-up comedy, Gregory's rage would, for a time, swallow the effectiveness his humor had in addressing issues of race.

Buoyed perhaps by an end to the days of viewing himself as a comedian, Gregory published *No More Lies* (1971) and sounded more like Malcolm X than Martin Luther King. The collection of essays includes his dissection of myths perpetuated by the United States. Among them: "White America's favorite myth is the myth of nonviolence, which really means that oppressed people should not use violence against the oppressor. Think of the only country in the history of the world that dropped atomic bombs on other human beings now coming to black folks, poor folks, and young folks telling them to be nonviolent!" (xiii). The assassination of King, the urban riots of the mid-to-late 1960s, and the emergence of the Black Panther Party and the philosophy of Black Power seemed finally to bring Gregory's militant rage out into the open. In *Lies* Gregory critiques white supremacy more extensively. There are moments of humor throughout the book, such as when he argues that the "biggest breakthrough" for African Americans came when "We got our first colored hurricane—*Beulah*. When you can integrate that big breeze, that's progress" (137). The majority of the book is virtually devoid of humor, replaced by Gregory's expressions of frustration over the growing unrest in predominantly African American urban areas, as well as his thoughts on constructions of whiteness and American imperialism. Describing the United States as a nation infected with a sickness, Gregory seems in sync with the thinking of African American political ideology of the late 1960s and 1970s; his comedy, however, had not progressed similarly. In *The Redd Foxx Encyclopedia of Black Humor*, Foxx argues that Gregory "became so wrapped up in the cause of racial equality that he began to lose sight of his humor" (181). Sacrificing the craft of humor in order to indict the racism that he encountered in his activism, Gregory's comedy suffered even as younger comics benefited from his mainstream acceptance and built on his foundation to incorporate a more aggressive and direct style. Unbound by the structure that Gregory pushed to its limits, younger comics successfully wove their style into their radical reimagining of American stand-up. Because the traditional stand-up structures made Gregory sound increasingly bitter, even Foxx would eventually complain that "Gregory was funny until he took his causes serious" (255). For Gregory, comedy's inability to temper his rage prevented him from expanding the possibilities of African American comedy to critique white supremacy. He could no longer see comedy as a mode of resistance and an effective avenue for expressing his long-simmering frustration.

Toward Comic Rage

Where *Nigger* contained the affability that made Gregory beloved by audiences, and *No More Lies* demonstrated the unrestrained rage that forced him to leave the stage, *Up from Nigger* (1976) attempts to blend the two sides of Gregory's life. Bolstered perhaps by a return to the autobiographical style of *Nigger*, Gregory traces his travels and experiences through the tumultuous years of the 1960s and 1970s. While the book is filled with the types of critiques that characterized *No More Lies*, Gregory capitalizes on his ability to address sensitive subjects with comic ease: "White folks praise Bob Hope for going to Vietnam and criticize me for coming to Mississippi. Well it's safer in Vietnam. At least there you know the government is on your side" (76). His return to stories about his performances and routines brought a welcome injection of humor into the work, a key absence in *No More Lies*, making his criticisms more poignant. Gregory's renewed appreciation for the role of comedy, and his individual importance, is documented in the chapter "Comedy and Conspiracy." Attending the Comedy Awards Show in Los Angeles in 1975, Gregory finds himself contemplative: "I realized that whatever else I've done or will yet do in my life, I'm first and foremost a comic. I was proud to be a comedian that night, proud of my profession, and proud of whatever contribution I've made to comedy" (239). We can view his respect for comedy as doubly important when, in the epilogue of *Up from Nigger*, Gregory contends that the "monster" that for so long lived within him has been bested. "I used to think my monster was a good thing. It gave me the drive to climb to the top. But now I realize that the monster was created within me by an oppressive and unjust social and political system" (249). Gregory correctly identifies white supremacist capitalist hegemony as the institution that affected his life, yet he also says at one point that "since the system created the monster, the system was in control" (249). Instead of viewing the monster inside him as militant and justified rage, he agrees with coauthor Robert Lipsyte that his "monster" was "a combination of ego and ambition" (249). Like the arguments of detractors that Gregory's involvement in demonstrations and marches was for publicity, this explanation casts his rage as more ego than resistance, classifying Gregory's efforts as a near-maniacal need to be recognized. Similarly Gregory's argument that "The life blood of the monster inside me was adrenaline, which filled my veins when there was a race to win, an audience to turn on, a civil rights struggle to engage in" (249). This explanation isolates Gregory from the individual and collective lives he touched. It robs him of the determination that rage fueled in him, instead positing that such rage and determination are responses to be ashamed of.

I am more persuaded by Gregory's argument in *Nigger* that leans toward a prideful viewing of his rage, one that has found a satisfying and effective expression in activism: "The monster. But it's not content to beat some mother's son in a foot race any more, and it's not satisfied to make people laugh and love me. Now it wants some respect and dignity, and it wants freedom. It's willing to die for freedom" (207–8). The previous appearances of his rage ineffectively contained the frustration that plagued him. His desire to win races displaced his rage toward a competitiveness and hate exacerbated by his economic status and capable of existing only within the confines of the track meet. He never connected his rage to the larger external, institutional forces of racial and class exploitation. The traditional structure of stand-up made comedy insufficient to fully utilize and express the direct racial critiques in African American comedic tradition. Gregory's use of comic rage stretched traditional stand-up beyond its boundaries because he rejected the traditional Freudian notion that humor hides or suppresses anger. His embrace of his anger collapsed the fundamental logic of humor. We can reject his abandonment of comedy as the "monster" temporarily overtaking him, and view it as a direct action that protested mainstream comedy's exclusion of distinctly African American comic tradition. In much the same way that the mainstream cast the activists of the early civil rights movement as radical in comparison to the racial discourse of the 1950s and 1960s, we can see Gregory's comedy as a groundbreaking performance fueled by a rage based not on pathology but on the segregation of comedy that Moms Mabley and Redd Foxx faced. In the struggle with his rage, Gregory recalls Ellison's narrator who throughout *Invisible Man* attempts, and frequently fails, to find paths to channel the rage that inevitably erupts in him. Most of the avenues that the narrator and Gregory take cannot contain their rage. While comedy provided a space for Gregory to make significant changes, as does the narrator's oratorical ability, the forces that surrounded comedy—white audience expectations, the growing intensity of the civil rights movement—allowed only a limited expression of rage. We must begin to view Gregory's "monster" as, for a time, simply lacking an appropriate avenue for its expression.

Gregory unleashed comic rage in the mainstream and found the stand-up genre incapable of sustaining his attempt to balance comedy and rage. Although he found a more suitable, militant space in the activism of the civil rights movement, his role as a stand-up comic remained an important part of his legacy and identity. By the time of *Up from Nigger*, the landscape of comedy had been permanently changed, as television and movies began taking advantage of the comic talents of Bill Cosby, Redd Foxx, and Richard Pryor. Nevertheless, Gregory's success made possible

comic critiques of racism in front of whites, complementing the protests and antiracist struggle that characterized the 1950s and 1960s. This
would expand the possibilities for expressions of rage and act as coun-
terbalance to the racial turmoil that seemed akin to tragedy. Nachman
contends that Gregory was at his best "as an astutely dry political comedian delivering firebombs about blacks and whites coexisting in America"
(482). The image that Gregory cultivated was one that directly challenged
popular notions of African Americans. Intentionally moving away from
the images that had been reinforced in movies and that had made racism and discrimination more acceptable, Gregory forced recognition of
the humanity of African Americans. Against the backdrop of the ongoing
civil rights movement, the change to the audience and politics of African
American comedy that Gregory popularized corresponded to the literary
possibilities that Ellison had opened up in *Invisible Man*. Influenced by
Gregory and the African American comedic landscape, African American
literature reflected the shift in African American political ideology in the
mid-1960s. Moving beyond opposing segregation and the lack of voting
rights, African American writers began focusing on white supremacist
capitalist hegemony. The militant spirit of Malcolm X, the formation of
organizations like the Black Panther Party, and the emergence of black
cultural nationalism would have a major influence on African American
writers, culminating in the Black Arts movement. The militant rage these
writers expressed mirrored the Black Power rhetoric that was becoming
the dominant political ideology by the late 1960s. More important, the
willingness of Gregory and the new comics to confront racism through
humor would continue to develop, creating a space analogous to what
writers were constructing in their works. Capitalizing on the spaces created by Gregory and Ellison, African American writers in the late 1960s
and 1970s provided uncensored and more aggressive expressions of
comic rage. Underneath a distinct nationalist declaration, many of these
works ridiculed racism and exposed the breadth of white supremacist assault. The development of African American comedic tradition, the expression of militant rage in black nationalism, and the onset of the Black
Arts movement formed the springboard for comic rage in the latter third
of the twentieth century, beginning in 1966 with Douglas Turner Ward's
critically acclaimed play *Day of Absence*.

☞ **3**

From *Absence* to *Flight*

The Appearance of Comic Rage in the Black Arts
and Black Power Movements, 1966–1976

Racial laughter as a weapon against racial injustice in the mainstream theatres is a recent sound, arriving only after the Supreme
Court decision on segregation, the Birmingham bus strike, the
Greensboro sit-ins, the success of *A Raisin in the Sun*, and the provocative speech of Dick Gregory and Malcolm X.

James V. Hatch and Ted Shine, *Black Theatre USA*

White People Do Not Know How to Behave at Entertainments
Designed for Ladies and Gentlemen of Colour

Placard allegedly posted by William Brown's African Grove Theatre

African American humor, as the previous chapter demonstrated, was un-
dergoing its own transition as Dick Gregory and the new comics overtly
engaged issues of race in their routines. In *Black Theatre USA: Plays By
African Americans*, Hatch and Shine note, "In the 1950s and 1960s, stand-
up comics like Dick Gregory, Moms Mabley, Shelley Berman, Redd Foxx,
Lenny Bruce, and later Richard Pryor, brought race and sex out of the toi-
lets and into nightclubs, onto records, and finally into television" (630).
The move by these comics into the mainstream represents an important
shift from the "'dementia praecox' humor" that Hamlin Hill in his 1963
essay "Modern American Humor: The Janus Laugh" describes as "ur-
bane, sophisticated, witty, reflecting the tinge of insanity and despair of
contemporary society" (92). In the middle part of the twentieth century,

with comics like Bruce and Foxx and the use of folk culture by Ellison and Hughes, we see a rise in "native humor" whose protagonist, according to Hill, "is less neurotic, more competent to face reality simply because he is prepared to accept its ugliness and to admit its brutality" (92). As more uncensored elements of African American comedic tradition replaced the remnants of the minstrel show in the public imagination, humor became a welcome and more frequent avenue for the expression of African American militant rage, and authors wove humor along with cultural/political nationalism into their work. However, humor's relationship to the Black Arts movement was not a natural symbiosis. Although the Black Arts movement scoffed at the idea of "protest literature," their embrace of Richard Wright as a literary forefather implicitly adopted that tradition's disinterest in the use of humor to articulate their critiques. In his 1968 essay "The Black Arts Movement," Larry Neal writes that "Black Art is the aesthetic and spiritual sister of the Black Power concept" and that "the political values inherent in the Black Power concept are now finding concrete expression in the aesthetics of Afro-American dramatists, poets, choreographers, musicians, and novelists" (1960). This does not mean, however, that the Black Arts movement was bereft of humor. In fact, say Hatch and Shine, the willingness to speak and "hear the forbidden spoken aloud in mixed audiences" that was "shocking enough to evoke laughter in both whites and Blacks" (630), was an important element of the Black Arts and Black Power movements' violent removal of the mask many African Americans had donned.

Although not new in African American literary history, the expressions of militancy become important for my purposes because the sociopolitical shift toward overt challenges to white supremacist capitalist patriarchy was augmented by a similar shift in African American literary production. Signaled by the 1964 Obie-winning play *Dutchman* by Amiri Baraka (then still called LeRoi Jones) and his subsequent essay "The Revolutionary Theatre," African American literature entered a transition similar to that initiated by Richard Wright more than twenty years earlier. In the development of comic rage as I trace it in this book, 1966 stands as a pivotal year. The newly minted chairman of the Student Nonviolent Coordinating Committee, Stokely Carmichael, coined the term "black power," which encapsulated the militant rage that was beginning to deviate from the more integrationist/nonviolent aspects of the civil rights movement of the 1950s and 1960s. That same year, the founding of the Black Panther Party for Self-Defense—of which Carmichael would eventually become a member—made clear that African Americans had found the previous generation's mode of resistance monolithic, if not ineffective. The urban riots that occurred throughout the 1960s revealed a black America that felt voiceless in the wake of the deaths of Martin Luther King Jr. and Malcolm X, despite the passage of the Civil Rights Act of 1964 and the Voting Rights Act of 1965. The militant rage that fueled the riots eventually found expression through black nationalist rhetoric and radical political ideology. The literature during the latter half of the 1960s and into the 1970s mirrored and embraced the political ideology by reimagining its works aesthetically and thematically. The Black Arts movement centered on what Larry Neal called being "radically opposed to any concept of the artist that alienates him from his community" and it "envisions an art that speaks directly to needs and aspirations of Black America" (1960).

The Black Arts movement's radicalizing impact on most, if not all, aspects of African American culture combined with American humor's shift to the more topical and taboo to produce sustained expressions of comic rage. The two works that this chapter examines, Douglas Turner Ward's *Day of Absence* (1966) and Ishmael Reed's *Flight to Canada* (1976), sit at opposite ends of the decade during which the Black Arts movement flourished, and through them we can view the progression of extended moments of comic rage from the beginning to the end of the Black Arts movement. Though both primarily depend on African American cultural tradition, their genres are also perfect for expressing comic rage because of the historical and contemporaneous legacy both had in depicting African Americans. Contrary to Hamlin Hill's belief that, for the "new" humorist in the 1960s, "social forces are too enormous and too impersonal, too much like a Juggernaut, for the individual to have any chance against them" (96), African American humor—and comic rage during this period—collectively engaged those forces. Unlike the dementia praecox humorist who, according to Hill, "admits by negation the loss of the humorist's role as satirist, his incapability of inventing homespun maxims about hundred-megaton bombs, or of feeling any native self-confidence in the face of uncontrollable fallout" (96), comic rage rejects ideas of timidity or insanity in favor of a bold confrontation of America's racial hypocrisy, rejecting the folly and danger of (white) mainstream narratives. For *Day of Absence*, it is the direct address of blackface minstrelsy onstage, the centrality of blackness, and the state of African American theater in the 1960s. Reed's novel, which is now considered part of the neo-slave narrative tradition, responded to William Styron's controversial 1967 novel *The Confessions of Nat Turner* by launching a no-holds-barred attack on Western mythmaking at large, in line with ideology at the height of black militancy. Yet the humor in Ward's play and Reed's novel embraces uncensored elements of African American comedic tradition, in an effective contrast with the Black Arts movement's unrelenting fury. Even though a major factor in the fusion of militant rage and humor was the Black Power and Black Arts movements' creation of a space to sustain its presence, works of comic rage during this period critiqued aspects both outside and, eventually, within the very movements that provided a radical interpretation of traditions and perspectives and thereby encouraged the development of comic rage. In the dichotomy of white subject and black object, the Black Power and Black Arts movements actively exploded the assumptions of both, eliminating the black object's longing to become the white subject by pointing out the rejection, indeed the erasure, of a distinct, celebrated African American culture. Often humor was seen as ineffective in challenging white supremacist hegemony, yet works of comic rage at this time went further than works of the Black Arts movement, because while works of comic rage similarly promoted collective acts of resistance—in literature and in society—they also questioned the symbols of power that nationalists myopically privileged and often replicated. The works of comic rage during this period, then, may be viewed as "the jettisoned object" which Kristeva says "is radically excluded and draws me toward the place where meaning collapses" (2). In challenging "meaning," *all* responses to white supremacy are open to interrogation in order to guard the reconfiguration of the hegemonic order. Works of comic rage are committed to breaking down traditional ideas and constructions that situate the creation of and response to white supremacist hegemony. So in Ward's play we can see an act of black consciousness initiated by the sudden disappearance of all the African Americans from a small Southern town, which forces a recognition of the fundamental role African Americans play in the construction and maintenance of (white) American identity. Reed's novel, coming at the end of the Black Arts movement, presents a fully realized consciousness that challenges black nationalist ideologies by suggesting that even flight from America itself does not guarantee escape from Western oppression. This chapter demonstrates how Ward's *Day of Absence* and Reed's *Flight to Canada* represent pioneering works of comic rage that emerge out of the Black Power and Black Arts movements' desire to express militant rage at white supremacist hegemony.

"Power to the People": The Roots of the Black Power and Black Arts Movements

The Black Arts movement employed a myriad of genres to capture the unique experience of blacks in America. A major result was an inherent variation of tone and style in the expression of militant rage. The central purpose of the Black Arts movement was, according to Neal, "to speak to the spiritual and cultural needs of Black people" by confronting "the contradictions arising out of the Black man's experience in the racist West" (1960). Although the movement claimed Wright as a forefather, it sought to separate itself from a key failing of the works of the Wright school. Larry Neal proclaims, "The Black Arts Movement eschews 'protest' literature. It speaks directly to Black people. Implicit in the concept of 'protest' literature, as Brother [Etheridge] Knight has made clear, is an appeal to white morality" (1961). Quoting Knight, Neal reveals this failing as the existence of a "belief that a change will be forthcoming once the masters are aware of the protestor's 'grievance' . . . Only when that belief has faded and protestings end, will Black art begin" (1961). The writer who best reflects the spirit of the Malcolm X militancy is, of course, Amiri Baraka.

Beginning with award-winning plays like *Dutchman*, *The Slave* (1964), and *The Toilet* (1964) and poetry from *The Dead Lecturer* (1964) to *It's Nation Time* (1970), Baraka became the best-known figure of the Black Arts movement. As coeditor (with Larry Neal) of *Black Fire: An Anthology of Afro-American Writing* (1968), Baraka helped demonstrate the versatility of Black Arts literature in addressing the concerns and expressing the rage of African Americans in unprecedented fashion. Not only did the Black Arts movement reject the black elite's perceptions of the literary and the political, but they also resisted the elite's idea of aesthetic assimilation. Primarily, resistance to traditional ideas of whiteness took the form of a celebration of blackness and the distinct physical and cultural characteristics of being a person of African descent in America. Whether it was Ron "Maulana" Karenga's creation of the African-centered

Kwanzaa holiday, the growth of Afros and natural hair as political statements, or the legitimizing of African American English, the celebration
of blackness became the foundation for an ideology that would dominate
the late 1960s and 1970s. One crucially significant element the political,
literary, and cultural nationalist movements shared was a Pan-African-
ism that embraced many Third World countries and cultures and reconfigured sociopolitical and cultural visions of race to move beyond Jim
Crow segregation and the suppression of voting rights. Thus America
was not the sole target of the Black Power and Black Arts movements. Instead, these movements sought to comment on the effects of colonialism
on oppressed peoples in Latin America, Africa, and elsewhere. The Black
Power and Black Arts movements, then, expanded the focus of militant
rage from the lives of African Americans onto white supremacist hegemony throughout the West. It comes as no surprise, then, that humor
would also be influenced by the ideological shift in African America.

However, in "Toward Vernacular Humor" (1970), James Cox argued,
"Whatever the sense of humor is, the non-sense of it is making it serious. Yet making it serious is the preoccupation of most critics—so
much so that they evade the reality of humor wherever they confront it
by means of shifty prepositional displacement, positing a prior reality
'behind,' 'beneath,' 'beyond,' or 'above' the humorous surface. And that
prior reality inevitably turns out to be dark, somber, tragic—most of all,
serious" (107). Like Cox, I see that, historically, "comic forms are considered lower in the genre hierarchy and thus need transfusions of value in
order to be elevated into the realm of serious art," which results in humor's being "tricked out as satire in many critical discussions, since satire, having ostensible moral purpose, is a more serious form" (107). Thus
we find novels in the Black Arts movement where humor is, in a limited
capacity, an element in expressing the sentiments of black political/cul-
tural nationalism. Writers during the Black Arts movement often used
humor as a way to reverse racist notions about African Americans, expose white supremacist hegemony, and ridicule African Americans who
supported what the authors saw as assimilationist ideology. Works like
William Melvin Kelley's *Dem* (1967), Sam Greenlee's *The Spook Who Sat
by the Door* (1969), and John O. Killens's *The Cotillion; or, One Good Bull Is
Half the Herd* (1971) reflected "serious" uses of humor in the Black Arts
movement. Not surprisingly, these novels involve either an unflinching

ridicule of the black bourgeoisie or, in Greenlee's novel, a militant revolt against the government that recalls Sutton Griggs's *Imperium in Imperio*.

So in *Dem*, the upper-middle-class African American protagonist has his "American dream" life slowly exposed as nightmare, while in Killens's *The Cotillion*, a soon-to-be debutante named Yoruba shocks the black elite in a hilarious satire about the folly of African American social climbing. And yet while I agree with Cox about the patronizing of the "just humorous" that is solely for pleasure, that assessment clearly ignores the history of African American comedic tradition's double-voiced presence in the mainstream that was enacted by comics like Moms Mabley and Dick Gregory. Works that did not fit the pattern of "serious" humor were virtually forgotten, as happened with Fran Ross's 1974 novel *Oreo*, which I will discuss in chapter 6. The story of a girl born to a Jewish father and black mother, Ross's novel uses the vernacular tradition of two cultures with an important, complicated, and contentious historical relationship. The absence of work on *Oreo* and on Ross, who once worked as a writer for Richard Pryor, demonstrates the limitations that comic rage critiqued in the Black Power and Black Arts movements, beginning with Ward's *Day of Absence*.

No Longer for Whites Only: *Day of Absence* and African American Theater

From the moment William Brown opened his African Grove Theatre in New York in 1820, an important dramatic counter to theatrical representation of African Americans was established. Ranging from the 1921 founding of the Colored Players Guild of New York through the 1929 appearance of the Negro Experimental Theatre, Negro Art Theatre, and National Colored Players to Baraka's establishment of the Black Arts Repertory Theatre in 1965 Harlem, African Americans sought to construct a space where African American life could be portrayed by and for African Americans. Brown's African Grove Theatre and its company eventually produced famed black actor Ira Aldridge as well as Brown's own *The Drama of King Shotaway* (1823), based on the 1796 uprising of blacks on the island of St. Vincent, which, although no longer extant, was most likely the first play written by an African American performed in the United States. The African Grove is especially important because we can see echoes of its intentions in Ward's *Day of Absence* and his Negro Ensemble Company.

Brown's theater emerged out of the African Grove, a pleasure garden that acted as a sociopolitical space for upper- and middle-class black New Yorkers. According to Marvin McAllister, the Grove was a place where "Afro-New Yorkers" could engage in acts of whiteface minstrelsy. In his interpretive history subtitled *William Brown's African and American Theater* (2003), McAllister defines whiteface minstrelsy as "extratheatrical, social performances in which people of African descent assume 'white-identified' gestures, dialectics, physiognomy, dress, or social entitlements. Whiteface is a mimetic but implicitly political form that not only masters but critiques constructed versions of whiteness" (15). Although McAllister recognizes how whiteface has been regarded as "simple mimicry," there is a danger involved when the performers do not, as McAllister says, create "hidden or private transcripts that contradict the public transcript and proffer alternative versions of civic order" (21). While the African Grove Company's initial performance of Shakespeare might arouse concerns about imitation and assimilation, Shakespeare's popularity continued to cross economic and artistic lines throughout the nineteenth century and thus "ushered [Brown's] company and its blackened versions of a beloved dramatist into the center of the majority culture's public space" (54). We can see the performances of Shakespeare in the theater and at the Grove as public acts of signifying, in which whiteness is publicly critiqued and revised. Likewise, expressions of comic rage radically critique whiteness, although its militancy seeks an explosion of traditional ideas rather than a revision.

Brown's theater signified on the practice of segregation, initially placing a partition in the *back* for whites and then racially integrating the house. Perhaps the most overt act by Brown and the African Grove Company, one with a comic element too significant to ignore, came after whites, angry at the company for performing Shakespeare, began a riot that closed the theater in the summer of 1822. In response, according to popular belief, Brown posted a sign that proclaimed, "White people do not know how to behave at entertainments designed for ladies and gentlemen of colour" (130). While McAllister points out that there is no proof such a sign ever existed, the legend has been passed on and reprinted by various figures, including Langston Hughes. McAllister believes that "writers perpetuated the legend because it spoke to their theatrical and historical communities as a statement of overt social and artistic resistance indicative of the more combative 'spirit' exhibited by 'New Negroes' of the 1930s and 1960s" (131). The sign ridicules assumptions of white superiority and privilege, while the very existence of the African Grove Company foreshadows the ideologies and practices deployed by many in the Black Power and Black Arts movements of the late 1960s and 1970s. The sign's first half humorously inverts stereotypes of black savagery and primitivism by playing on the fact that whites instigated the riot. The second half makes clear that the African Grove sought to provide work specifically tailored for a black audience, a sentiment expressed by Baraka's Black Arts Repertory Theatre and Ward's Negro Ensemble Company (NEC) in 1967.

Douglas Turner Ward's pair of one-act plays, *Happy Ending* and *Day of Absence*, earned him Vernon Rice and Obie Awards for writing and acting, respectively. In the 1971 drama collection *Contemporary Black Drama*, editor Clinton Oliver informs us that the double bill "became the third time plays by a new black playwright ran long enough to be considered a success in theater terms (the other two were *A Raisin in the Sun* and *Dutchman*), which means that they ran for over a year and made their investment back" (318). As important, in response to a request to write an article on race and theater, Ward presented a vision of African American theater that complemented, in part at least, the Black Arts movement's desire for control over their own images and eventually resulted in the formation of the NEC. His famous *New York Times* article of August 14, 1966, "American Theater: For Whites Only?," charges that mainstream American theater—Broadway, Off-Broadway, and even Off-Off-Broadway—suffered from an unwillingness to produce plays that examined the human condition beyond a privileged few. He labels American theater "A Theater of Diversion—a diversionary theater, whose main problem is not that it's too safe, but that is surpassingly irrelevant." Within this framework Ward includes the exclusion of African American playwrights, save a few successful names, from the American stage. The isolation of African American writers could be solved, according to Ward, by making "the most immediate, pressing, practical, absolutely minimally essential active first step . . . the development of a permanent Negro repertory company of at least off-Broadway size and dimension. Not in the future, but now." Ward's article, while not as militant in tone as Baraka's theatrical manifesto "The Revolutionary Theatre," mirrored Baraka's belief that African American theater should address the specific problems of African Americans and actively seek to appeal to African American audiences.

One difference, however, is the extent to which Ward viewed humor as a weapon attacking white supremacy.[1] James Cox writes of "the miracle of humor, which, far from being serious or evasive, is an invasion into the very temple of seriousness, reducing us, as working adults, to the helpless laughter from which our seriousness happily cannot save us. To be so reduced is not to be transported back to childhood where play was reality, but forward toward the last possibility of adulthood" (120). My examination of comic rage continues humor's invasion of the serious, viewing how humor transforms rage into an expression that resists its consumptive, destructive tendencies. Yet along with the reduction that Cox sees, the response of African American audiences to expressions of comic rage is a recognition of their own rage and the appreciation of the artist's ability to convey that rage constructively. In commenting on the importance of integrated audiences at African American plays directed toward a black audience, Ward's article points to an important effect on whites: "With Negroes responding all around, white spectators, congenitally uneasy in the presence of Negro satire, at least can't fail to get the message." This is not to suggest that Ward was overly concerned with tailoring his works for whites in the way that protest literature sought to do. In fact, initial reviews of Ward's plays demonstrated that the majority culture had not "gotten it." Martin Gottfried commented that Ward's use of whiteface "could only be conceived by a royal artist like Genet. Ward's borrowing of it was presumptuous and his application of it to a play whose attitude basically is peevish, makes it obscene. *Day of Absence* is an elaborate pout" (Hatch and Shine 2:265). The reference to the use of blackface and whiteface in Jean Genet's play *The Blacks* is partially understandable, especially given that Ward was a participant in the 1961 production along with other prominent black actors like James Earl Jones. However, Gottfried's attitude seeks to privilege Western inspiration, instead of the horrific legacy of blackface minstrelsy, as the genesis for Ward's play.

Moreover, along with the awards the plays garnered, its run of 504 performances proved that Ward had found an audience that responded to the frustration underlying its entertaining humor. "Like Hughes," says Oliver, "Ward uses sardonic humor and caustic laughter to attack the

shrewdly observed ways of white folk and is, underneath it all, brood-
ingly bitter at the oppression and exploitation of black folk by white folk
in the American scheme of things" (318–19). In Hoyt Fuller's 1968 essay
"Towards a Black Aesthetic," he mentions that both "*Day of Absence* and
Happy Ending . . . were tolerated as labored and a bit tasteless. . . . Ward
had dealt satirically with race relations, and there were not many black
people in the audiences who found themselves in agreement with the
critics" (1815–16). The play's aggressive tone confronts complex racial relationships while lambasting racial discrimination. Ward recognizes that
the white audience's understanding "the message" is a possible, but not
primary, result. White audiences might not fully understand the rhetoric of comic rage, but the response of black audience members to the
play might exacerbate what Ward calls the whites' congenital uneasiness,
particularly if the whites fear they are the targets of the play's humor.
Moreover, the presence of the African American vernacular tradition—
which, like the vernacular humor that Cox examines, "converts [loss]
into the gain of purest pleasure" (120)—makes possible comic rage's simultaneous expression of militancy and humor. As opposed to existing
"beneath" or "beyond" humor, militant rage, especially during the Black
Arts movement, exists *alongside* humor. Ward's plays, then, like William
Brown's African Company, inject comic rage into the majority culture's
public space without concern for that culture's response.

In *Day of Absence*, a small, nameless southern town awakens to discover that its African American population has disappeared. The play
opens with two white men, Clem and Luke, engaged in their morning
ritual of sitting outside and talking as people go to work. As they begin
to realize that they have not seen one "Nigra," the play shifts to capture
the reactions of the white townsfolk, who deduce, almost all at once,
that there are no African Americans to be found. Their immediate panic
becomes more amusing as their desperation grows. Ward's play interrogates the historical significance of African Americans by depicting the
total racial separation that many white politicians and black militants
previously promoted—by emigration to Africa, separate black states, or
complete annihilation. Ward's play, despite its seemingly absurd premise, demonstrates more clearly (and comically) the centrality of African
Americans to the very identity of American culture. Picking up, concep-
tually if not ideologically, where Schuyler left off in *Black No More*, Ward
imagines a world devoid of African Americans. While Schuyler's solution

called for the abandonment of a distinct African American art in favor of assimilation into white America, the characters in Ward's play engage in a conscious and overtly political act, leaving the town for the one day as an assertion of their understanding of whites' dependence on their presence. Ward's play dramatizes Ralph Ellison's belief in the centrality of race in America and reverses the destructive portraits of blackness that artists of the Black Arts movement completely abandoned.

In his 1970 essay "What America Would Be Without Blacks," Ellison points out the contradictory desire of whites (and some blacks) to rid America of a group of people that have been vital to its construction and identity. Noting that the "fantastic vision of a lily-white America appeared as early as 1713, with the suggestion of a white 'native American,' thought to be from New Jersey, that all the Negroes be given their freedom and returned to Africa," Ellison effectively conveys the "complex and confounding role" African Americans played "in the creation of American history and culture" (105, 107). Ellison sees the placement of race as a key factor in American identity dating back to early America, stating that "white Americans have suffered from a deep inner uncertainty as to who they really are" (110). One solution, according to Ellison, "has been to seize upon the presence of black Americans and use them as marker, a symbol of limits, a metaphor for the 'outsider'" (110–11). In her 1992 collection of lectures, *Playing in the Dark*, Toni Morrison goes a step further to argue that American obsession with race permeates the social and literary imagination. While discussing America's initial fears of limitless freedom in "Romancing the Shadow," Morrison argues that "Black slavery enriched the country's creative possibilities. For in that construction of blackness *and* enslavement could be found not only the not-free but also, with the dramatic polarity created by skin color, the projection of the not-me. The result was a playground for the imagination" (38). In Ward's play we can still see remnants of the early 1960s protest through the African American community's collective act of absence. A similar concept is the basis of William Melvin Kelley's 1962 novel *A Different Drummer*, in which the African American community methodically and individually decides to leave a mythical southern town amid white racial violence. But here there is a clear transition to the militant rage of the Black Power Movement in the black community's immediate and collective desire to cause physical and psychic damage to the white community. There is, in fact, a hint of the radical separation one finds in

Griggs's *Imperium*, Garvey's Back-to-Africa Movement, and the Nation of Islam's call for a separate black nation. Ward's play, by contrast, reveals itself as an expression of comic rage in its eschewing of the militaristic violence often advocated by black nationalist groups and instead drapes itself in the spirit of nonviolent marches and sit-ins. Extending the idea of black absence to its logical conclusion, the result is hilariously enacted chaos. The rage, however, becomes unmistakable in the portrait of the white characters and the complete breakdown of the town.

The response of John and Mary, a young white couple, to the absence of their trusted nursemaid Lula is taken to its outlandish end, in which the parents are helpless in dealing with their own child. The scenes with John and Mary call attention to the construction of the mammy figures in *Gone with the Wind* and *Beulah*, in which the African American women seem inseparable from the white family, acting as marriage counselor, surrogate mother, and emotional center. Recalling the mammy figure that Moms Mabley subverted in her comedy routine, *Day of Absence* plays on white expectations of African American female servitude. While Mabley co-opted the image of the mammy in order to explode it with her famous "I don't do no domestic" claim, *Absence* lambastes the reliance on, and ensuing construction of, the mammy in white bourgeois culture. The play exposes the idealized white middle-class family as fractured, tense, and loveless. Mary, in contrast to mainstream ideas of a pure, pious, and virginal white female, is lazy, boozy, and shrill. One telling moment occurs when Mary, who according to the stage directions is at the end of her patience, cries, "SMOTHER IT!" (38). Of course, under other circumstances such a comment might seem frightening or abhorrent. In this play, however, Mary's scream can elicit laughter because it highlights the absence of Lula and Mary's inability to relate to her child, whom she not-so-lovingly refers to as "it." As John and Mary begin to realize that Lula may not show up at all, Mary laments, "How am I gonna git through the day? My baby don't know *me*, I ain't acquainted wit' *it*. I've never lifted cover off pot, swung a mop or broom, dunked a dish or even pushed a dustrag" (40). Her dependence on Lula is less about the romanticism fostered in the "friendship" between Scarlett and Mammy in *Gone with the Wind* than it is about Mary's virtual uselessness. As her husband exits, his sardonic question encapsulates the Mary-Lula relationship: "Are you sure you kin make it to the bathroom wit'out Lula backing you up?!!!" (38). John, of course, is not blameless in the construction of the mammy figure. Primarily concerned with maintaining an edge at his office through the "mostest brown-nosing you ever saw" (37), John's expectation of a peaceful domestic home is based on Lula's efficiency in a distinct racial and gender hierarchy.

As in Schuyler's *Black No More*, the absence of African Americans exposes other forces at work in the lives of Americans, namely class and religion. Yet while Schuyler's elimination of race engages a larger argument about class and religion, *Day of Absence* places race at the center of America's identity. Race, then, is not the avenue through which class discrimination is enacted, but a construction whose existence pervades America's very construction, including class and gender. So the proclamation by the character known as the Businessman that "customers are not only not purchasing—but the absence of handymen, porters, sweepers, stock-movers, deliverers and miscellaneous dirty-work doers is disrupting the smooth harmony of marketing" (41) signifies on the role of race in class hierarchy. With African Americans relegated to lower-wage work, their absence leaves no one employed in service jobs, jobs that primarily operate for the benefit of whites. Ward reverses notions that suggest an absence of race would reveal historical class distinctions and virulent gender discrimination. Although it is necessary to reveal the connections between race, gender, and class oppression, *Absence* rejects the idea that race can be so easily removed from our consciousness. In *Black No More*, Schuyler operates from the position that racial categories—and the inevitable racial hierarchies—would be created even if every African American disappeared. At times, however, Schuyler's novel seems to suggest that racial hierarchies exist solely for the maintenance of class inequality, especially in the South. The novel collapses traditional meanings and boundaries that frequently inform our discussions of race, class, gender, and religion. Comic rage works in *Absence* by conveying the pervasiveness of race in American society *through the use of* class, gender, and religion. Put more simply, race does not exist so that class inequity can be maintained. It exists as a necessary part of America's perceptions of itself, regardless of class and/or gender concerns. Ward's play renders mainstream narratives abject by collapsing the meanings encouraged by those narratives—namely that blackness can, and should, be easily cast away—in the service of a more "universal" American identity or in favor of more "fundamental" concerns of class or gender.

One example occurs when the Announcer, who has been covering the story, interviews Mrs. Aide, the town's social welfare commissioner. In another play, the elimination of the "Negro problem" might see Mrs. Aide emerge as a catalyst who initiates resistance against the class and gender discrimination that underlie the town's focus on race. Instead she bemoans their absence, rationalizing that her organization's plans for "helping Nigras help themselves by participating in meaningful labor" (47–48) have been thwarted. She promotes the Protestant work ethic, a pull-yourself-up-by-the-bootstraps ideal to which she believes African Americans should aspire, primarily by serving whites. For her and her constituency who "volunteer" to accept the labor of African Americans, the placement of African Americans at the bottom of the class hierarchy is necessary for the lifeblood of the community. In a moment made comic by her blunt self-interest, Aide uses the importance of class distinctions to cover the white supremacy underneath. It is possible to conceive in *Absence*'s world that, if class were eliminated, a racial stratification would remain to determine advancement, power, and status. Here there are echoes of the late nineteenth century's consolidation of white southern power across class lines in order to continue the promotion of white supremacy. Recalling the Secret Nine of Wilmington, North Carolina, portrayed as the Big Three in Charles Chesnutt's *The Marrow of Tradition*, the elimination of class distinctions reveals the necessity of racial hierarchies to the maintenance of power and identity. As the tension across the town continues to build, the play shifts to focus on the influential members of the community who are pressured by the Announcer to explain the absence of black people.

Similarly, *Absence* uses these characters to engage in national debates about the implications of race. Mr. Council Clan, for example, is an obvious reference to the Ku Klux Klan and the legacy of racial violence in the South. However, it is revealed in the play that Clan has run as an opponent of the Mayor several times, losing each time. Clan's participation in the politics of the town—and the Mayor's need to appeal to those who might support Clan—negate the notion that the ideology and practice of the Klan were confined to the South's extremist wing. More likely, while the Klansmen may not have held high political office, they continued to directly influence mainstream sociopolitical life. Whether that influence took the form of participation in community activities or joining the police force, the Klan exercised power in ways that often went beyond the power wielded by political offices. Clan's first name references the White Citizens Councils founded by businessmen and leading civic figures in many southern towns as a response to desegregation efforts. Often considered "respectable" in comparison to the Klan, the White Citizens Councils' ability to discriminate openly was demonstrated in their use of economic pressure (employment, bank loans) to dissuade African Americans from voting or supporting integration. So we can view Mr. Clan as representative not only of the Ku Klux Klan but of race's importance in white political life.

Clan's belief that the black population "Ain't supposed to do nothing 'til we tell 'em. Got to stay put until we exercise our God-given right to tell 'em when to git!" (47) highlights an important synthesis of race, religion, and nation. In the play we see this synthesis represented through the figure of Reverend Reb Pious. In "Three Black Playwrights: Loften Mitchell, Ossie Davis, Douglas Turner Ward," C.W.E. Bigsby points out that whites of the town are so dependent on African Americans "in the construction of their mechanical Eden [that they] are prepared not only to exploit the Negroes but even to justify their actions by reference to a pliable religion. The Reverend Reb Pious appeals to them to fulfill their usual passive role, quoting in the process a fraudulent line from Booker T. Washington, whom he predictably calls 'one of your greatest prophets'" (165). Pious may not be involved in the political life of the town, although religious leaders were sometimes members of the White Citizens Council, but he represents a clear example of the pervasiveness of white supremacist hegemony. Similar to Reverend McPhule in *Black No More*—in their ironic naming if nothing else—Pious is exposed by comic rage for his usage of religion to morally justify racist oppression.

The presence of Pious signifies on the historical use of religion that began before slavery, from the Myth of Ham to the forced conversion of slaves to Christianity. Focusing on the obedience of slaves to their masters, white religious leaders sought to convert slaves without allowing religion to become a space for radical political action, such as the Nat Turner insurrection. Instead, Christianity was used to quell the possibility of African American uprisings, a practice that continued into the civil rights movement with the promotion of nonviolence. Addressing the white clergymen who had criticized him, Martin Luther King Jr. took the white church and its leaders to task in "Letter from Birmingham Jail." In the essay, he expresses his disappointment at the white church's failure to argue the case for equality: "I have heard numerous southern religious leaders admonish their worshippers to comply with a desegregation decision because it is the law, but I have longed to hear white ministers declare: 'Follow this decree because integration is morally right and because the Negro is your brother'" (96). Chastising the members of the white church who do not become involved in the struggle for civil rights or who seek the "absence of tension" over the "presence of justice," King concludes by asking, "Is organized religion too inextricably bound to the status quo to save our nation and the world?" (97–98). Almost as a response to King's question, Pious manipulates Booker T. Washington's famous Atlanta Exposition Speech of 1895, which urged African Americans to "Cast down your buckets where you are" instead of opposing segregation and the suppression of civil rights. Pious, in his message to the town's blacks, proclaims, "I say to you without rancor or vengeance, quoting a phrase of one of your greatest prophets, Booker T. Washington: 'Return your buckets to where they lay and all will be forgiven'" (49). Through Pious the play exposes traditional ideas of Christianity. The black population's rejection of Pious's reference to Washington represents the shift away from Washington's philosophy. Despite its use of humor, in the tradition of Robert F. Williams and the Deacons for Defense and even King himself, *Day of Absence* reflects the expression of rage by African Americans in the South through a commitment to radical action in opposition to the traditional adoption of Washington's conservative racial ideology.

It is the Mayor, however, who reveals the depth of the play's rage and the effectiveness of comedy in conveying it. Played by Ward in the original production, the Mayor, appropriately named Henry R. E. Lee, represents in a single figure the blend of the personal and the public, the political, religious, and economic white world which has been inescapably affected by the absence of the black population. Although the name also recalls Henry "Light Horse Harry" Lee of the Revolutionary War, Ward's naming of the character is a clear reference to Robert E. Lee, the Confederate commander who was a hero to many white southerners both during the Civil War and during the civil rights movement. The play ridicules the Mayor's unsuccessful attempts at maintaining order and inducing the town's African Americans to return while it also broadcasts its unmistakable rage at racist perceptions of African Americans on a national level, especially given the significance of African Americans to national identity. To be sure, the Mayor's own personal life has been thrown into disarray by the disappearance of the African Americans. His complaints are a litany of examples of the vital presence of African Americans in the white private space: "Already had to dress myself because of JC, fix my own coffee without MayBelle, drive myself to work 'counta Bubber, feel my old Hag's tits after Sapphi—NEVER MIND!" (38). Ward's reference to contemporaneous African American figures confronts the historical ideas of African American servitude. For instance, Big Maybelle, who was a popular blues singer during the 1950s and 1960s, is relegated to a typical maid role, and Sapphire, the wife of Kingfish in *Amos 'n' Andy*, is cast as the Mayor's mistress. The play seems to be suggesting that African Americans have not yet, in the white mind at least, moved out of the stereotypical roles of subservience to whites. The Mayor responds to the Announcer's questions by reporting, "The President of the United States, following an emergency cabinet meeting, has designated us the prime disaster area of the century—National Guard is already on the way" (50). The Mayor's reference to the president and the National Guard is a clear reversal on the presence of the federal government that the South reviled in the 1950s and 1960s. The South, angered by the 1954 *Brown v. Board of Education* decision, famously resisted desegregation on numerous occasions, including attempts by the Little Rock Nine in 1957, James Meredith's integration of the University of Mississippi in 1962, and the integration of the University of Alabama in 1963 when George Wallace personally attempted to block the doors. The National Guard, sent in 1957 by President Eisenhower and in 1962 and 1963 by President Kennedy, was necessary in each case to prevent white violence. The Guard's presence highlighted the South's promotion of states' rights and initiated a growing disdain there for the intervention of the federal government in solving the "Negro problem." Thus the Mayor's claim that he is relying on the help of the federal government is an important reversal that ridicules the Mayor even as it recalls violent white responses to attempts at racial equality.

The Mayor turns to a direct appeal when his initial plans, which include an even more hilarious appeal to the NAACP, are thwarted by the refusal of the other states to lend any African Americans and by the "mysterious" disappearance of any African Americans who approach the town. The Mayor's speech, which is a culmination of the stereotypes that have been paraded throughout the play, is intentionally immersed in the African American sermonic tradition. Although not possessing the rhythm or call-and-response that characterize African American sermons, the speech seamlessly shifts from empathetic petitions to fire-and-brimstone apocalypse to attempts at humor to personal testimony. At one moment the Mayor is reminiscing that "the one face I will never be able to erase from my memory is the face—not of my Ma, not of Pa, neither wife nor child" but "the full face of my dear old . . . Jemimah— God rest her soul . . . Yes! My dear ole mammy, wit' her round ebony moonbeam gleaming down upon me in the crib, teeth shining, blood red bandana standing starched, peaked and proud, gazing down upon me affectionately as she crooned me a Southern lullaby" (53–54). The figure of Aunt Jemima, specifically the highly stereotypical and detailed description, is laced with the degrading portrait of African American women as servants for the upbringing of southern whites. In fact, I argue that the Mayor's remembrance is not of a specific person but of the face on the Aunt Jemima syrup bottle! Although the role of female servants to whites has already been dramatized in the John and Mary scenes ridiculing the young white couple, the Mayor's remembrance engenders an audience response of fury. The national implications of the mammy figure are played out, as Aunt Jemima becomes the mammy for the entire nation. The next moment of the Mayor's speech finds him demanding "Come on back, YOU HEAR ME!!!" and threatening that "The city, the state and the entire nation will crucify you for this unpardonable defiance!" (54–55). Reduced to hilarious pleas and guarantees to "kiss the first shoe of the first one 'a you to show up . . . *I'll smooch any other spot you request*" (55), the climax of the Mayor's speech departs from the crescendo of African American sermons, in which the minister and the audience are in sync rhythmically as the minister reaches the apex of the sermon and the congregation's excitement peaks. The Mayor's speech, after that peak, sputters to a pitiful ending, and the townspeople's excited response is rioting, followed by abrupt silence and darkness.

After the riot in what the Announcer calls "The Face Of A Defeated City," the next day finds Clem and Luke in the same positions as at the start of the play. Seeing one African American approaching, they seize upon him, demanding to know where he and others have been. The man, Rastus, blandly says he has no knowledge of missing a day. As the rest of the African American population begin to return, Luke hopefully comments, "There's the others, Clem . . . Back jist like they useta be . . . Everything's same as always . . ." (57). Clem's response, however, is not as certain: "???. . . . . Is it . . . Luke . . . !" (57). Clem's doubt highlights the departure of Rastus, shuffling away from them with, according to the stage directions, "*a flicker of a smile playing across his lips*" (57). Clearly masking for the benefit of Clem and Luke, Rastus represents to the audience a new ideology that does not simply seek to prove the humanity of African Americans but exposes their significance to America's very existence. In the play, the absence of the African American population demands a reexamination of traditional ideas. Rastus's smile reflects the African Americans' consciousness not only of what they have done but of its effect and of the power they have to force change. Continuing the play's reference to stereotypical portraits of African Americans, the name Rastus evokes fictional figures who appeared in minstrel shows, in Joel Chandler Harris short stories, and on Cream of Wheat boxes at the end of the nineteenth century. Ward transforms Rastus into a character who represents the black consciousness and solidarity that Ward seeks with the presentation of his play. Its appeal to black audiences does not lie in the confirmation of African Americans' importance to whites, as some critics might argue. Instead, the play seeks to convey the possibility of black collective resistance against white supremacy.

What truly separates Ward's work as one of comic rage is the requirement that the white characters be played by African American actors in whiteface. Recalling the Happy Hill lynching party at the climax of *Black No More*, Ward presents the most fearless indictment of the blackface minstrel show tradition through the enactment of a reverse minstrel show. The play's signifying on blackface minstrelsy goes beyond Schuyler's similar reversal in the novel's climactic episode to take center stage in *Day of Absence*. In her master's thesis, Rozell Renée Duncan posits that the play's reverse minstrel show "adds a new dimension to minstrelsy" because "here we have Black men portraying whites and presenting stereotypes as white men would present them" (16). The play itself becomes an act of comic rage, a political act in and of itself, continuously signifying on American racial history and the construction of racial identities. Moving beyond the whiteface minstrelsy presented in the African Grove by William Brown's company, the performance of Ward's play in whiteface is a direct challenge to the stereotypical depiction of African Americans.

The play is, as Henry Louis Gates might label it, "an extended linguistic sign" on the blackface minstrelsy and white American theater that have been central in contributing to negative stereotypes of African Americans. Ward's "Notes on Production" begin the process of signifying: "If any producer is faced with choosing between opposite hues, author strongly suggests: 'Go 'long wit' the blacks—besides all else, they need the work more'" (29). The explanation of Rastus as the only black character similarly exposes Ward's larger comment on the dearth of work for African American actors. Ward, in a magnificently sarcastic tone, responds to possible concerns about his desire for an all-black cast: "Before any horrifying discrimination doubts arise, I hasten to add that a bonafide white actor should be cast as the Announcer in all productions, likewise a Negro thespian in pure native black as Rastus. This will truly subvert any charge that the production is unintegrated" (29). Ward's requirement that all who perform the play, including whites, do so in whiteface renders the idea of minstrelsy a crucial point in the telling of the story. African American actors, Ward writes, are "urged to go for broke, yet cautioned not to ham it up too broadly. In fact—it just might be more effective if they aspire for serious tragedy" (29). Here Ward reveals the necessity of balancing humor and drama, which would prevent the play from falling into farce and irrelevancy. Also, Ward's suggestion that the actors "aspire for serious tragedy" conveys the feeling that Ward wishes such a response by whites to be taken as a legitimate possibility. The underlying rage that permeates the play becomes visibly militant when we begin to consider who and what the white characters represent. The system of control that the whites employ has previously made African Americans the sufferers of abjection. In the play, however, such systems are collapsed by the abjected race's planned disappearance, which exposes the class discrimination, sexual abuse, religious manipulation, and black accomodationism the white townspeople use to hide their practical and symbolic dependence.

Day of Absence's engagement of the history of blackface minstrelsy would influence African American artists for decades as they sought to revise and critique historical depictions of African Americans. Although the plays do not all exclusively deal with minstrelsy, they mirror Ward's thematic examinations of masking, stereotyping, and resistance. A later work that seems influenced by *Day of Absence* is Carlyle Brown's play *The*

Little Tommy Parker Colored Minstrel Show (1992). Brown, who later dramatized the pioneering efforts of William Brown's African Grove Theatre in *The African Company Presents King Richard III* (1994), tackles the issue of blackface minstrelsy in a comic tone similar to Ward's. Including Brown's play, the works range from George C. Wolfe's *The Colored Museum* (1986), Suzan-Lori Parks's *The Death of the Last Black Man in the Whole Entire World* (1990), and Breena Clarke and Glenda Dickerson's *Re/Membering Aunt Jemima: A Menstrual Show* (1996) to Spike Lee's remarkable film *Bamboozled* (2000). *Day of Absence* becomes a necessary step, then, because once the consciousness of the community was realized, which Ward's essay and the formation of the NEC sought to institutionalize, African Americans began the process of constructing collective, militant responses to hegemonic oppression.

Debunking His/tory: *Flight to Canada* and the Reimagination of History

A collective, militant response would be given a target when, in 1967, William Styron's *Confessions of Nat Turner* appeared to critical acclaim, eventually winning the 1968 Pulitzer Prize for Fiction. However, the accolades Styron received from the mainly white press were contrasted by the furious response of African Americans, especially in the literary and intellectual community. Aside from the novel's seemingly oblivious attitude to the heroism in the 1800 Gabriel Prosser revolt, as dramatized in Arna Bontemps's novel *Black Thunder* (1936) or in the black collective spirit of Margaret Walker's *Jubilee* (1966), *Confessions* transforms Turner from a defiant revolutionary into a self-doubting Uncle Tom figure whose psychosexual desire for a white woman is the basis for his actions. The best-known critical response to the novel came a year after its publication in *William Styron's Nat Turner: Ten Black Writers Respond*. Edited by John Henrik Clarke, the essays in the collection are, without a doubt, one of the more uncensored, explicit collective expressions of black rage in African American letters. As Clarke notes in the introduction, "In addition to reducing Nat Turner to impotence and implying that Negroes were docile and content with slavery, Styron also dehumanizes every black person in the book. Nat's mother, according to Styron's account, enjoys being raped by a drunken Irish overseer" (viii). The writers charged that Styron was incapable of exploring Turner as a revolutionary black leader because his portraits remained consistent with historical, destructive notions of African Americans in the white imagination.

Perhaps more important, Styron co-opts the slave narrative form which, in addition to providing the template for African American literary tradition in general, was a form of counter-history, a rebuttal of the claim that slaves were property instead of human beings. Styron's novel, on the other hand, fits squarely within the historical tradition of white images of blackness that justify oppression. Nat Turner's 1831 slave revolt becomes, for many whites, a confirmation of African American barbarism instead of a legitimate act of rebellion. The renewed embrace of Turner in the late 1960s made Styron's portrait—and the mainstream's celebration of that portrait—that much more controversial. Clarke argues that the press lauded Styron's novel because it allowed them to ignore the legitimacy of black militancy during their time: "Have they failed to see Nat Turner as a hero and revolutionist out of fear that they might have to see H. Rap Brown and Stokely Carmichael the same way?" (ix). It was popular, then, as Charles Hamilton writes in the collection, precisely because "the ultimate treatment reinforces what white America wants to believe about black America. The treatment, in other words, turns out right for whites" (73). Styron's novel revealed that many of the assumptions that the slave narratives had attempted to counteract still existed in the late 1960s, and those assumptions affected both the construction of history and contemporaneous ideas about African Americans. However, the collective critical response announced that previous constructions of blackness would not be passively tolerated, but actively resisted.

Artistically, the response to Styron's novel similarly influenced a collection of works now referred to as neo-slave narratives, of which Ishmael Reed's *Flight to Canada* is an important example. Though Walker's *Jubilee*, which many consider the first neo-slave narrative, preceded *Confessions*, a number of these works emerged in order to directly challenge Styron's novel as part of their overall artistic project. Sherley Anne Williams in *Dessa Rose* (1986), for instance, informs us in an author's note that she was "outraged by a certain, critically acclaimed novel of the early seventies that travestied the as-told-to memoir of slave revolt leader Nat Turner" (ix). Though the publication of Styron's novel was in the late 1960s, it is clear that Williams is referring to *Confessions*. Reed's novel indeed responds to Styron's in the tradition of *Dessa Rose*; however, *Flight to Canada* has other reviled figures and themes on its mind besides Styron and his novel. Unlike other neo-slave narratives that possess moments of comic rage, Reed's *Flight to Canada* adopts comic rage as a tone that flows throughout the entire novel, refusing to spare any character or ideology that enters Reed's imagination. The story of Raven Quickskill's escape from slavery along with two other slaves and his attempts to reach Canada as his master Arthur Swille doggedly pursues him is a slave narrative redux, bursting from the pages with a voice filled with fury and wit. Moving back and forth between Quickskill's travels from the mythical Emancipation City to Canada and his life on the Virginia plantation from which he escaped, *Flight to Canada* launches a no-holds-barred assault on Western history, culture, and ideology. Reed eschews the more subtle jabs and knifings found in Ellison's *Invisible Man* in favor of a veritable signifying sledgehammer in his critique of white Western hegemony. Though primarily set during the years of the Civil War, Reed's novel is loaded with anachronisms that help collapse time and juxtapose myth, reality, and fantasy in depicting the historical and contemporaneous effects of white supremacist oppression. Thus Quickskill escapes slavery on a jumbo jet while the mistress of the plantation watches *The Beecher Hour* on TV with great anticipation. The seemingly loyal slave Uncle Robin uses the telephone to place orders from the slave quarters, and the Swille family travels around in limousines.

Some have argued that *Flight to Canada* parodies the slave narrative tradition, but to some extent that suggests a ridiculing of that important form. Instead I view the novel as a freeing of the voices contained within that genre, specifically from the constraints placed on it by the limitations of nineteenth-century white society. Two of those limitations related to construction and audience. In *Contemporary African American Fiction* (1998), Robert Butler writes: "Whereas most of the nineteenth-century slave narratives were directed at a white audience, edited by a white editor, and introduced by a white abolitionist who would verify the 'authenticity' of the text, Reed consciously purges these conventions of traditional slave narratives" (106). Reed's insertion of modern conveniences and contemporaneous themes into the slave narrative form seeks to connect slavery to the continued oppression of African Americans. The poem that begins the novel rejects typical slave narrative beginnings despite the significance of slave narratives to African American literature. Butler notes that the novel "opens up with a black poem that completely subverts the standard expectations of the introductions found in nineteenth-century slave narratives" because instead of a white abolitionist promoting the legitimacy of the "respectable" slave telling the story, we find "a much less manageable black rebel who wants to poison his master after drinking his best liquor, stealing his money, and sleeping with his 'prime Quadroon'" (106). The poem, also titled "Flight to Canada," announces that the novel will not fit into traditional ideas of literature. Most likely the transference of the oral to the written, in Reed's mind, cannot be contained by traditional Western constructions. What results is perhaps the epitome of a work of comic rage that reimagines constructions and perceptions of race with a fearless, and hilarious, confrontation of white supremacist hegemony.

That *Flight* might serve as the embodiment of comic rage should not be considered a radical idea, especially given its author. It has been clear for a number of years that the foremost humorist in African American literature in the last half century is Ishmael Reed. With ten novels to his credit, Reed has consistently shown a desire to engage his topics and themes in the most daring of comic voices. Michael G. Cooke in *Afro-American Literature in the Twentieth Century: The Achievement of Intimacy* comments that "Reed has taken the underground mischief that marks the entertainer's humor of Chesnutt and Hughes and made it almost volcanic" (34). Cooke's words seems as accurate as possible in describing what comic rage does, especially in linking the African American vernacular used in the humor of Chesnutt and Hughes to the unflinching rage in Reed's work that Cooke appropriately labels "volcanic." Reed uses a comprehensive array of comic weapons, ranging from outlandish and amusing tales to venomous condemnation. Reed's method involves the overt ridiculing found in the best African American comics' routines and the most dependable extended signifying since Ralph Ellison. Although a clear descendent of Schuyler in his comic tone, Reed goes beyond Schuyler's traditional satire by questioning the very standards that Schuyler promoted, namely white Western assimilation.

Much critical attention has been devoted to Reed's third novel, *Mumbo Jumbo* (1972), because of its overt challenge to white Western hegemony, chiefly through its destruction at the hands of the mysterious force Jes Grew. In this novel Reed's promotion of his "Neo-HooDoo" aesthetic, which is the black American manifestation of the African-inspired HooDoo, appears at its most overt. Existing outside the written word in the oral, the performative, and the spiritual, Neo-HooDoo is, as Reed says in his "Neo-HooDoo Manifesto," "a litany seeking its text / Neo-HooDoo is a Dance and Music closing in on its words / Neo-HooDoo is a Church finding its lyrics" (2300). As such, Neo-HooDoo fits perfectly within the versatility of form and genre that was vital to the Black Arts movement. Although not the thematic focus of the novel in the way that it is in *Mumbo Jumbo*, Neo-HooDoo permeates *Flight to Canada*. The construction of Reed's mixture of "part prose fiction, part literary historiography, part poetry, part drama, and part autobiography" (63), as Joe Weixlmann describes the novel, merges written forms with uncensored African American humor and challenges American literary ideas of genre and canon. Traditional literary forms are disrupted, replaced by a text that is self-aware, radical, and distinctly African American.

Reed's infusion of Neo-HooDoo into his novels represents another synthesizing in African American literature of the written and the oral. Henry Louis Gates's discussion of *Mumbo Jumbo* in *The Signifying Monkey* is important to understanding comic rage in *Flight to Canada*. Returning to Bakhtin's belief that an "inner dialogization" takes place between "parodic speech acts" and "hidden polemic" when the two overlap, as they do in *Mumbo Jumbo*, Gates sees "curious implications, the most interesting, perhaps, being what Bakhtin describes as 'the splitting of double-voiced discourse into two speech acts, into two separate and autonomous voices'" (112–13). However, aside from the traditional problem of the devaluing of works labeled "polemic," my concern here lies with the separation of the voices of "parody" and "hidden polemic," which for me are representative of comedy and rage. While I agree that such an "inner dialogization" takes place when polemic and parody overlap, two separate voices do not always emerge. Such an assumption would ignore, first and foremost, African American comedic tradition which has inherently contained attacks on oppressive forces couched in humorous depictions. Comic rage, which partially emerges out of that tradition, is a *fusion* of humor and resistance in which these two elements in African American culture speak as one voice against hegemonic onslaught. It is this fusion that leverages the abject, as works of comic rage confront racist assumptions and respond to the abject's challenge to "borders, positions, rules." In *Flight*, not surprisingly, roles are not merely reversed or revealed but reimagined.

For Reed, no topic is sacred. There is no person or subject above Reed's imaginative aim. He signifies constantly on the history/mythology about race and America. As part of his anachronistic strategy, he argues that Edgar Allan Poe should be the chief historian of the Civil War, replete with the terror of whiteness in *The Narrative of Arthur Gordon Pym* (1838), the obsession with blood and purity found in "The Fall of the House of Usher" (1839), and the violence and death beneath the decadence in "The Masque of the Red Death" (1842). Arthur Swille, who the novel claims mourns the death of his sister/lover Vivian, refers to the South as "Camelot." Swille's reference reflects the South's nostalgia for the antebellum period, which led to the post-Reconstruction backlash against African American political power, the heroic portrayal of the white South in the novels of Thomas Dixon and the movie *Gone with the Wind*, and the South's resistance to integration and equality during the civil rights movement. Building further on the theme, Quickskill, while speaking to his lover Quaw Quaw Tralaralara, expands the idea of Camelot to encompass the entire nation: "Camelot. Camelot West, Camelot East, Camelot South. One big fucking Camelot. With darkies and Injuns to set places, pour and serve at the Round Table. Playing on the lute and reciting verse, doing court dances" (98). This expansion of Camelot can certainly be seen as a play on America's version of Camelot perpetuated through the Kennedy family's mix of majesty, romance, and tragedy, especially throughout the 1960s. However, in this vision of Camelot the minorities, here African and Native Americans, are given a specific place in the racial hierarchy, of servitude and entertainment, in order to definitively establish the ideal society. The vision of America as Camelot is a major reason that Quickskill seeks to escape to Canada; it also directly informs Quickskill's opposition to the prostitution and pornography mail-order business in which his fellow escapee Stray Leechfield is involved and his criticism of Quaw Quaw, whose "exotic" dancing and performance are in high demand by the white mainstream. In the novel, comic rage, through Quickskill's comments, reimagines "Camelot" and the actions of Leechfield and Quaw Quaw as extensions of hegemonic oppression that confirm perceptions of white superiority.

When Quickskill visits 40s, the other slave who escaped with him and Leechfield, another metaphor similar to "Camelot" is revealed. Upon realizing that 40s has a shotgun aimed at his head, Quickskill comments,

"'Aw, 40s, put it away. We're not in Virginia no more.' 40s spat. 'That's what you think. Shit. Virginia everywhere. Virginia outside. You might be Virginia'" (76). Virginia, of course, is where Quickskill, Leechfield, and 40s were enslaved. However, 40s's comment casts Virginia beyond its literal role in the novel toward its historical role. The state's status as the site of the first colony, the birthplace of George Washington and Thomas Jefferson, and the capital of the Confederacy for the bulk of the Civil War highlights the contradiction of America itself. Although the birthplace of two of the chief proponents of (white) American democracy and freedom, Virginia also became a major site of the oppression of an entire populace. Virginia, then, comes to represent the institution of slavery and, because of its historical significance to the founding of the country, the broader promotion of white supremacist hegemony. Representations of Virginia are thus not restricted to one individual or one race. For 40s the agents of oppression, "Virginia" as he labels them, can come from anyone or anywhere. The paranoia of 40s is no doubt fueled by the presence of Mammy Barracuda and Cato the Graffado, slaves who act to ensure the system, maintaining order among the slaves, informing on their activities, and forcing them to adopt Christianity, referred to in the novel as "the Jesus cult."

While attacking both institutions and mythology, Reed reserves his most obvious expressions of comic rage for real-life figures. Swille claims that Quickskill, 40s, and Leechfield escaped because they suffer from dysaesthesia aethiopica, a malady invented in 1851 by a Dr. Samuel Cartwright, who diagnosed slaves' desire to escape as a form of mental illness. One of the fiercest objects of Reed's portrayal is Abraham Lincoln, as the novel seeks to destroy the myth of Lincoln as the Great Emancipator. Despite labeling the second part of the novel "Lincoln the Player," Reed equally casts Lincoln as an inept country bumpkin. After a meeting with Swille, Lincoln asks his aide if Camelot is a town in Virginia. In a wry play on the masking that has been a hallmark of African American humor and negotiation, Lincoln says: "Curious tribe. There's something, something very human about them, something innocent and . . . yet I keep having the suspicion that they have another mind. A mind kept hidden from us" (46). Reed also challenges the notion that Honest Abe's abolitionist convictions were one reason for the Civil War by having Lincoln comment, "We change the issues, don't you see? Instead of making this some kind of oratorical minuet about States' Rights versus the

Union, what we do is make it so you can't be for the South without being for slavery!" (49). The quote reminds readers that, although he supported abolition, Lincoln argued in 1858 that African Americans should not be considered equal to whites. At the next moment, Lincoln seeks to take full advantage of the signing of the Emancipation Proclamation by telling his aide, "'Call in the press. Get the Capitol calligrapher who's good at letterin to come in and draw this Proclamation. Phone the networks. We'll put an end to this Fairy Kingdom nonsense. Guenevere, Lancelot, Arthur and the whole dang-blasted genteel crew" (49). Lincoln's signing of the Emancipation Proclamation elevated him to a celebrated place in African American cultural history and memory. During the twentieth century, Lincoln became an example of white America's racial tolerance—as the Union/North stood in heroic contrast to a South stuck in the past—that camouflaged the virulent system of segregation and the erosion of civil rights that began with the end of Reconstruction. The novel even foreshadows the assassination of Lincoln unsympathetically by depicting his presence at the theater as a political move: "I might need Swille's support some more and so I'm going to start doing more for culture. . . . I want you to get me and Mary Todd some tickets to a theatre from time to time and invite Ulysses and his wife" (46). What becomes abundantly clear through the ridicule of Lincoln and others is the novel's desire to rip down previous representations of white historical figures and their role in African Americans' freedom struggle.

Traditionally, Lincoln is thought of as one of the nation's greatest presidents because of his role in the preservation of the Union, his legacy raised alongside the lofty status of George Washington and Thomas Jefferson, with the Emancipation Proclamation taking its place next to the Constitution and the Declaration of Independence as the key documents in American political and moral identity. In the second part of the novel, Reed methodically destroys that image, casting Lincoln as a figure who exploits the issue of slavery and African Americans to exert political and moral power. For example, *Flight to Canada* interrogates the specifics of the Emancipation Proclamation to critique Lincoln's defining act. Lincoln's signing of the document has been remembered as the equivalent of Thomas Jefferson's authorship of the Declaration of Independence. The proclamation "all men are created equal" has frequently been cited to highlight the inequalities African Americans faced. Sitting in bed with her husband, Robin, Aunt Judy refuses to toast the Emancipation:

"Won't do us any good. He freed the slaves in the regions of the country he doesn't have control over, and in those he does have control over, the slaves are still slaves. I'll never understand politics" (59). Matthew R. Davis suggests that Reed "never reconciles Lincoln as either a player or a fool" (744). This seems purposeful. Through Lincoln the novel's use of comic rage questions how history is constructed and remembered, especially with regard to America and its treatment of race.

Though Reed makes demystifying Lincoln a chief concern of the novel, he embeds *Flight to Canada* with the demonizing of Harriet Beecher Stowe. The novel's first section is labeled "Naughty Harriet," and after Quickskill's opening poem, it launches into a fiery ridiculing of Stowe and her place in history. The novel charges that her 1852 novel *Uncle Tom's Cabin*, one of the benchmark texts of the American literary canon, was stolen from the 1849 autobiography *The Life of Josiah Henson*, which she manipulated to create the figure of Uncle Tom. Quickskill, who narrates the first part of chapter 1, accuses Stowe of writing the novel not in protest against slavery but because she "only wanted enough money to buy a silk dress" (8). He reduces her to a second-rate story-stealing "spinster" who committed what the novel sees as an unpardonable crime. Quickskill informs us that Henson's autobiography was "Seventy-seven pages long. It was short, but it was his. It was all he had. His story. A man's story is gris-gris, you know. Taking his story is like taking his gris-gris. The thing that is himself" (8). We can therefore view Reed's novel as an attempt to return the story of Josiah Henson to its owner and right a historic wrong. As for Stowe, who is also charged with building a Virginia plantation in New England with the proceeds of Henson's "borrowed" story, the novel issues a warning: "Harriet paid. Oh yes, Harriet paid. When you take a man's story, a story that doesn't belong to you, that story will get you" (8). Reed's novel is invested in making Stowe pay. It takes frequent shots at both Stowe the individual and her novel. Whether suggesting that Stowe spread rumors that Lincoln was illiterate or ridiculing Stowe's exclusionary feminism, Reed is relentless. The novel suggests that Henson's hand guides the story's attack on Stowe as a way to recover what was taken from him. As with the portrayal of Lincoln, the ridicule of Stowe exemplifies the novel's larger target, specifically the Western construction of history which manipulates African American life for the promotion of white supremacist rule.

The novel is, in some ways, an extended linguistic sign on *Uncle Tom's*

Cabin, in much the same way *Day of Absence* signifies on blackface minstrelsy. It is through the attack on *Uncle Tom's Cabin* that *Flight to Canada*, as a neo-slave narrative, simultaneously comments on contemporaneous ideas about race. Aside from the effect of the Black Arts movement, the novel's treatment of Stowe parallels the critique of William Styron's aforementioned "theft" of Nat Turner's life and story. Just as Stowe's novel robs Henson of his "gris-gris," Ashraf Rushdy believes, Reed "continues the work of the Black Power intellectuals who had also claimed that Styron's use of Nat Turner constituted a 'deliberate attempt to steal the meaning of a man's life.' Indeed, Reed is implicitly critiquing Styron's cultural appropriation by revisiting the analogous case of Stowe's act of appropriating Henson's narrative" (102). Reed achieves his critique through his use of the slave narrative tradition and his (re)construction of the Uncle Tom figure. Challenging the genesis of Uncle Tom, which emerges out of the same belief in African American docility that permeates Styron's portrait of Turner, Reed meanwhile addresses the labeling of African Americans considered "Uncle Toms," who were often so defined by many in the Black Arts movement for their lack of overt militant resistance.

The character that Reed uses to develop this debate is Uncle Robin, the loyal servant of Arthur Swille. Although the Uncle Tom figure, made famous by Stowe's novel, was initially credited with helping whites understand the evils of slavery, over the years the image has become vilified in the African American community as someone who has willingly adopted a white supremacist ideology that increased his individual benefits. Though the perception of this figure has changed as well as the specifics of his role, his ceaseless loyalty to his white master remains constant. *Flight to Canada* does not intend to destroy "Uncle Toms" as a Black Power/Black Arts ideology might dictate. Instead the novel destroys the *idea* of the Uncle Tom figure at its root, namely though Uncle Tom in Stowe's novel, by focusing on the character upon whom the figure is based: Josiah Henson. Henson's escape from slavery represents one of the most radical acts of resistance, perhaps second only to insurrection, and reveals the Uncle Tom figure as a fictional creation that became a locus of nostalgia for white southerners after the Civil War rather than a realistic depiction of the slave/master relationship.

Through the character of Robin, and Quickskill to some extent, "Reed uses that conventional dichotomy of the sixties—Uncle Tom and Nat

Turner—to show that those who seem to be Uncle Toms in their bourgeois values can sometimes turn out to be Nat Turners in their dedica-
tion to concerted and planned revolutionary action, including strategic
violence" (110), according to Rushdy. This may seem to be a traditional
form of masking, part of the negotiation of rage and pain that Ellison
hails as important in "Negro" American culture and that Ward conjures
when he defends the word "Negro" in the NEC because it "had a long,
honored" history" (Hatch and Shine 2:265). Influenced by the Black Arts
movement, however, *Flight to Canada* adds a new dimension to those
ideas of masking, instead using it as an offensive weapon. The radicalizing of comic rage, then, moves it from a cultural form that is part of
African American nonviolent negotiations of rage to a more active attack on oppression and its byproducts. Quickskill's escape, made possible
by his time as Swille's bookkeeper, is the most obvious example of the
proactive use of masking. However, Uncle Robin becomes a figure just
as important, especially since we see his role as "Uncle Tom" played out
throughout the novel. Although Robin "is required to dress up as a Moor-
ish slave to satisfy one of Swille's cravings" (18), his position remains
among the most powerful on the plantation. He makes trips across the
country for Swille, handles the financial affairs, and is considered one
of Swille's most beloved servants. Reed makes clear that this is only a
façade, and the novel presents several moments where Robin uses his
mask to ridicule whites and comment on white supremacy. In one encounter with the white slave Mr. Moe, Robin responds to Moe's comment "No wonder they call you an Uncle Tom" (41) by firing a deadly shot
at the heart of white supremacy:

> "You are a white man but still you a slave. You may not look like a
> slave, and you dress better than slaves do, but all day you have to run
> around saying Yessuh, Mr. Swille and Nossuh, Mr. Swille and when
> Mitchell was a child, Maybe so, l'il Swille. Why, he can fire you any-
> time he wants for no reason."
> "What! What did you say? How dare you talk to a white man like
> that!"
> "Well, sometimes I just be reflectin, suh. Ain't no harm in that." (41)

Robin's suggestion that he "just be reflectin" hides his critique of class
and white expectation of privilege. Nevertheless, he blatantly comments
on the legacy of white solidarity that began at the end of Reconstruction,

one that hid class discrimination in favor of the oppression of African Americans. His friendship and collaboration with Quickskill, who agrees to write Robin's story, deviates even further from the Uncle Tom figure. Traditional ideas of Uncle Toms suggest that these figures abandoned the idea of escaping and typically disassociated themselves from slaves planning to do so.

Reed engages the debate over the construction of Nat Turner and Uncle Tom figures through the use of violence, although not in the sense of Turner's insurrection, but in comic rage's overt tone that forces a reassessment of the docility of Uncle Tom. Rushdy notes, "In situating violence, particularly violence against slavemasters, so centrally in his novel, Reed is contributing to the dialogue over political activism emerging from Black Power and the sixties debate over the inefficacy of nonviolence" as well as "alluding to one of the basic feature of Styron's novel (the confusion of violence and sexuality, which Swille the masochist exemplifies)" (110). Thus Reed extends his reworking of Uncle Tom to Quickskill in his encounters with 40s and Leechfield, both of whom Quickskill goes to warn once he discovers that Swille has sent slave catchers after them. In an argument with the field slave Leechfield, Quickskill reveals the house slaves' attempts to keep their fellow slaves from the wrath of the master: "We covered for you all the time—made excuses for you and sometimes did the work ourselves that you were supposed to do" (73). Leechfield would stereotypically be one of the models for the Black Arts and Black Power movements' idea of African American resistance. One of the most popular slaves on Swille's plantation because he stole hens and went into business for himself, he eventually escapes with 40s and Quickskill. However, Quickskill finds Leechfield profiting by making pornographic movies and involved in a mail-order business that offers him as a "slave for a day." He becomes the epitome of the hypersexualized black man—and another example of the confusion of violence and sex that Rushdy references—as opposed to Quickskill's comic and militant resistance. Leechfield privileges money by assuming that payment to Swille will allow him to remain free, a belief that is proven wrong when he is captured by Swille's slave "tracers." Although 40s's possession of a rifle and willingness to murder the slave catchers is reminiscent of the violent militancy of the Black Power movement, his paranoia and mistrust have isolated him from any collective African American resistance struggle. The presence of the gun does not automatically reflect revolutionary intent, especially when it is disconnected from collective cultural forms of expression. Here we see comic rage moving beyond only targeting whites to critiquing black ideas of revolutionary figures and actions. The progression of comic rage, then, moves from Ellison, who parodied Booker T. Washington, to Ward, who questioned ideas of appealing to white audiences, to Reed's direct examination of flaws in black socio-political ideology. Quickskill and, eventually, Robin emerge as the truly revolutionary figures despite their status as house slaves.

Although Matthew Davis contends that Reed "never fully distinguishes between Raven's narrative and that of Robin" (744), Quickskill drives the action of the novel and, separately, stands as a literary character from which we can examine comic rage at its greatest potential. First, Quickskill's presence and flight allow Reed to pull from the slave narrative tradition. Mirroring the stories of literacy, consciousness, and escape that often characterize slave narratives, the novel depicts Quickskill as a character for whom flight from slavery seems inevitable. In Reed's continuing critique of contemporaneous ideas of the house slave/Uncle Tom figure, the novel augments Swille's confusion over Quickskill's escape with the claim that "Raven was the first one of Swille's slaves to read, the first to write and the first to run away" (14). More specifically, as Davis argues, Quickskill can be connected to Frederick Douglass and William Wells Brown through his "chosen profession as an anti-slavery lecturer and writer" (748). Though the slave quarters are named the "Frederick Douglass houses," Davis believes that "*Flight to Canada* relies upon themes, stylistic devices, and characters introduced and developed in the works of William Wells Brown, revealing an affiliation between Reed and Brown in their individual belief in HooDoo, their use of anachronism, their particular political and social views, and, importantly, their styles" (744). It is, after all, Brown that Quickskill meets toward the end of the novel, at which point Quickskill compliments Brown as a premier satirist. Thus we can see Quickskill as a figure that uses comic rage to signify on Swille's oppression and express cynicism about white America.

Brown, who Davis argues changed a number of historical facts throughout his three autobiographies, can also be considered a manipulator of history in the same vein as Reed.[2] Davis, however, sees another connection to Brown. In contrast to Douglass's dismissal of the "root" he is given before his memorable fight with the slave breaker Edward Covey, Davis contends that "Brown's willingness to accept the possibility of HooDoo and his disavowal of literacy, as opposed to Douglass's disbelief in magic and his celebration of literacy, allow Reed to argue that writing itself is a form of HooDoo" (748). Davis astutely points out that it seems "paradoxical" that Quickskill would "assert faith in HooDoo and conjure while relying nearly completely upon the written word, his literacy, for his escape, buying his passage to Canada with proceeds from the sale of his first poem" (748). Yet where Davis believes that Quickskill "downplays the significance of the author's learning throughout," I am persuaded that Quickskill does not minimize the importance of his education, but instead uses his book knowledge to complement his embrace of HooDoo. A critical example appears when Quickskill considers his poem "Flight to Canada," which has earned him both money and a trip to the White House: "'Flight to Canada' was the problem. It made him famous but had also tracked him down. It had pointed to where he, 40s and Stray Leechfield were hiding. It was their bloodhound, this poem 'Flight to Canada.' It had tracked him down just as his name had" (13). That danger, Reed seems to be suggesting, lies in the dependence on the written, in not fusing it with the oral, the Neo-HooDoo.

Again, we can see an important contrast in Cato the Graffado. The explosion of the Uncle Tom myth by Robin and Quickskill does not mean that there were not African Americans who fit black popular definitions of an Uncle Tom. These figures are completely assimilated into hegemonic culture, and they are viewed with great disdain in the novel. Cato has earned a PhD, acts as a spy for Swille, and seems to celebrate all things Western. One of the many subversive and overt shots the novel takes occurs when Arthur Swille looks at Cato and sees someone "who bears a remarkable resemblance to himself, in fact, could be a butterscotched version of him" (51). So committed that "he volunteered for slavery, and so dedicated he is to slavery, the slaves voted him all-Slavery" (34), Cato uncritically espouses Western ideology at the expense of African American cultural tradition like HooDoo. It is in the effective transference to the written, in which traditional ideas are revised and critiqued, that Neo-HooDoo, the black American manifestation of HooDoo, maintains its power. So while the novel does proclaim that, for Quickskill, "writing was his HooDoo," Quickskill seeks to write Robin's story because "'You put witchery on the word,' Robin said. He would try to put witchery on the word" (13). Like the transfer of African American orality in the works of Sutton Griggs, the poetry of James Weldon Johnson and Langston

Hughes, and the novels of Zora Neale Hurston and Ralph Ellison, *Flight to Canada* uses the *written* word as an expression of a distinctly African American *voice*. Contained within that voice is a mixture of humor and rage that views America from the unique perspective of being of African descent in America.

Quickskill differs from Schuyler's Max/Matthew in his conscious, radical acts in defiance of white supremacist assault. Quickskill's poem declares its intent to assault his master's fantastical vision of race. The novel does not cast Quickskill's poem and his flight as evasions or sub-versions of oppressive assault as in Max/Matthew's transformation. Instead the poem directly engages byproducts of oppression through comic attack and sets the tone for the comic rage that suffuses the novel. Quickskill boasts to Swille that he has "snuck back to / The plantation 3 maybe 4 times" and claims: "Last night I slept in / Your bed and sampled your / Cellar. Had your prime / Quadroon give me / She-Bear. Yes, yes" (15). Quickskill's references suggest an inversion of the traditional power dynamic that renders Swille powerless. Quickskill becomes the master, sleeping in the master's bed and reaping all the master's benefits. Thus the novel does not simply become the traditional slave narrative that details the horrific treatment by the master in contrast to the heroic self-actualization of the slave. Quickskill's action goes beyond the slave's journey of self-discovery. Indeed, this novel begins with its protagonist already having reached the point of awareness and resistance. In addition, the title suggests that Quickskill rejects the post-slavery adoption of idealized standards of the white mainstream through American de-mocracy. Whereas Max undergoes the surgery offered by Junius Crook-man primarily to find the white woman who rejected him, Quickskill's escape acts as part of the larger resistance the slaves on Swille's planta-tion carry out. The critical awareness of Quickskill seems absent in Max, who, out of greed, helps recruit for the racist, Klan-like Knights of Nor-dica. His use of the white fear at the Black-No-More treatments amounts to a desire to play a practical joke. By contrast, Quickskill undermines the institution of slavery beyond his own benefit. "Fooled around with my books," Swille complains, "so that every time I'd buy a new slave he'd destroy the invoices and I'd have no record of purchase; he was also writ-ing passes and forging freedom papers" (35). His decision to emigrate to Canada rejects America's projection of itself as exceptional and adopts one of the most radical of African American nationalist ideologies.

Ultimately the novel's attack on Stowe and *Uncle Tom's Cabin*—and its realization as a work of comic rage—rests on Uncle Robin's entertaining subversion, and eventual abjection, of the Uncle Tom character. After the murder of Swille, most likely achieved by the hyper-fast Pompey, Robin's manipulation of the will leaves him with control of the plantation and Swille's estate. The doctored will establishes a school for freed slaves, leaves Cato nothing, and, in Reed's final nod to Poe, directs that Swille be buried with his sister in an illustrated Kama Sutra position at which "the Judge blushed" (169). In the final pages, with Quickskill finding disappointment in the physical space of Canada, Robin emerges as the novel's triumphant voice. Highlighting the Uncle Tom/Nat Turner dichotomy that the novel seeks to complicate, Robin muses, "Now Nat's dead and gone for these many years, and here I am master of a dead man's house. Which one is the fool?" (178). He becomes the abjection that breaks down the lines—and the lens—that informs the debate between revolutionaries and sell-outs Simplistic racial stereotypes and dichotomies are essential to white supremacist hegemony and provide a rationale for the demonization and expulsion of African Americans who complicate mainstream portraits of race. The presence of Robin, who represents the abjected race that cannot be expelled, threatens the fundamental assumptions and discourses that relegate African Americans to second-class citizens. So when Robin's wife asks about his practice of bringing Swille slave mothers' milk, he tells her that it was never milk but rather Coffee Mate, which, because of the poison he had been giving Swille, would eventually have killed the slave master. Combining this revelation with his rejection of Harriet Beecher Stowe as the ghostwriter of his autobiography in favor of Quickskill, Uncle Robin protects his story from the crime that Stowe committed on Josiah Henson and secures for it the "witchery" Quickskill will put on it: "Quickskill would write Uncle Robin's story in such a way that, using a process the old curers used, to lay hands on the story would be lethal to the thief. That way his Uncle Robin would have the protection that Uncle Tom (Josiah Henson) didn't" (11). Reed's reimagining of these historical figures reflects comic rage's willingness to engage, to challenge, and to reject traditional ideologies about race and identity. So while a satire, especially one influenced by the Black Arts movement, may have called for a return to the ideology of Nat Turner, *Flight to Canada* questions the (white) construction of divergent figures like Nat Turner and Uncle Tom. Just as Quickskill has begun the novel in the first person, Robin ends it there, a final merging of the Uncle Tom and the Nat Turner characters present throughout the novel and finalized with Quickskill's return to the plantation.

Quickskill's return signals the novel's critique of traditional ideas about emigration, freedom, and the Promised Land. At the end of *Black No More*, Max/Matthew leaves America and lives happily with his white wife and their child, even as he confesses to them that he is African American. This is consistent with Schuyler's belief that America would be incapable of overcoming its obsession with race. In *Flight*, Quickskill and Quaw Quaw make it to Canada but begin to realize that discrimination has not stopped at the borders of America. When they run into a friend named Carpenter, he informs them that he is returning to Emancipation City. Having been beaten and denied a hotel room, Carpenter reports, "Man, they got a group up here called the Western Guard, make the Klan look like statesmen," and "of the ten top Canadian corporations, four are dominated by American interests" (160). Once in Canada, Quaw Quaw's celebrity continues to be based on her exoticism, even as she is mistaken for Japanese. This eventually alienates her from Quickskill, who becomes depressed that he has not found the Promised Land for which he has been searching. Robert Butler sees the idea of a "promised land" as another difference between *Flight* and traditional slave narratives. "Although both take the form of flight from a condition of servitude in the South to a kind of liberation in the North, Reed's novel expresses a radical disillusionment with any actual places outside the South," he suggests, and "Reed depicts all places as various kinds of betrayals" (106). Adding to Butler's argument, the novel returns to the racist but romanticized vision of the South that extends beyond regional and even national borders when, upon Mrs. Swille's release from the sanitarium after she has been acquitted of murdering her husband, she gets a job in Canada to create "a replica of a Virginia plantation" (172). Here we see an extension of the metaphor of "Virginia" and "Camelot" beyond the United States. More important, we see the novel's use of comic rage to render assumptions about the Promised Land and antebellum slave narratives abject. *Flight* rejects the limited critique of the North and Canada found in nineteenth-century slave narratives, exposing the limitations placed on African American voices by white editors and abolitionists.

Therefore, in the demystifying of Canada, a place considered throughout African American history as the quintessential refuge from oppression, comic rage gets fully realized in the novel through its commentary on *Western* hegemony's construction of race. As a physical and geopolitical space, Canada replicates Western ideas and practices that marginalize minority groups. The destruction of Canada as a physical space for freedom solidifies the parameters for Reed's work as an act of comic rage. At the beginning of the novel, Quickskill, most likely at the end of his journey like Ellison's Invisible Man in the prologue, asks, "Who is to say what is fact and what is fiction?" (7). By questioning fact and fiction, myth and reality, the novel challenges readers' previous notions of history and avoids satire's tendency to call for the return to a specific standard that may have not been met in the first place. At the end of the novel, with Quickskill's disappointment in Canada revealed and Robin's voice completely uncensored, Robin declares that "Canada, like freedom, is a state of mind" (178). The statement reflects nationalist ideas of emigration and separation, exposing Western hierarchal notions of oppression—"good" versus "bad" slaves, or Canada versus North versus South—and redirects the path for African American freedom and resistance by reclaiming history, culture, and language, made possible by humor's creation of a space where rage can be channeled into an effective assault on traditional ideas.

From *Absence* to *Flight* and Beyond

Despite the heavy influence of the Black Arts movement on *Flight to Canada*, the novel is not a consistently loyal follower of the movement. Aside from the critique of Nat Turner, Reed's novel appeared at a time of great flux in African American literature. Ashraf Rushdy reports, "The year 1976 also marked the end of the Black Arts movement, the cultural arm of Black Power. Ceasing publication in 1976, *Black World*, the major journal of the Black Arts movement, issued key statements critical of the cultural values and literary production of the Black Power sixties" (98). Reed's own shifting allegiances with the Black Arts movement, from affiliation to disenfranchisement to appreciation, play out in the novel. According to Rushdy, "Reed persistently criticized Black Power advocates for failing to appreciate the extent to which previous African American cultural movements and political figures had also struggled to achieve the same social freedoms for which Black Power advocates were striving" (101). The Uncle Tom/Nat Turner exploration exemplifies

Reed's recognition of the multitude of ways African Americans resisted oppression. Here the novel recalls Ellison's belief in the transcendence of the blues, masking, and deflection of pain. Reed, as Rushdy suggests, disagreed with "Black Power advocates for their reluctance to appreciate the diverse political styles within the black community, their inability to accept the complex aesthetic values beyond protest fiction, and their unwillingness to revere cultural formations from the past" (101). Humor in attacking racist oppression sits at the center of a literary debate that Ward and Reed navigate in their works. Reed, in his "Harlem Renaissance Day" speech, referred to some Black Arts writers as the "sullen, humorless critics of the Black Aesthetic movement" (297). Yet while comic rage may have been at odds with the Black Arts movement, it still shared much of its impetus and ideals.

Similarly, in regard to *Day of Absence*, Clinton Oliver notes that while "Ward's work has the sting of sharp and sophisticated humor, it is not propelled by the violence and fury so characteristic of the work of LeRoi Jones, James Baldwin or Ed Bullins" (318). Ward's play is not, like *Flight to Canada*, considered a work of the Black Arts movement. Its chief act of resistance, absence, is not the militant challenge to white society that the artists of the Black Arts movement considered preferable. However, the play's demonstration of the African American community acting with a solidarity befitting an awakened black consciousness, and its construction for an African American audience, are elements influenced by, and some would say forecasting, the parallel desires that characterize the works of the Black Arts movement.[3] The point here continues to be that comic rage can be influenced by, even as it also critiques, the movement(s) of which it is a part. So although comic rage emerges out of the spirit that spawned the Black Arts and Black Power movements, it is not necessarily *of* those movements, particularly because of the Black Arts movement's aversion to comic attacks on racism.

To be sure, expressions of comic rage remain intricately tied to the historical moment and politics of the African American community. In particular, the works of comic rage openly challenge traditional forms. Thus we see Ward presenting a "reverse minstrel show" and Reed combining genres and historical periods. Those challenges to form remain, even when we see a discernible shift in expressions of comic rage from the unabashed militancy of the late 1960s and early 1970s to the inward turn in the 1980s and 1990s that reflects the changing face of black

America with its emergent middle class. As a natural progression away from protest literature that was concerned with the perceptions of white audiences, African American literature became more internal, examining specific problems within the African American community. Among those issues were the internalization of stereotypes, the controversial debate between black men and black women, and the black middle class's relationship to the African American underclass. African American literature continued to address the conflicts between the African American community and white supremacy. In fact, in the face of a conservative counterrevolution that peaked with the Reagan/Bush era of the 1980s and early 1990s, African American literature often turned to humor as a way of debunking stereotypes as well as commenting on the reconfiguration of white supremacist oppression. Newer works of comic rage demonstrate its versatility during these years, ranging from moments in neo-slave narratives like Sherley Williams's *Dessa Rose* and Charles Johnson's *Middle Passage* (1990) to plays like Carlyle Brown's *Little Tommy Parker Colored Minstrel Show* and Robert Townsend's movie *Hollywood Shuffle* (1987) to Reed's novels *The Terrible Twos* (1982) and its sequel *The Terrible Threes* (1989). The black middle class's exponential growth contrasted with the explosion of crack in the inner cities, placing black America in the unique position of having segments of its population moving in significantly different directions. With the appearance of Trey Ellis's "New Black Aesthetic," a new breed of African American writer emerged and comic rage seemed to find a place among those writers. Works that encapsulate the shifting literary, sociopolitical, and economic dynamics of African American life include George C. Wolfe's play *The Colored Museum* (1986), Trey Ellis's *Platitudes* (1988), and Paul Beatty's *White Boy Shuffle* (1996).

4

Fury in the "Promised Land"

Comic Rage in George C. Wolfe's *The Colored Museum*
and Paul Beatty's *The White Boy Shuffle*

Rock the hard jams—treat it like a seminar
Teach the bourgeois, and rock the boulevard
Public Enemy, "Don't Believe the Hype"

By the time Reed's *Flight to Canada* appeared in 1976, the benefits of the
civil rights movement were becoming apparent. Although African Americans were central in the development of American culture before the
decades of the civil rights movement and after, their imprint during the
1960s and 1970s would become indelible. Whether it was the election of
Carl Stokes as the first African American mayor of a major city, in Cleveland in 1967, or Shirley Chisholm's historic run for president in 1972, the
1965 Voting Rights Act led to the realization of African American political power unseen since the days of Reconstruction. Yet, as at the end of
Reconstruction, white supremacy began to respond by adjusting itself
to fit the new racial dynamic. One of the primary mechanisms to effect
such an adjustment was national politics, specifically the conservative
"counterrevolution" that began with Republican Barry Goldwater's failed
presidential campaign in 1964. Augmented by George Wallace's virtual
splintering of the Democratic Party in his attempt to win the party's
nomination that same year, Goldwater's opposition to the Civil Rights
Act of 1964 initiated a process through which the white South would begin to gravitate toward the Republican Party in national, and eventually

local, elections. President Nixon's election in 1968 and reelection in 1972 were based in large part on his so-called southern strategy, which signaled racial conservatism through coded language in hopes of winning moderate whites in border states alongside the "foam-at-the-mouth segregationists" who had supported Goldwater. The promotion of the Republican Party as more concerned with law and order, more connected to the religious revivalism of the 1970s, and more in favor of a "color-blind" society culminated in the election of Ronald Reagan in 1980. Underneath Reagan's optimistic vision, new members of the African American elite struggled with the decision to assimilate like black neoconservatives. Meanwhile the African American underclass became increasingly disenfranchised and voiceless. Although the elite and the underclass continued to enact racial solidarity publicly and politically, specifically in Jesse Jackson's bid for the presidency in 1984 and 1988, their modes of expression reflected the divergent states in which the two classes existed.

Artistically, African Americans in the 1980s and 1990s built on the traditions of the Black Arts movement and the emergence of black female writers even as they began to distinguish themselves through their varied modes of expression. This new generation was encapsulated in Trey Ellis's 1989 essay "The New Black Aesthetic." Incorporating figures from virtually every sector of black popular culture, from the movies of Robert Townsend to the essays of Lisa Jones or the music of Public Enemy, Ellis posited that the "cultural mulattoes" who dominated the New Black Aesthetic, or NBA, "no longer need to deny or suppress any part of our complicated and sometimes contradictory cultural baggage to please either white people or black" (235). The resulting freedom allowed artists of the NBA to engage in debates within the African American community more explicitly than any other movement in the twentieth century. For instance, Trey Ellis's first novel, *Platitudes* (1988), seeks to address the discourse on gender within the African American community by having an African American male and female coauthor a novel. The cultural mulattoes, defined as African Americans who were raised and educated in integrated settings, critiqued images of blackness constructed by the white mainstream, as well as the counterimages produced by African Americans that fail to examine the multiplicity of African American characters and responses. To be sure, this comprehensive, and often controversial, viewing of race in America had been previously expressed through humor, as in works by Ralph Ellison and Ishmael Reed. Given the influence of Ellison on Reed, and of Reed's ensuing impact on the NBA, it comes as no surprise that NBA artists made significant use of humor in expressing dissatisfaction with the state of post-civil-rights America.

The New Black Aesthetic thus became a space where comic rage could flourish, particularly when we consider the genres in black popular culture where the NBA was manifested. In his acclaimed play *The Colored Museum* (1986), George C. Wolfe demonstrates how the promotion of positive one-dimensional images can result in a loss of identity and a co-optation by white supremacist hegemony that reconfigures those images to confirm traditional stereotypes. Throughout his play Wolfe slays *any* image of African Americans that does not embrace the complexity of African American culture and experience. Ellis's inclusion of rap music, which had become the primary expression for African American underclass youth by the mid-1980s, reveals the importance of the cultural tradition that continued to link African America. The rhetorical play that characterizes rap music, which has its roots in the Black Arts movement's performance poetry, infused African American literature, moving from celebration to fury to humor within albums and even singles. Mirroring African American sermonic tradition, rap maintained the symbiotic relationship between black oral culture and black literary production that lies at the center of the development of comic rage. The novel that demonstrates rap's influence in moving beyond the comic rage seen in the works of Ellison, Ward, and Reed is Paul Beatty's *The White Boy Shuffle* (1996). Beatty's novel skewers white and black culture by examining the criteria of authenticity and credibility that both sides require of African American leadership. Transferring the intensity, bluntness, and versatility of rap, Beatty wields humor as a weapon from which no one escapes unscathed. This chapter argues that Wolfe's play and Beatty's novel, in their respective uses of parody and rap rhetoric, represent the maturation of comic rage, made possible by the NBA's embrace of humor in examining post-civil-rights America.

Disturbing Tha Peace: The New Black Aesthetic and Trey Ellis's *Platitudes*

In *The Great Wells of Democracy*, Manning Marable observes: "White middle-class suburban voters and white ethnic voters in urban areas, concerned about issues such as busing to achieve school desegregation, affirmative action, welfare, and crime, began consistently to vote Republican" (72). The twelve years from 1980 to 1992, which saw the reelection of Reagan in 1984 and the election of the first President Bush in 1988, represent a time when the black militancy of the 1970s was quelled in favor of celebrating the appearance of the black middle class. Perhaps more important, African American political power continued to grow, reaching a zenith in the presidential runs of the Reverend Jesse Jackson in the 1984 and 1988 elections. Jackson, who had been an important aide to Martin Luther King during the civil rights movement, built a "rainbow coalition" of groups in his attempts to win the Democratic nomination. His efforts helped increase black registered voters by the millions and solidified African Americans as an influential presence in the Democratic Party and mainstream American politics. Ronald Walters notes in *White Nationalism, Black Interests* that while "group solidarity was the central factor that led Black voters to support him, more importantly, it established that this expression of Black political solidarity reflected a broader phenomenon of African American life consistent with Black identity: the rejection of an exclusively individualistic ideology" (255). If nothing else, Jackson's bids proved the power of African Americans to shape national politics. Therefore, when Bill Clinton ran for president in 1992, in addition to his famous appearance on *The Arsenio Hall Show* and his condemnation of Sister Souljah, he tapped Jackson as a way to prove himself empathetic to the African American community. More specifically, Jackson's presence announced that the black middle class had become a significant force in an increasingly integrated America. At work and school, as peers or superiors, middle-class African Americans helped change perceptions about African Americans through their interactions with whites and the power they were able to wield in an integrated society.

However, while the black middle class was being held up as proof that African Americans as a group could achieve success in America—especially with the phenomenal popularity of television's *The Cosby Show*—the African American underclass was decimated in the 1980s by the crack epidemic, the erosion of civil rights legislation, and the elimination of government jobs that employed significant numbers of African Americans. The "cultural mulattoes" that Ellis saw as a dominant force in "The New Black Aesthetic" were forged during this complex time when some African Americans lived in predominantly white neighborhoods while others were falling into a frightening system of poverty and despair.

Appearing in the journal *Callaloo* in 1989, Ellis's essay boldly proclaimed the NBA to be part of "a minority's minority mushrooming with the current black bourgeoisie boom" which sought to bridge the gap between the different classes, sexes, and genders within African America. "The culturally mulatto *Cosby* girls," Ellis suggested, "are equally as black as a teenage welfare mother. Neither side of the tracks should forget that" (235). Like Richard Wright's "Blueprint for Negro Writing" or Larry Neal's "The Black Arts Movement," Ellis's "The New Black Aesthetic" outlines the new perspective of its generation in part by comparing itself to previous movements, ones intimately connected to African American cultural tradition. Eric Lott wrote in his "Response to Trey Ellis's 'The New Black Aesthetic'" that "Optimism and desire burst so infectiously from Trey Ellis's essay that you want to forget its occasional glibness" and that "Ellis touches on much of the work as well as the crucial black institutions that support it, and that is a welcome thing" (245). Unlike Wright's and Neal's virtual rejection of the thematic and political ideology of their forefathers, the NBA acknowledged the influences of literary booms that preceded it.

For instance, like the novels of the Wright school, the NBA does not seek to separate art from protest, as Ellis informs us that the NBA "is not an apolitical art-for-art's-sake fantasy. We realize that despite this current buppie [black yuppie] artist boom, most black Americans have seldom had it worse. But what most all the New Black Artists have in common is a commitment to what Columbia University philosopher Arthur Danto calls 'Disturbatory Art'—art that shakes you up" (239). The recognition by NBA artists of the plight of underclass African Americans, and the role of white supremacy in their status, allows its middle-class artists to avoid the assimilationist politics of some members of the black elite, namely the black neoconservatives that emerged during the Reagan-Bush era. In his "Response" Lott notes that "these black artists, like most young artists, almost ritualistically castigate their buppie contemporaries—misguided alter egos—that have turned themselves into investment banker/Republicans" (250). The belief by African American neoconservatives that race no longer mattered, that race-conscious policies should be eliminated, and that the advancement of the race rested solely on the personal responsibility of African Americans was contested by middle-class NBA artists who connected their rage to the reconfiguration of white supremacy.

The NBA was influenced by the Black Arts movement spiritually and historically. In particular, Ellis notes its importance in shaping part of the ideology of the NBA: "Nationalist pride continues to be one of the strongest forces in the black community and the New Black Aesthetic stems straight from that tradition" (239). But the NBA was not a mere extension or spinoff of the Black Arts movement. Its very embrace of the middle class, or the ideas of cultural mulattoes, contrasts with the Black Arts movement's denunciation of the black elite. The artists most influential in the NBA were those who were often relegated to the margins of the Black Arts movement. As Ellis states, although "during the mid-seventies they were a minority of the black-arts community, branded either counter-revolutionary, too artsy, or just not good propagandists, nevertheless avant-garde artists like novelists Ishmael Reed, Clarence Major, Toni Morrison, and John Edgar Wideman" in addition to "Richard Pryor with his molten parodies of black life on his early albums and short-lived television show" all "helped forge our current aesthetic" (237). In fact, Ellis cites Morrison's 1977 novel *Song of Solomon* as a possible starting point for the NBA, though he maintains that NBA artists had not gained enough collective power and leverage to enact their projects until the 1980s. For this study, however, it is the NBA's use of parody that becomes important. The use of parody is, to be sure, sometimes oppositional to comic rage. Its use by NBA artists coincided with a national obsession with the form. In 1984 in "The Future of American Humor: Through a Glass Eye, Darkly," Hamlin Hill reported, "We live in an age of parody" (221), citing Mel Brooks's *Blazing Saddles*, Philip Roth's *The Great American Novel* (1973), and Joseph Papp's production of the Gilbert and Sullivan operetta *Pirates of Penzance*. Yet, Hill believes, "Parody is the emotional opposite of satire. It lacks satire's indignation and anger; it exaggerates the model it is based upon without wishing to reform it. It mocks, where satire ridicules; it teases, where satire taunts" (221). Certainly a number of artists of the NBA fit the description, including Eddie Murphy and Keenan Ivory Wayans. However, Hill's essay misses the importance of the historical moment for African Americans. Both in the African American elite, whose "pain" Ellis Cose identified in *The Rage of a Privileged Class*, and in the crisis-ridden underclass, parody serves as a crucial vehicle through which comic rage can be manifested. Hill notes that "theoretically, [parody] flourishes in periods of tranquility, while satire reigns in periods of turmoil. In either case, parody equates with complacency"—but he ignores the tensions between classes and genders in African American culture and literature as well as their collective tension with America itself.

Despite such turmoil, parody is definitely present in the work of NBA artists. Here I return to Ellis's citing of Reed and Morrison as important sources for the emergence of the NBA; both artists utilize aspects of the African American cultural and vernacular tradition so important to comic rage. Reed's body of work, in particular, consistently deploys comic rage. Naming Reed as an influence situates comic rage next to parody, resulting in an African American humor that comes closer to the "satire" that Hill explains. Thus the parody we see from artists like Trey Ellis, George Wolfe, and Paul Beatty maintains "its spirit, its will to fight" (221), which Hill argues it does not have and which I label comic rage. Regardless, Ellis's promotion of humor as an important element separates the NBA from black literary movements that rejected comic articulations of anger at racism. Also, Ellis recognizes Reed's presence along with Morrison's on the outskirts of the Black Arts movement. Both authors, however, are clearly impacted by the Black Arts movement, and we can use their relationship to help explain the rejection by works of comic rage of attempts by the mainstream to assimilate them fully into the majority culture. So, while comic rage was certainly radicalized because of the militancy of the Black Arts movement, it did not suffer from the limited ideas of blackness that the movement often perpetuated. The resistance to assimilation was, similarly, a key aspect of the NBA as it moved to challenge the limitations it saw in previous literary movements.

Obviously, one of the works reflective of the NBA's use of humor is Ellis's own novel *Platitudes*. When Ellis's protagonist, the bourgeois, (white)-mainstream-minded DeWayne Wellington, joins forces with the militant black feminist Isshee Ayam, a literary comic war ensues as they seek to collaborate on Wellington's failing novel about two middle-class black teenagers, Earle and Dorothy. As Christian Moraru notes in *Rewriting: Postmodern Narrative and Cultural Critique in the Age of Cloning*, the novel "stages an entire comedy of contending styles, discourses, and their underlying value repertoires. Invited to this contest are established and not-so-established storytelling forms and signifying systems from pop culture to computer software to sentimental prose to talk shows, fashion, and metafiction" (118). The novel throws itself full-force into the debate within the post-1970s African American literary community, as the emergence of female writers met with a critical backlash from many male writers because of their portraits of African American men. As J. Martin Favor posits in "'Ain't Nothin' Like the Real Thing, Baby': Trey Ellis' Search for New Black Voices," we find Wellington's focus on Earle's middle-class status faltering because Wellington seeks "to make white and black the same in regard to social interaction, something clearly not in line with the New Black Aesthetic project aimed at unique expression rather than assimilated identity" (698). Wellington's unpublished manuscript *Hackneyed* embraces the literary experimentation of writers like Ishmael Reed and Clarence Major but possesses none of the militant cultural consciousness that drove their challenging of white cultural norms. His work, including his Earle and Dorothy story, is left virtually unreadable. By contrast, the entrance of Ayam, whose letters castigating Wellington are unmistakable moments of comic rage, presents a radically different set of politics. Author of novels titled *Good Lord, Gimme A Good Man!* and *My Big Ol' Feets Gon' Stomp Dat Evil Down*, Ayam is clearly meant to signify on African American females writers of the 1970s and early 1980s. Announcing her presence with a literary sledgehammer—"I must have been naïve to have believed that after comparing my work with your own puerile, misogynistic, disjointed, and amateurish ejaculations (and I use that last word deliberately), you would have never again dared to defile the temple of black literature" (39)—Ayam challenges Wellington's ability to produce an "authentic" African American novel with the first chapter of her own version, typically titled "Rejoice!" As Favor notes, "Authenticity, Isshee suggests, lies in the 'folk' (or at least one particular representation of it), and particularly the poor women of the folk" (699). Ellis ridicules the politics of both characters to reveal how detrimental the myopic representation of African Americans can be to producing a text that examines the multiplicity of subjectivities in African American life.

The back-and-forth between Wellington and Ayam produces important comic moments that parody both sides of black literary production, and thereby promote Ellis's New Black Aesthetic. As an example of comic rage, the novel is unafraid to signify on those figures influential to the development of the NBA, specifically Morrison and Reed. Moraru asserts, for instance, that Isshee Ayam's character I. Corinthians is "an allusion to Morrison's *Song of Solomon*" (123), while Isshee's own name "arguably anagrams Ishmael Reed's and possibly Alice Walker's, ironically endowing the author of *Mumbo Jumbo* with a feminine identity and thus hinting at Reed's disputes with black women writers, Walker included" (119). *Platitudes* merges the two worlds in a celebration of the multi-vocality that he views as central to his NBA. Thus, while Ayam's initial letters serve to render black machismo virtually helpless, Wellington's experimentation helps expand the possibilities of African American literary style and subject. Even though Favor sees a problem in Ellis's construction of the NBA's "diversity" in that although "Isshee and Dewayne are set up as two completely different types, they come together because of their similarities" (703), I see the investment of those "bourgeois artists" in African American cultural traditions as a necessary step in counteracting the historical impulses of the black elite to create a world separate from the black underclass. It is for lack of such investment that E. Franklin Frazier chastised the black elite, and many in the African American middle and upper classes struggled with that lack throughout the decades that followed the civil rights movement. Like Reed's examination of the Uncle Tom/Nat Turner dichotomy in *Flight to Canada*, comic rage in the work of NBA artists questions white stereotypes as well as black counter-stereotypes that are equally one-dimensional. As Ellis's essay states, "No longer are too many black characters either completely cool (*Sweet Sweetback's Baadasssss Song*) or completely loving and selfless (*Sounder*)" (237). The NBA began the process of deconstructing the racial dichotomy that only further contributed to white supremacist constructions of blackness, often through the use of humorous confrontations that exposed and critiqued. Thus the comic rage in *The Colored Museum* and *The White Boy Shuffle* was part of the NBA's move toward exploring the multiplicity of African American culture and experience, with all of its complexity and contradictions. The rage that exists in both works was aimed at white supremacy in post-civil-rights America, whether that lens was pointed at blacks or whites.

Nothing Is Sacred: George C. Wolfe's *The Colored Museum*

One of the artists that Ellis specifically names as part of the NBA is writer-director-producer George C. Wolfe. In discussing the period of the NBA, Ellis states, "I agree with playwright George Wolfe: 'This is an incredible time'" (243). Likewise, Wolfe accepted Ellis's ideas about the NBA and its rejection of the pleas of protest literature and the isolation of the

Black Arts movement. Instead, Wolfe states, "I'm coming from a place of casual arrogance because I feel that black culture is one of—if not the—most dominant forces in American culture. Even if people don't admit to it, they snap to it, they watch it, they dress like it" (51). By directing both parts of Tony Kushner's Pulitzer Prize–winning *Angels in America* (1993), Wolfe demonstrated his status as a cultural mulatto, and he became the first African American director to win a Tony—for *Angels in America: Millennium Approaches*—for directing a "white" play. Despite this success, an unmistakable desire to chronicle African American life dominates his writing. Wolfe's belief in the power of African American culture is easily seen in his adaptation of three Zora Neale Hurston stories in *Spunk* (1990), the telling of the story of jazz artist Jelly Roll Morton in *Jelly's Last Jam* (1992), and his celebration of tap dancing in his musical *Bring in 'Da Noise, Bring in 'Da Funk* (1996). His first critically acclaimed play, *The Colored Museum* demonstrates Wolfe as a chief explorer of the complexity of African American experience. Kim Euell in "Signifyin(g) Ritual: Subverting Stereotypes, Salvaging Icons" writes: "In recent decades, at least one groundbreaking work of black theater has caught fire, engendering a new genre and/or body of work. The 1950s yielded *A Raisin in the Sun,* the '60s *Dutchman*, the '70s *for colored girls who have considered suicide/when the rainbow is enuf*, and the '80s *The Colored Museum*" (667). The difficulty with these successes, however, is that each work becomes the representative piece for its literary era, and the characters created within the works become commodified to represent all African Americans. Wolfe's *The Colored Museum*, aiming to counteract the tendency to limit the voices of minorities, takes on not just one or two specific stereotypes within the black community but as many as Wolfe is able to fit in.

As Euell writes, "The premise of *The Colored Museum* involves exhibiting culturally specific characters, situations, and behaviors with the goal of having African Americans evaluate them to determine which are assets and which are detrimental to our progress" (667). Through a series of eleven vignettes, in which each of the museum exhibits speaks, Wolfe speaks to a large number of black stereotypes. In this play the sometimes subversive signifying seen in *Invisible Man* takes a furious and direct tone. As Henry Louis Gates points out about Reed, "parody and hidden polemic overlap, in a process Bakhtin describes as follows: 'When parody becomes aware of substantial resistance, a certain forcefulness and profundity in the speech act it parodies, it takes on a new dimension of complexity via the tones of the hidden polemic'" (112). With *The Colored Museum*, according to Euell, "a new body of work has emerged that 'talks' to earlier works between works, both critiquing and revising themes and characters, while revisiting and reexamining the theatrical and cultural past" (668). Taking a cue from Ishmael Reed, Wolfe begins the play with an anachronistic field day in the first vignette, "Git On Board." The play calls for slides of African slaves being captured, tortured, and placed on slave ships, to be shown at a rapid pace as live drums are being played. Soon, however, an enthusiastic African American stewardess named Miss Pat appears, welcoming everyone aboard the plane "Celebrity Slave-ship, departing the Gold Coast and making short stops at Bahia, Port au Prince, and Havana, before our final destination of Savannah" (1). The play situates the beginning of white control over African American images at the moment of capture and enslavement in Africa. Of key importance is the suppression of drums, which play sporadically throughout Miss Pat's speech. The drums, a part of many African cultures' mode of communication that has carried over to contemporary America, highlight the significance of orality and performance in African American culture. As signals of events taking place in the community—birth, marriage, death—the drums are similar in their versatility to the black vernacular expression they augment. They can act as modes of celebration, ritual, and resistance, but they ultimately establish the distinctiveness of their culture. Miss Pat's attempts to convince the passengers that there are no drums, even when they momentarily overwhelm her, signal Wolfe's recognition of the importance of black forms of expression to African Americans' history of resistance and survival.

Miss Pat's sunny optimism, similar to the Mayor's in Ward's *Day of Absence*, masks a harrowing and violent chronicle of oppression. In one instance Miss Pat seems reassuring as she informs her passengers, "the songs *you* are going to sing in the cotton fields, under the burning heat and stinging lash, will metamorphose and give birth to the likes of James Brown and the Fabulous Flames. . . . And just think of what *you* are going to mean to William Faulkner" (3). Miss Pat's recognition and casual dismissal of that oppression differs from the Mayor's in that it represents a post-civil-rights shift that downplays the lingering effects of past racist oppression in favor of African American successes. Miss Pat is even able to admit, "All right, so you're gonna have to suffer for a few hundred years, but from your pain will come a culture so complex"—she holds up a basketball—"with this little item here . . . you'll become millionaires!" (3). Miss Pat's comment reveals an important correlation between Ellis's naming of the NBA and the National Basketball Association. While Ellis does not specifically mention the professional basketball league in his essay, there is an inherent signifying that exposes the interrelation of sports and race. Embodied by the racially charged Magic Johnson–Larry Bird rivalry that dominated the 1980s, the racial symbolism of the NBA was simultaneously used to promote equality and to expose the maintenance of white supremacist hegemony. The increasingly wealthy African Americans who made up the majority of the players contrasted starkly with the predominantly white coaches and the all-white team owners. This disparity, like the persistent whiteness of baseball's managers and football's quarterbacks, promoted the underlying assumption that African Americans were superior physically but were incapable of handling the mental rigors of the game. The Magic/Bird debate, for instance, often centered on Magic's "natural gifts" and "instincts" as opposed to Bird's "hardworking" and "cerebral" approach. Moreover, while Ellis's NBA engaged issues of racial politics, major sports in the 1980s were becoming an increasingly depoliticized space, where African American athletes were marketed as commodities for mass celebration and devotion.

Exuding an optimism that rivals Miss Pat and the Mayor, Aunt Ethel enters the next vignette, "Cooking with Aunt Ethel," with a smile and a bandanna around her head in an obvious reference to the Aunt Jemima figure. As the star of the cooking extravaganza "The Aunt Ethel Show," Aunt Ethel heavily signifies, like many of the other fictional characters in this study, on the mammy figure. While serving hearty helpings of food, she details a list of ingredients that represent the African American cultural experience: "NOW YA ADD A HEAP OF SURVIVAL / AND HUMILITY, JUST A TOUCH / ADD SOME ATTITUDE / OOPS! I PUT TOO MUCH" (7). The ingredients that Aunt Ethel lists, though, are not merely re-creations of stereotypical African American behavior. What "Cooking" actually does is list the avenues of expression by which African Americans have resisted racist assault and nihilistic threat. For example, Aunt Ethel's "AND NOW A WHOLE LOT OF HUMOR / SALTY LANGUAGE, MIXED WITH SADNESS / THEN THROW IN A BOX OF BLUES / AND SIMMER TO MADNESS" (8) indicates the responses that have been historically used against racism, from the African American comedic tradition to Ellison's "tragic-comic lyricism" to the militancy of the Black Arts and Black Power movements. After she has made a "batch of Negroes," Aunt Ethel warns not to "ask me what to do with 'em now that you got 'em cause child, that's your problem" (8). Picking up where the first vignette ends, "Cooking with Aunt Ethel" thus deploys comic rage to trace the "ingredients" found in African American culture and experience that have historically constituted the response to racist oppression. Aunt Ethel's final comment reflects the ambivalence African Americans have created in the United States as figures of fascination, anxiety, and reliance.

Whether African American responses to oppression were ultimately destructive or constructive often depended on their purpose. Thus the choices African Americans make become a significant theme in the play, addressed in "Photo Session" and "Soldier with a Secret." In the latter a soldier kills the black members of his unit to spare them the pain of their lives back in segregated America. In "Photo Session" we find two bourgeois African American characters, one male and one female, who have created an escapist world promoting a "positive" middle-class image that appeals to whites and eliminates black pain. The success they seem to embody, however, has been bought at a heavy price. The two characters admit, "The world was becoming too much for us," and inform us that they have been unable to resolve "the contradiction of our existence" or "yesterday's pain" (9). Their solution, then, is to give away their lives and "now live inside *Ebony Magazine*" (9). The vignette is a clear commentary on the African American elite that E. Franklin Frazier examines in *Black Bourgeoisie*. Playing on the positive, simplistic images of success and beauty that appear in black middle-class magazines like *Ebony*, *Jet*, and *Essence*, the scene skewers the world that African American elites seek to construct in response to racist stereotypes. However, the characters' willingness to buy into the world of "make-believe," as Frazier has termed it, leaves them unable to participate in any activity that might contradict their counterimage, such as a social life or sex. Yet by the end of the scene, it becomes clear that the veneer they have built is falling apart. The two characters reveal that "everything is rehearsed, including this other kind of pain we're starting to feel," which is the "kind of pain that comes with feeling no pain at all" (10). The scene critiques the rejection of methods of resistance that African Americans have engaged in, including comic rage, by claiming a loss of pain and rage that clearly exists.

The three scenes after "Git on Board" trace the complicated history of African American responses that forged the culture's varied avenues for negotiating racist oppression. However, where "Git on Board" combines the history of racist oppression with the humor of Miss Pat's presentations, the three vignettes that follow run the gamut from the joviality of Aunt Ethel to the aloofness of "Photo Session" to the tragedy of "Soldier with a Secret." Those elements coalesce into an explosive mix of comic rage in "The Gospel According to Miss Roj," in which a drag queen performs at The Bottomless Pit, "the watering hole for the wild and weary which asks the question, 'Is there life after Jheri-curl?'" (14). "The Gospel According to Miss Roj" challenges stereotypical ideas about black homosexuality, particularly as it relates to the Black Arts and Black Power movements. Wolfe moves beyond NBA brethren Spike Lee (in his early work), Eddie Murphy, the creators of the 1990 movie *House Party* Reginald and Warrington Hudlin, and Professor Griff from Public Enemy, all of whom, despite their various uses of humor, are criticized as continuing to promote a hostile atmosphere for African American gays and lesbians. Comic rage in "Miss Roj" allows Wolfe to engage a topic that is either taboo or condemned in the African American community. Most members of the Black Arts and Black Power movements viewed homosexuals, particularly men, with disdain. References to "faggots" were frequent, and Eldridge Cleaver in his 1968 autobiography *Soul on Ice* unleashed a furious attack on James Baldwin and black male homosexuals. Characterizing black homosexuals as "outraged and frustrated because in their sickness they are unable to have a baby by a white man" (128), Cleaver paints Baldwin's attack on Richard Wright as a de facto promotion of whiteness, an attitude he imputes to all black gay men.

Similarly, black mainstream portraits of the drag queen are distorted to represent the whole of black homosexuality. Harry J. Elam states, "Historically, the drag queen has existed on the margins of black culture, a figure of ridicule and derision" (294). African American drag queens, like African Americans in general, are reduced to stereotypes that serve to entertain the majority culture and confirm the culture's oppressive values and ideologies. Black homosexuality is viewed through a reductive lens that simultaneously eliminates the racial, sexual, and gendered critique that drag queens often embody. Elam notes, "Despite the complexity of black homosexual experience, the effeminacy of the drag queen has become the representative image, a stereotypical comic figure" (294). Ironically, while Cleaver declares that "Richard Wright reigns supreme for his profound political, economic, and social reference" (134), there are echoes in "Miss Roj" of the cross-dressing Carl/Lucy from the story "Man of All Work" in Wright's 1961 collection *Eight Men*. In addition, Cleaver's former Black Panther Party leader Huey Newton once demanded, "Whatever your personal opinion and your insecurities about homosexuality and the various liberation movements among homosexuals and women . . . we should try to unite with them in a revolutionary fashion" (281). "The Gospel According to Miss Roj" builds off the complexity that Wright infuses into his portrait of Carl/Lucy, as well as Newton's desire to include gay liberation in the radical struggle against white supremacist capitalist hegemony.[1] Wolfe's command of humor allows him to address homosexuality in general in black America, fundamentally challenging ideas of black masculinity by taking the "comic figure" of the drag queen and transforming it into a distinctive voice of black rage.

Although Miss Roj's performance begins with the sexual patter and musical interludes typical of drag shows, there is an immediate shift in both tone and subject. While generally inverting or challenging traditional ideas about gender and sexuality, the show delivers a sermon to the audience. However, Miss Roj avoids being preachy through a volatile mix of sass, charisma, and wit, announcing, "I ain't just your regular oppressed American Negro. No-no-no! I am an extraterrestrial. And I ain't talking none of that shit you seen in the movies! I have real power" (14–15)—thus warning that what the audience is about to witness is unlike anything seen before and that we must discard previous notions about race, gender, and sex. This, of course, is only part of the message, the "truth." More specifically, Miss Roj seeks to inform the audience of its impending doom, like a prophet warning against millennial apocalypse: "I was placed here on Earth to study the life habits of a deteriorating society, and . . . New York is doing a slow dance with death" (15). The warning indicts the city and America at large for its myopic views that have led to oppressive policies in the past and present. A significant part of that oppression is reflected in the country's myriad contradictions. Miss Roj provides a litany of images and examples: "A high-rise goes up. You can't get no job. . . . A whole race of people gets trashed and debased. . . . Some sick bitch throws her baby out the window because she thinks it's the

Devil" (17). In detailing America's deterioration, Miss Roj employs the most powerful weapon to augment the telling of that gospel: snapping.

Elam argues, "The gesture of the 'Snap!' has been cultivated within the black gay community as a form of visual signifyin' similar to the black tradition of playing the dozens on the street corners" (294). As a Snap Queen, Miss Roj should be immediately considered a threat to all. Yet in the mainstream, snapping has become an empty, depoliticized, comic representation of African American homosexual behavior. As recently as the late 1980s and 1990s, as Elam notes, "the image of the drag queen has been appropriated and abused by more mainstream black media and culture. On the prime-time variety program 'In Living Color' as well as the extremely successful touring black comedy, 'Beauty Shop,' stereotypical gay caricatures swish, sashay and snap to the laughs and pleasure of the audience" (295). Wolfe reclaims the political and cultural significance of snapping, and indeed anticipates works that examine black gay men, including Marlon Riggs's 1989 documentary on race and the homophobia that black gay men face, *Tongues Untied*, and Jennie Livingston's 1990 documentary about Harlem drag balls thrown by African American and Latino men in the 1980s, *Paris Is Burning*. Snapping in "The Gospel According to Miss Roj," then, becomes not simply an aesthetic performance but, like signifying, a cultural act of significant power. And like signifying in general, snapping is notable for its versatility. As Riggs's essay "Black Macho Revisited: Reflections of a Snap! Queen" states, "the SNAP! contains a multiplicity of coded meanings" and "can be as emotionally and politically charged as a clenched fist, can punctuate debate and dialogue like an exclamation point, a comma, an ellipse, or altogether negate the need for words among those who are adept at decoding its nuanced meanings" (294). Therefore, while Miss Roj's initial use of the "Snap!" may appear to confirm comic assumptions, it merely serves one of the many purposes consistent with a complex language.

Very quickly Miss Roj reveals uses of the "Snap!" that fit with her explosive mix of rage, humor, and tragedy. Miss Roj claims, "Everytime I snap, I steal one beat of your heart. So if you find yourself gasping for air in the middle of the night, chances are you fucked with Miss Roj and she didn't like it" (16). Here the snap possesses the ability not only to ridicule but to destroy. In doing so, snapping takes on added power as an expression of rage and an act of resistance. Snapping funnels Miss Roj's volatility and acts to highlight oppression and hypocrisy. At the same time, snapping can be a weapon. On the one hand, Miss Roj claims that after a man on a beach called her a "monkey coon in a faggit suit" he snapped him to death: "A heart attack, right there on the beach" (16). Yet knowing that this scene can be distorted to emphasize the humor, Miss Roj also uses snapping to overtly challenge the contradictions in white bourgeois values: "Snap for every time you walk past someone lying in the street, smelling like frozen piss and shit and you don't see it. Snap for every crazed bastard who kills himself so as to get the jump on being killed. And snap for every sick muthafucker who, bored with carrying around his fear, takes to shooting other people" (17). Although Miss Roj's show retains aspects of the drag queen as comic, each act is layered with underlying meaning that reflects the rage at the oppression she witnesses. As the scene ends with Aretha Franklin's "Respect" playing, Miss Roj demands that the audience dance, although she warns, "don't be surprised if there ain't no beat holding you together 'cause we traded in our drums for respectability. So now it's just words" (17). The drums that Miss Pat attempted to suppress throughout the first vignette have been, according to Miss Roj, sacrificed in the post-civil-rights desire for legitimacy and assimilation into the white mainstream. "The Gospel According to Miss Roj" demonstrates Wolfe's desire for the destruction of simplistic, stereotypical images of African Americans that have arisen in the absence of those drums. Also, the vignette's synthesis of music, sermon, and stand-up represents the NBA's permeation through various forms of African American cultural expression that make comic rage's presence in each of those forms possible.[2]

The manifestations of rage and resistance in the first half can seem sparing, appearing most notably through the drumming Miss Pat attempts to suppress and the snapping Miss Roj employs. However, as Frank Rich notes in his review of the play, "There comes a time when a satirical writer, if he's really out for blood, must stop clowning around and move in for the kill. That unmistakable moment of truth arrives about halfway through 'The Colored Museum'" (17). When the vignette "The Last Mama-on-the-Couch Play" opens with the Narrator's proclamation "We are pleased to bring you yet another Mama-on-the Couch play. A searing domestic drama that tears at the very fabric of racist America" (24), it becomes clear that an extended uncensored assault has been launched. The main target of this vignette is Lorraine Hansberry's

A Raisin in the Sun, especially the family at its center, the Youngers. Signifying heavily on Hansberry's opening stage directions, the Announcer
intones, "Lights up on a dreary, depressing, but with middle-class aspirations tenement slum. There is a couch, with a Mama on it. Both are well-
worn" (24). The obvious reference is to the Younger family's pursuit of a
bourgeois, middle-class aesthetic, from Mama's desire to move into the
all-white, middle-class neighborhood to Walter Lee's attempts to own a
liquor store and Beneatha's work to be a doctor. Much as novels of the
Wright school appeared after *Native Son*, the success of Hansberry's play
led to a long line of works that employed the same stock characters, particularly long-suffering mothers—who always seemed to sitting stoically
on couches in low-rent "tenement slums"—and troubled, brooding sons.

When Mama's aptly named son Walter-Lee-Beau-Willie Jones (also referred to as Son) enters, Wolfe's signifying on Hansberry's play continues
with overt hilarity: "He is Mama's thirty-year-old son. His brow is heavy
from three hundred years of oppression" (24). The interactions of Mama
and Son encapsulate the disenchantment of Hansberry's Walter Lee. For
example, in the vignette, Mama's demands that Son "wipe his feet" actually comes from *Raisin*'s scene in which Walter Lee's wife Ruth, over his
expression of desire to move beyond being a chauffeur, tells him to eat
his eggs. Son's questioning of God and Mama's ensuing slap recall a similar scene between Mama Younger and her daughter Beneatha. Thus when
Son's wife enters after Mama receives an award from the Announcer for
her performance, one expects more signifying on Hansberry's play, a
reenacting of the Walter Lee–Ruth Younger relationship. Instead Wolfe
now has a second play in his sights. With the name of Son's wife, the
Lady in Plaid, Wolfe is signifying on the characters from Shange's *for colored girls* (Lady in Red, Lady in Yellow, . . .). Her speech pattern—"She
was a creature of regal beauty / who in ancient time grow the temple of
the Nile / with her womanliness / But here she was, stuck being colored
/ and a woman in a world that valued neither" (26)—imitates the cho-
reopoem style that Shange uses. Also, the Lady in Plaid shares the thematic concern of *for colored girls*, as well as other works by black female
authors, to reflect the experiences of all African American women. The
Lady in Plaid's monologues, counterpointed by her husband's increasing
anger that she has not cooked dinner, become expressions of an entire
black female urban community who "knew, as she, that their souls be-
longed / in ancient temples on the Nile" even as "their life has become /

one colored hell" (27). Wolfe re-creates the climactic scene in *for colored girls*, "Nite with Beau Willie Brown," in which Lady in Red is terrorized by her on-again, off-again lover Beau Willie who, in an enraged argument with her, drops their two children out the window.

In the "Mama-on-the-Couch" scene, Son, true to his Beau-Willie name, retaliates for his wife's refusal to make dinner by holding two black dolls out the window and dropping them amid his wife's shrieks. The Announcer responds by taking the award from Mama and giving it to the Lady in Plaid, who immediately recovers from her "pain." Wolfe's anger at simplistic images of African Americans is driven forward by Mama, her Juilliard-trained daughter Medea, and the Lady in Plaid, even as Walter-Lee-Beau-Willie Jones remains the focal point off of whom all three play. So although the Lady in Plaid and Medea represent a shift away from the male-dominated views of race, they maintain a construction of black masculinity that is similarly limited. While the Lady in Plaid provides a less sympathetic vision of *Raisin*'s Walter Lee in the form of "Beau Willie," Medea urges her brother to "not let thy rage choke the blood which anoints thy heart with love" and believes that her "speech, like my pain and suffering, have become classical and therefore universal" (28). Like the couple in "Photo Session," Medea's assimilation and adoption of Western cultural values reject African American culture and resistance, only enraging her brother further. His proclamation "This is my play. It's about me and the Man. . . . It's about me. Me and my pain! My pain!" (28–29) is eerily similar to the protest novels of the Wright school that often exclude all voices except black heterosexual males that are overly concerned with the clash between African American men and white America.

The response to Walter Lee's bid for the spotlight is not an award but a reproach from the Voice of the Man, who accuses him of "overacting" (29). Going to the window to confront the Man, Walter Lee is shot. In her mourning, Mama confesses that she now wishes "he had been born into an all-black musical" because "Nobody ever dies in an all-black musical" (29). The actors break out into a dance number that encompasses African American musical experiences similar to those that Aunt Ethel named in the second vignette, namely gospel, jazz, and blues. As Walter Lee springs to life and the cast dances in celebration, Wolfe initiates the final slaying of "dead" images. His inclusion of the African American musicals, like 1921's *Shuffle Along* and 1978's film adaptation of the

Broadway hit *The Wiz*, concludes with the cast desperately working to please a presumably white audience. Standing frozen, the cast simply and eerily sings "IF WE WANT TO LIVE / WE HAVE GOT TO / WE HAVE GOT TO / DANCE . . . AND DANCE . . ." (32). The stage directions indicate that when dancing resumes, the characters evoke minstrel show performers while "images of coon performers flash as the lights slowly fade" (32). The final part of the vignette suggests that such simplistic images are easily digested and manipulated by the white mainstream to become versions of old stereotypes. Thus Mama eventually begins to resemble the traditional mammy figures, and Son becomes the epitome of the black masculinity that justifies white fear.

In constructing a scene that so blatantly reflects his rage through ridicule, "The Last Mama-on-the-Couch Play" is the point where *The Colored Museum* moves beyond satire to become a work of comic rage. Moreover, Wolfe's primary purpose for writing the play becomes clear. As he once stated, "I wanted to remove these dead, stale, empty icons standing in the doorway, blocking me from my truth" (Wolfe, qtd. in Kroll, 85). The characters' overblown performances bear strong resemblances to the African American actors' "go for broke" whiteface performances in Ward's *Day of Absence*. Both reveal an unmistakable rage at the traditional images of African Americans by taking ideologies to their extreme conclusion. While Ward uses the disappearance of the town's black population to point up white American dependence on racist hierarchies, Wolfe ridicules overused African American stock characters in order to clear the way for newer, complex images. As Rich comments, in "The Last Mama-on-the-Couch Play" Wolfe "says the unthinkable, says it with uncompromising wit, and leaves the audience, as well as a sacred target, in ruins" (17). Using this vignette as its jumping-off point, *The Colored Museum* takes on a distinctly more aggressive tone as its characters become incapable of suppressing the contradictory elements of African American culture and experience. So, in "LaLa's Opening" the international superstar making her American debut, LaLa Lamazing Grace, struggles to maintain the image she has constructed. Her white lover Flo'rance's cheating on her with black women (which mirrors the white Western exoticizing of blacks), the presence of her daughter, and her underclass roots under her real name Sadie all impede LaLa's desperate attempts to maintain her celebrated status. Although there are clear allusions to Josephine Baker, who LaLa claims was a French resistance fighter with her mother, the vignette also makes connections to Paul Robeson and other African Americans forced to find success outside America.

In keeping with Wolfe's purpose—the birth of newer and more complex African American representations—the egg that the naïve Normal Jean Reynolds lays in the next-to-last scene, "Permutations," is representative of a new breed of artists and images, embodying Ellis's NBA. Freed by the efforts of artists of the 1960s and 1970s, Wolfe seeks to create characters "the likes of which nobody has ever seen" (49). He articulates his vision through the aptly named Normal, and his characters reflect a multiplicity of behaviors, ideologies, and struggles, as their "skin is gonna turn all kinds of shades in the sun and their hair a be growin' every which-a-way. And it won't matter and they won't care 'cause they know they are so rare and special" (49). Normal Jean's description represents Ellis's own belief in the growing collective awareness of the NBA as they come "together like so many twins separated at birth—thrilled, soothed, and strengthened in finally being reunited" (234). The characters that have been marginalized in previous works of African American literature, if they even existed, make up the core of Wolfe's play. In addition, the play, like Ellis's NBA, re-visions white and black constructions of race through the presentation of comprehensive aspects and characteristics of African America, whether the work contained the ridiculing humor that complicated traditional selfless nobility or militant rage alongside integrationist ideology. For this book's purposes, however, one of the most significant vignettes in the play comes immediately after "The Last Mama-on-the-Couch Play."

A character named Man discards objects in "Symbiosis" that distress the second character in the scene, the Kid. Those objects include clothes, record albums, and photos. The Kid, who represents Man's rage, objects to Man's actions that are meant to ease his assimilation into the white world. Unlike the earlier scenes, "Symbiosis" is overtly political and directed toward the attempts by many in the post-civil-rights African American community to "integrate" into the mainstream society. Seizing on the opportunities provided by the *Brown* decision, the Civil Rights and Voting Rights Acts, and affirmative action policies, post-1970 African Americans entered mainstream America, particularly corporate America, in unprecedented fashion. Man represents this wave, who are perhaps not the first African Americans at their jobs, but for whom race

remains at the forefront of their interactions with their peers. As Elam
notes, "Man's dilemma" is "critical to contemporary African American
discourse as well. Ambitious and educated African Americans ponder the
question: Must success in corporate America necessitate the sacrifice of
African American cultural identity?" (297). Besides donning a corporate
suit, Man seeks to dispose of any items that might be considered "racially distinct," which has become synonymous with controversy. Objects
that are distinctively black, highlight racial difference, or demonstrate
clear expressions of rage at white supremacy are especially targeted.

So, as the dismayed Kid watches, Man reels off a list of items: "My
first Afro-comb. Gone. My first dashiki. Gone. My autographed pictures
of Stokely Carmichael, Jomo Kenyatta, and Donna Summer. Gone" (33).
As Man continues his litany, which includes replacing Eldridge Cleaver's
Soul on Ice with Alice Walker's *The Color Purple*, it becomes apparent that
Man seeks to eliminate the Kid and his representation of the historical
racial conflict between African Americans and whites.[3] Saying that "the
Ice Age is upon us," Man explains that "the climate is changing, Kid, and
either you adjust or you end up extinct. A sociological dinosaur" (34).
Here we see the reconfiguration of white supremacy that perpetuates assimilation of African Americans under the guise of integration. Those
African Americans, like the neoconservatives, are rewarded for their
wholesale adoption of white bourgeois values and ideology, much of
which maintains white privilege and is hostile to antiracist work and legislation. Despite the Kid's attempts to entice Man to keep him around,
primarily through the singing of the Temptations hit "My Girl," a physical confrontation ensues between the two. Choking the Kid unconscious
for a moment, Man decides "Being black is too emotionally taxing; therefore I will be black only on weekends and holidays" (36). However, before
he is able to throw the Temptations album away, the Kid awakes and,
with a smiling "What's happening?" (37), locks Man in a death grip as the
scene ends.

Elam astutely notes that, in "Symbiosis," "rage cannot be left behind.
The legacy of the past remains a part of The Man's contemporary identity" (297). A similar theme runs throughout the play itself, with characters attempting to jettison unsavory parts of themselves as a way of
negotiating the integration/assimilation of African Americans into the
post-civil-rights white mainstream. Although the attempts vary from
scene to scene, they all involve attempts to reject the pain and rage that

befall them as African Americans. They do so not only to achieve success in an America that promotes itself as having become color-blind, but as a way of ignoring the contradictions they would inevitably recognize in America's claim and their own individual compromises. However, as Elam points out, in "Photo Session," "Symbiosis," and "LaLa's Opening" none of "the characters escape from their African-American past. These exhibits establish that cultural denial or escape should not be a viable option for African Americans today" (297). Thus by the time we reach the final vignette, titled "The Party," we see a myriad of African American figures from the play and from history reflecting the contradictions of African American cultural experience. With sacred icons broken down and others unable to separate themselves from the complexity of African American life, we see a veritable merging, one that is commensurate with the humor and militancy that permeate the play itself.

"The Party" is hosted by Topsy, the character from Harriet Beecher Stowe's *Uncle Tom's Cabin* who popularized the "pickaninny" stereotype associated with young black children. Topsy announces that she has just been to the "largest gathering of black/Negro/colored Americans you'd ever want to see," in which she saw "Nat Turner sippin' champagne out of Eartha Kitt's slipper. And over in another corner, Bert Williams and Malcolm X was discussing existentialism as it relates to the shuffle-ball-change" (50). Wolfe returns to the anachronistic impulse that begins the play in order to celebrate the complexity of African American history and culture. Thus Topsy can relate with glee that "Aunt Jemima and Angela Davis was in the kitchen sharing a plate of greens and just goin' off about South Africa" (50) because the play has created a space where African Americans can produce images without fear of subscribing to stereotypes. The creation of such a space, one in which comic rage can flourish, is based on the disregarding of white mainstream perceptions. Topsy informs us, "whereas I used to jump into a rage anytime anybody tried to deny who I was, now all I got to do is give attitude, quicker than light, and then go on about the business of being me. 'Cause I'm dancing to the music of the madness in me" (51). The play ends as it begins, centering on the question that Frank Rich recognizes as dominant throughout the play: "How do American black men and women honor the legacy of suffering that is the baggage of their past?" (17). We discover that the drums that Miss Pat attempted to suppress, and that Miss Roj claimed had been sacrificed, remain crucial to black life and survival. The discovery provides a key element in negotiating the complex, sometimes contradictory, images and expressions in African American culture and experience. Unable to "live inside yesterday's pain" as the cast states they "can't live without it" (52), one might get the feeling that we have come to the end in the same state as at the beginning. Yet Topsy encourages all to celebrate the madness that can result, realizing that her "power" lies in that madness "And my colored contradictions" (53). In *The Colored Museum*, Wolfe has produced a work that embodies the strengths of the NBA's philosophy and, in keeping with the NBA's willingness to parody whites and blacks, unleashes comic rage at post-civil-rights America.

Ready to Die . . . But Before I Go: Paul Beatty's *The White Boy Shuffle*

Topsy's proclamation that she is "dancing to the music of the madness in me" centralizes music as part of African American cultural expression. The ongoing negotiation between African American music and white fascination with black cultural production in general has often led to an uneasy, even hostile relationship. However, as is the case with comic rage, whites rarely come away from these interactions unscathed. In fact, they often come away from them racialized in ways they had not intended. The phrase "white boy shuffle" plays on the idea that white men are incapable of dancing. Like the stereotype that white men cannot jump, fed by the perception in the 1980s of white basketball greats Larry Bird and Kevin McHale, the white boy shuffle highlights racial difference while placing African Americans as the creators of the musical culture that whites historically co-opt, exploit, and commodify. Still, the idea of the white boy shuffle robs whites of being completely able to "get down." Although there are a number of definitions for the phrase, Nick Charles in "The Suicide Hip-Hop" comes closest with "that halting side-to-side sway, which pays no mind to a tune's bass line and double-times on the Joe Walsh-like riffs. It's common to whites who haven't been to Dead concerts or caught Tom Jones on the tube—which means most of them mofos—and blacks whose exposure to music has been limited to Dennis Day and Anthrax" (30). Refusing to exclude African Americans who only need the opportunity to participate in African American cultural traditions, Charles in defining what it means to "be down" captures the necessity of recovering "drums"—and the influence of African American musical expression—in Paul Beatty's 1996 novel *The White Boy Shuffle*.

Beatty's novel tells the story of Gunnar Kaufman, a young African American male who is abruptly moved from his predominantly white Santa Monica neighborhood to the predominantly black West Los Angeles neighborhood called Hillside. Unable to communicate with his underclass black schoolmates, Gunnar connects through his unexpected ability to play basketball. He wins the admiration of his community, authors a collection of poetry called *Watermelanin*, which sells 126 million copies, and is "anointed" the messiah of African America, to whom he eventually suggests mass suicide. In his review of the novel, Charles asserts: "This is exactly what black folks may need: their own culturally displaced, ethically challenged Jack Kevorkian, a juiced-up euthanasiast promoting the ultimate remedy" for "disillusioned, 40 Acres & a Mule-less African Americans prone to mantra-ing about some 'dream' and 'by any means necessary'" (30). The novel is a comprehensive critique of the reconfiguration of post-civil-rights white supremacy. In true NBA fashion, Beatty uses the black middle and upper class as a site from which the two extremes of America's reductive racial dichotomy, namely the white middle class and the black underclass, can be examined. By doing so, Beatty also re-visions the black middle class to contrast traditional labels of the black elite, specifically the "make-believe" of Frazier's *Black Bourgeoisie* and the "sell-outs" that drew the wrath of the Black Power and Black Arts movements. Like other works of comic rage, the text itself becomes a significant mechanism of expression. The novel mixes poetry and prose in a manner similar to Reed's *Flight to Canada*. Its collapse of traditional forms—music, monologue, prose, and poetry—is at the core of spoken word performance, which can be traced back to the 1968 formation of the poetry/performance group Last Poets, often called the "godfathers of rap." Beatty's own role in this tradition is clear, particularly when we consider the oral intent of his two books of poetry, *Big Bank Take Little Bank* (1991) and *Joker, Joker, Deuce* (1994), and his anointing as the "premier bard of hip-hop" (*Newsweek*). In *Shuffle*, Beatty adopts the language of rap and hip-hop that has dominated young African American speech patterns since the 1980s. The use of the rhetoric of rap provides the template for the use of comic rage. Hip-hop culture, which emerged out of the late 1970s, mirrors the Black Power and Black Arts movements' embrace of African American culture, history, and traditions. For instance, Michael Eric Dyson in "'Speech Is My Hammer': Black Preaching, Social Justice, and Rap Rhetoric" explains, "As a rhetorical form, hip-hop has a lot in common with a variety of antecedent oral and musical practices, whether it's signifying within street discourse, the articulation of playful hyperbole around sex in blues culture, the poetic musings of Gil Scott-Heron, Bessie Smith rapping to a beat, or Lou Rawls and Isaac Hayes weaving extended monologues into their music" (296). Rap, which is one of the four major elements that make up hip-hop, is heavily influenced by the spoken-word artists who redefined African American poetry during the Black Arts movement. Those artists, like Beatty himself, constructed poetry that was intended to be performed for an audience. Artists like the aforementioned Gil Scott-Heron and the Last Poets often set their poetry to music, anticipating the relationship between rapper (or MC) and deejay that was central to early hip-hop music.

Gunnar's story is revealed in equal parts prose, poetry, and confessional letter. Poems appear in the middle of paragraphs, and Gunnar's letters to various people are often more revelatory than his narration. The novel's mixture maximizes opportunities for wordplay and signifying. Perhaps most important, *Shuffle's* use of comic rage explores race in post-civil-rights America by setting the novel in the present. Although its challenges to history, literature, and identity are apparent, the novel's direct confrontation of the contemporary effects of white supremacist hegemony typifies works of comic rage in the post-civil-rights era. Also, while Reed's challenge to traditional narrative structure maximizes the knifelike signifying by presenting characters whose militancy resembles that of the Black Power and Black Arts movements, Beatty's novel attacks racist oppression from the ultimate insider position that the black elite gained in the 1980s. The narration is more traditional, but only because the infusion of the rhetoric of rap makes the novel album-like, as the portraits of rage, pain, joy, and laughter that Gunnar paints burst from the pages from moment to moment, single to single. Methodically delivering body blow after body blow to post-civil-rights assumptions, figures, and ideologies, the novel's comedy and rage become unmistakably clear. Gunnar's placement as the quintessential cultural mulatto rips the myth of a color-blind America apart from the inside, as the African American vernacular tradition that influences Gunnar disrupts white bourgeois ideology.

The novel does not appropriate the language of rap; instead, it epitomizes the complexity, versatility, and expressiveness that characterize hip-hop culture in the depiction of African America in the post-1970s

United States. As the rhetorical arm of the four elements of hip-hop culture—rapping (also known as MCing), deejaying, break dancing, and graffiti art—rap music employs a number of responses that emanate from the severe disenfranchisement that many in the African American underclass experienced during the 1980s. Additionally, it includes the consciousness and overt critique of racist oppression that is influenced by 1970s nationalist pride and reflected in NBA artists and the rap group Public Enemy. According to Michael Eric Dyson, "First, rappers deploy rhetoric as a means of self-expression; second, rappers deploy rhetoric as a means of social critique; and third, rappers deploy rhetoric as a means of ethical engagement and moral suasion as they make assertions about the way life is and the way it ought to be" (296). The novel's infusion of the rhetoric of rap informs Gunnar's storytelling and interactions. As a classic NBA character, Gunnar in his use of language can mask the influence of rap. Yet even before he and his family move to Hillside, black dissatisfaction with the racist politics of culture from which hip-hop emerges is present in Gunnar's mind. In one letter to a friend, Gunnar informs us that in debates with his white Jewish friend David Schoenfeld "I stumbled across my first black heroes: the Tuskegee airmen, the Redball Express, some WAC nurses from Chicago, Brigadier General Benjamin O. Davis, Sr., Jesse Owens, and the mess cook who shot down a couple of [Japanese] zeroes from the sinking deck of the *Arizona*. I kept these discoveries to myself" (40). In naming these previously unknown or forgotten figures, Beatty, like Ellison and Reed before him, creates an insider/outsider relationship that forces the reader to examine figures significant to American and African American history. The marginalization of these figures is often reflective of the racial politics that continues to exist in constructing American history and identity.

Gunnar's confession bears a striking resemblance to one that Trey Ellis makes in "The New Black Aesthetic." Citing the moment when he realized he was cultural mulatto, Ellis tells of how a white friend questioned his knowledge of black culture. In response, Ellis writes that his friend "didn't know I was reading *Soul on Ice*, *The Autobiography of Malcolm X* and listening to Richard Pryor's *That Nigger's Crazy* after school. I didn't share them with him, one of my best friends" (235). Like Man's decision in the "Symbiosis" vignette to "only be black on weekends and holidays," both Gunnar and Ellis are forced to make decisions on the extent to which they can reveal their blackness in front of whites. The myth of integration and a color-blind America promotes the idea that the African American presence in the majority culture is acceptable. Yet this applies only to African Americans "acceptable" to whites—in other words, black folks that make white people comfortable by not talking about race too much. Man's decisions about assimilation are what form the central argument between him and the Kid, while Gunnar's withholding gives way to his more militant attitude after moving to Hillside. For Ellis, the texts he mentions in his essay reflect the combination of militancy and humor that form the core of the NBA and, more important, comic rage. Even though the nationalist pride in the autobiographies of Malcolm and Cleaver are parodied by some NBA artists, the militant expression of rage at white supremacy pervades the NBA. The complexity that runs throughout these works—the transformations of Malcolm and Cleaver as well as Pryor's uncensored humor—complements an unmistakable immersion in African American cultural tradition that is a central tenet of the NBA. Beatty's novel thus situates itself squarely in the tradition of comic rage and the NBA's creation of a space that allows comic rage to thrive.

So, in keeping with the NBA's cultural mulatto ideology, Beatty does not limit the novel to postindustrial, urban African American English. Instead, he also includes traditional Western speech, academic analysis, and rural "homespun" wit. In its exploration of cultures, the novel ranges from Gunnar's self-proclamation as the "black Orestes in the cursed House of Atreus" to his fascination with German culture to the pervasiveness of Asian culture. Beatty employs both linguistic and cultural references in a freewheeling, unpredictable style similar to Ishmael Reed's. Gunnar can at one moment speak to his white classmates in elementary school and college in language that recalls Chris Rock and Chuck D, and the next moment speak to his "ghetto peers" in the language of Shakespeare or Bakhtin. The prologue's first two sentences reveal the alternating style that Beatty maintains throughout the novel: "On one hand this messiah gig is a bitch. On the other I've managed to fill the perennial void in African-American leadership" (1). Gunnar begins his journey by revisiting the past, and disrupting traditional African American notions of selfhood along the way. Starting the first chapter with the lines "Unlike the typical bluesy earthy folksy denim-overalls noble-in-the-face-of-cracker-racism aw shucks Pulitzer-Prize-winning protagonist mojo magic black man, I am not the seventh son of a seventh son of a seventh son. I wish I were, but fate shorted me by six brothers and three uncles" (5), Gunnar takes aim at African Americans' construction of their own image in the twentieth century, usually considered to have begun with W.E.B. Du Bois's *Souls of Black Folk* in 1903 and continuing to the 1980s with references to Alice Walker's *The Color Purple*. He replaces these images, which seem to be the same simplistic and overly "positivist" ones that Wolfe seeks to demolish, with a radical signifying. Gunnar himself confesses in the opening pages, "I am the number-one son of a spineless colorstruck son of a bitch who was the third son of an ass-kissing sell-out house Negro who was indeed a seventh son but only by default" (5). As Gunnar recalls the family history of the Kaufmans, it becomes apparent that he is heir to a house that radically dislodges the nobility, militancy, and perseverance that characterize the images in African American literature.

Instead we are witness to a host of fast-talking charlatans and cowards, beginning with Gunnar's great-great-great-great-great-great-great-grandfather Euripides Kaufman who "artfully dodged a redcoat's musket shot with his name on it and Crispus Attucks woke up in nigger heaven a martyr" (9). Here the novel, like Reed's *Flight to Canada*, re-visions both American and African American history through a significant event and figure, in this case Attucks and the 1770 Boston Massacre, which Beatty recasts as having begun because Euripides "deftly redirected the scorn of his colonial rabble-rousing shipmates from him onto a lone adolescent redcoat" (10) eventually avoiding the shot that struck Attucks, who was Euripides's "ace boon coon since childhood" (9). Gunnar traces his family line down through Swen Kaufman, who, like Cato the Graffado in Reed's *Flight*, ran away into slavery, to Gunnar's father Rolf, who serves as a sketch artist for the much-hated LAPD. Along the way, Gunnar rewrites the next two hundred years of American history and inverts popular images of African Americans in the process. Whether serving as the source of *Amos 'n' Andy* or helping in the assassination of Malcolm X, the Kaufman men—"There are no comely Kaufman superwomen" (23)—play an unexpected and undesirable role in race relations in America. Gunnar's anger and disgust with his lineage permeates both the opening chapter and the novel as a whole. This is especially evident in his relationship to his father, toward whom Gunnar has adopted a simple mantra: "Fuck that nigger." That anger, however, highlights his interactions with whites, whom he sees as "embarrassingly like myself but with whom somehow I had nothing in common" (179). His attempts to avoid the fate of his ancestors result in a number of subversive moments as well as direct comic confrontations.

Gunnar's general enthusiasm for language reflects the novel's larger engagement of African American vernacular culture. As he is being confronted by the LAPD almost immediately after moving to Hillside, Gunnar's adoption of "local catchphrases" stems from his recognition that "Language was everywhere. Smoldering embers of charcoal etymology so permeated the air that whenever someone opened his mouth it smelled like smoke" (48). However, his attempts to master the language of his new environment also serve to maximize the text's parodying of urban black life and speech. When the police question him about his gang affiliations, Gunnar answers, "You know, it's me, my homegirl Jiang Qing, Wang Hongwen, Zhang Chuqiao, and my nigger even if he don't get no bigger Yao Wenyuan. Sheeeeit, we runnin' thangs from Shanghai to Compton" (47). Soon after, Gunnar relates, "Call information and the operator answered the phone with a throaty 'Who dis?' Nothing infuriated my mother more than me lounging on one elbow at the dinner table slinging my introductory slang with a mouth full of mashed potatoes: 'Sheeeeit, Ma, I'm running thangs, fuck the dumb'" (48). His initial use of language does not reflect an immersion but an awkward co-optation in order to survive.

While he is able to use performance and language as a way to respond to the police and annoy his mother, obvious outsiders to the rhythms and speech patterns of the neighborhood, he is initially unsuccessful at convincing his new African American peers. After he and his sisters receive a "full-scale beatdown," Gunnar notes, "In a world where body and spoken language were currency, I was broke as hell" (52). Yet eventually Gunnar becomes the neighborhood's urban griot, a storyteller using the language of rap to reveal underclass black America in stunning urban decay. A large part of gaining legitimacy comes from his use of poetry, specifically the spoken-word poetry he sprays on the walls that surround Hillside. He becomes like the "best rappers" who, according to Dyson, "are not interested in generating speech for its own sake, but in crafting superior rhetorical vehicles to articulate their distinct worldviews" (296). Like those rappers, Gunnar uses "a variety of rhetorical strategies and verbal practices—enjambment and clever rhyme schemes, for example—to achieve these ends" (296). In addition, his friendships with Psycho Loco, the leader of the dance-troupe-turned-gang Gun Totin' Hooligans, and street basketball legend Nicholas Scoby help gain him credibility throughout the neighborhood. His relatively easy adjustment is due both to his understanding of the differences between him and his white friends before his move and to the novel's embrace of the rhetorical play embedded in hip-hop culture.

One of the most telling aspects of the novel is Gunnar's attitude toward his own life and the events that surround him. While other characters we have encountered, like Schuyler's Matthew/Max, Ellison's Invisible Man, and Reed's Raven Quickskill, are heavily invested in the stories they tell, Gunnar remains just beyond the emotional pull of his own tale. Indeed, there is an aloofness running through his observations that at first seems antithetical to an expression of comic rage. He dismisses his sisters' pregnancies too quickly, disturbed only that they are having the babies at the same time, and fails to view his friendship with Psycho Loco with the caution one would normally expect, even as his "back yard became a burial ground for missing evidence; warm guns and blood-rusted knives rested in unmarked graves under little mounds of dirt" (97). The most obvious manifestation is Gunnar's seeming disinterest in relationships or marriage, which leads Psycho Loco to set him up with a Japanese mail-order bride named Yoshiko as an eighteenth-birthday present. Not surprisingly, when asked if she speaks English, she climbs on a table in the Kaufman house and, in a hilarious nod to the global influence of hip-hop culture, spouts Run DMC lyrics: "I'm the king of rock—there is none higher! Sucker MC's must call me sire!" (170). To which Gunnar deftly responds: "Anyone know how to say 'I love you' in Japanese?" (170). It becomes apparent, however, that Gunnar's perspective enhances the impact of his observations. His casualness emphasizes the myriad responses to white supremacist oppression. When confronted by gang members who flash their handguns, Gunnar shows them "a paperback copy of Audre Lorde or Sterling Brown and a checkerboard set of abdominal muscles" while commenting, "You niggers ain't hard—calculus is hard'" (96). Gunnar's tone also contrasts with those of the other characters in the novel, chief among them Gunnar's good friend and basketball teammate Nicholas Scoby. An admitted jazz lover, Scoby seeks "to listen to everything before 1975 in alphabetical order. No white band leaders, sidemen cool. No faux African back-to-the-bush bullshit recorded post-1965" (67), signifying on the co-optation of jazz by the white mainstream and the pseudo-nationalist portrait of Africa. Unlike Gunnar, however, Scoby is close to the "noble-in-the-face-of-cracker-racism" that Gunnar rejects at the beginning of the novel. He is an almost magical character, highlighted by his status as a street ball legend because, as Gunnar comes to realize, "he never missed. I mean never" (94). Through Gunnar, we see Scoby as a character in search of his identity, constantly swayed by outside forces from one extreme to the next, like the jazz albums he listens to. At one point, for instance, as Gunnar and Psycho Loco mourn the death of a friend, Psycho Loco asks Scoby's whereabouts. Gunnar responds, "He's listening to Miles Davis and refuses to come outside" (99). Appropriating Davis's notoriously famous antisocial behavior, Scoby is unable to separate himself from whatever forces influence him at any given moment. By contrast, Gunnar seems regularly unaffected, and his constant incredulity makes the comic rage in the novel that much funnier and the rage that permeates the novel that much blunter.

More specifically, as Charles notes, "it isn't apathy for apathy's sake that unmotivates Gunnar"; instead Gunnar suffers from "the curse of the third eye; his b.s. detector is always on high and at every turn the shit is beeping" (30). So when Gunnar does seem emotionally invested, his commentary becomes doubly poignant. Aside from his response when he realizes what kind of place his mother has moved them to in Hillside— "Ma, you done fucked up and moved to the 'hood!" (41)—Gunnar's moments of emotional engagement provide the impetus from which *The White Boy Shuffle* emerges as a work of comic rage. Primary among those is the moment when Gunnar and Scoby find themselves in the middle of the 1992 Los Angeles riots, as Gunnar mixes humor with a distinct desire for retribution. Signifying heavily on the actual riot sparked by the Rodney King verdict, Gunnar and Scoby watch the half-black, half-Korean Ms. Kim burning her own store, receive a car alarm and air fresheners from one store, and help Psycho Loco steal a mobile safe from Montgomery Ward. At one point Gunnar confesses, "I wanted to taste immediate vindication, experience the rush of spitting in somebody's, anybody's, face," and at the next, he and Scoby beat a white man "silly with pillows of white bread until it snowed breadcrumbs" (132). Here we can see echoes of Ellison's Invisible Man, whose rage in the prologue almost leads him to kill the anonymous white man who bumps into him, but whose laughter emerges to direct that rage away from murder.

For Gunnar, the riots unearth important responses, as he sits in an unknown man's house and admits, "I never felt so worthless in my life" and "my pacifist Negro chrysalis peeled away, and a glistening anger began to test its wings. A rage that couldn't be dealt with in a poem or soothed with the glass of milk and glazed doughnut offered by our kind host" (130–31). Most significantly, Gunnar comes to recognize the limits of his poetry. Before the riot, he has become the unofficial poet laureate for the neighborhood, and his placement of poetry at various public places around the town mirrors the public display of graffiti art that is one of the significant elements of hip-hop culture. However, in the face of a clear example of the rage of the voiceless, Gunnar muses, "Even at its most reflective or its angriest, my poetry was little more than an opiate devoted to pacifying my cynicism," as opposed to Psycho Loco's criminal behavior which gave his friend "the satisfaction of standing up to his enemies and listening to them scream, watching them close their eyes for the last time" (131). Gunnar's feeling about the ineffectiveness of his poetry is confirmed when he begins to recite the Langston Hughes lines "What happens to a dream deferred? Does it dry up like a raisin in the sun?" and Scoby, influenced by the rioters' rage, exclaims, "Fuck Langston Hughes. I bet when they rioted in Harlem, Langston got his" (134). Hughes's poem "Harlem," which predates Hansberry's *A Raisin in the Sun* by some eight years, reflects the play's middle-class desire, which seems irrelevant during the riot, a manifestation of rage found in the underclass. Instead of repeating the last two lines of the actual poem— "Maybe it just sags like a heavy load. / Or does it explode?"—Gunnar signifies on the poem, revealing comic rage as a response to his frustration: "Does it dry up like a wino in rehab? Or gesture like a whore, reeling from the pimp's left jab?" (134). With the riot situated as a moment where a myriad of Gunnar's emotions are expressed, it comes as no surprise that he encounters his father, one of the few subjects about which Gunnar is never emotionally neutral. Helping Psycho Loco escape with the mobile safe, Gunnar finds himself on the other side of his father's nightstick, sparking memories of his father's violence to both him and his mother.

The riot, then, becomes a site where comic rage fully emerges, like "The Last Mama-on-the-Couch Play" in *The Colored Museum*. By funneling militancy into signifying critiques, the novel avoids the promotion of violence without dismissing the rage that results from racist oppression. Ultimately, Gunnar comes to believe, "The day of the L.A. riots I learned that it meant nothing to be a poet. One had to be a poet and a farmer, a poet and a roustabout, a poet and a soon-to-be revolutionary" (132). Gunnar's realization mirrors the NBA's connection of art to the larger projects of exploring African American culture and resisting the effects of white supremacist hegemony. In his "Response to NBA Critiques," Trey Ellis notes, "We realize that a poem, no matter how fiery, isn't going to feed a homeless black child or make a black junkie clean his syringe. But it can perhaps disseminate some small corner of truth—either political, historical, or psychological—stumbled upon by the young artist" (250). I argue, then, that Gunnar underestimates the impact of his poetry, especially in contrast to Scoby. Even though Gunnar sees himself at times only saying "enough scholarly bullshit to keep from getting my head chopped off" (105), poetry serves as a space from which he can funnel his rage in a constructive, uncensored manner.

For Scoby, no such possibility exists. While basketball and sports in general have historically been a space where African Americans promoted racial equality, post-civil-rights America has depoliticized sports and its participants. Figures like Bill Russell, Jim Brown, and Muhammad Ali who used their standing as celebrated sports figures as a platform to expose racist oppression have given way to apolitical African American athletes packaged to appeal to a broader (white) audience. Beginning with the mainstream's embrace of the "raceless" O. J. Simpson in contrast to the militancy demonstrated by black athletes in the 1968 Olympics, the mass marketing of politically neutral athletes like Michael Jordan initiated the formation of the black athlete as multicultural messiah. Here again we can see Ellis's New Black Aesthetic signifying on the complex workings of race in the National Basketball Association and America's general obsession with sports. In attempting to explain his unhappiness to Gunnar, Scoby notes, "Man, I'm tired of these fanatics rubbing on me, pulling on my arms, wishing me luck. I can't take it. People have buttons with my face on 'em. They paint their faces and stencil my number on their foreheads. One idiot showed me a tattoo on his chest that said, 'Nick Scoby is God'" (118). The novel examines this sports phenomenon, which in recent years has included Tiger Woods and LeBron James, through Scoby's discomfort with the role. Basketball, and by extension sports, becomes a co-opted space where African American resistance is neutralized and the "mainstreaming" of black athletes promotes the myth of a color-blind society.

The celebration of Scoby is overwhelming for him because he is easily influenced by outside forces and cannot escape the identity that others have constructed for him. When Gunnar suggests that he "miss once in a while," Scoby confesses, "I can't. I can't even try. Something won't let me" (118). With the recognition of the absence of basketball as a site of resistance and refuge, Gunnar begins to understand—and reveal to the audience—the price of Scoby's success: "Watching his hands shake, I realized that sometimes the worst things a nigger can do is perform well. Because then there is no turning back. We have no place to hide, no Superman Fortress of Solitude, no reclusive New England hermitages for xenophobic geniuses like Bobby Fischer and J. D. Salinger" (118–19). Gunnar connects the celebration of Scoby to the expectations of American society on the African American body: "Tote that barge, shoot that basketball, lift that bale, nigger ain't you ever heard of Dred Scott?" (119). Such expectations get played out as the white mainstream, usually in sports, comedy, and music, continually makes demands on African American figures for its own consumption and entertainment.

Although Gunnar is subject to a similar following through his own success at basketball, it is not his primary form of expression or resistance. His intellect, which frequently reveals the brooding consciousness beneath his casual veneer, becomes the avenue through which he gains entrance into Boston University. His consciousness is made manifest in his poetry, which, like comic rage, constantly subverts any outside forces that might seek to define him. Gunnar's use of hip-hop's often disruptive rhetoric provides him the opportunity to define himself. Gunnar's reentrance into predominantly white schools reveals the extent to which he must negotiate his intellect and consciousness in the white mainstream. Moreover, his attendance at a predominantly white high school for his last two years and his time at Boston University produce comic critiques that establish how the riot shifts the novel into a work of comic rage. The moment when comic rage is fully realized, the riot permeates Gunnar's interactions with his white classmates and teachers. As Gunnar states, "If you want to raise the consciousness of an inner-city colored child, send him to an all-white high school" (153). In contrast to his naive acceptance of white cultural behavior and values during his days in Santa

Monica, in high school and college Gunnar views his conversations with whites with a critical and defiant eye. While he maintains white speech patterns, he recognizes the racial politics and masking involved in the performance of race. Referring to his African American classmates, Gunnar states, "It was sad to watch us troll through the halls, a conga line of burlesque self-parody, all of us affecting our white-society persona of the day. Most days we morphed into waxen African-Americans" (154). Like the whiteface minstrelsy adopted by Afro–New Yorkers at William Brown's African Grove in the nineteenth century, Gunnar recognizes the importance—and danger—of appropriating certain masks and injecting such performances into the presence of majority culture.

In keeping with comic rage's critique of African Americans, the novel parallels the NBA's assault on the assimilationist-minded black elites. As he observes the African Americans at his high school, Gunnar points out, "Those niggers most afflicted by white supremacyosis changed their names from Raymond to Kelly or Winifred to Megan. They walked around campus shunning the uncivilized niggers and talking in bad Cockney accents" (154). Unlike Gunnar, who adopts white cultural behavior strategically, the students he criticizes do so out of an internalization of white supremacist values and ideologies. Gunnar views the adoption of an entirely new identity by those "afflicted by white supremacyosis," people like the black conservative bankers that Ellis references in his essay, with a spirit of rage instead of tragedy. Here we return to Nick Charles's review and his belief that the novel confirms that, regardless of political ideology or community status, "The same size twelves are on Clarence Thomas's napes as Jesse's. Clarence just has a matching suit" (30). Conversely, Gunnar views African Americans who seek to appropriate blackness with equal disdain. Encouraged to join an organization on BU's campus because he is not attending classes, Gunnar attends a meeting of Ambrosia, the black student union, a group that "was originally called Umoja, but the name was changed because of the whites' inability to pronounce the Swahili word for unity." At the meeting Gunnar observes that "Harvard, BU, MIT Negroes were wearing loud African garb over their Oxford shirts and red suspenders, drinking ginger beer, and using their advertising skills to plan how best to package the white man's burden" (183). The president of Ambrosia, Dexter Waverly, draws particular attention from Gunnar, who sees him as a "charlatan" who only dates white women. Despite his opinions, Gunnar confesses to being "awestruck at how such an ugly motherfucker, with an eczema condition so severe that when he furrowed his brow tiny flakes of skin fell to the lectern, could hold an audience spellbound with a single gesture" (183). The novel's target is thus expanded to include those who appropriate blackness— "keeping it real" as it is termed in the hip-hop community—while still subscribing to white supremacist values.

The group's discussion of a fashion show–literacy program ridicules the simplistic, overly positivist rhetoric that NBA artists frequently parody: "There'll be booty and learning for days. You think when the boys go to the bathroom and start beating off they going to be saying, 'Goddamn, that bitch is fine'? No. They gone be pulling on their growing black manhood saying, '*I* before *e* except after *c*'" (185). Despite his being unable to find a group with which he can identify, the popularity of *Watermelanin* results in a speaking engagement at a rally protesting South Africa's apartheid. Deciding he would want to hear "candor," Gunnar launches into a speech that criticizes the audience's commitment and, referencing a Martin Luther King inscription he claims no one reads, signifies on King's famous quote "If a man hasn't discovered something he will die for, he isn't fit to live." Declaring that "I want them niggers to get theirs, but I am not willing to die for South Africa, and you ain't either," and that "today's black leadership isn't worth shit, these telegenic niggers not willing to die," Gunnar confesses, "I ain't ready to die for anything, so I guess I'm just not fit to live. In other words, I'm just ready to die. I'm just ready to die" (200). In the ensuing and ironic celebration of Gunnar as the "new black leader," the novel's critique of African American leadership becomes abundantly clear. Like the faux multiculturalism taught in Gunnar's elementary school and the multicultural messiah role that is forced on Scoby, the novel sees African American leaders as ultimately reinscribing white supremacist values, most notably in their failure to address the institutional racism that has devastated the African American underclass while forcing the African American elite into a state of near schizophrenia.

The novel's ridiculing of leaders reflects a general disenchantment with the state of black leadership in the post-civil-rights era. This results in part from the failure of African American leaders to adopt strategies and ideologies that are specific to the reconfiguration of white supremacy after 1970. As Robert C. Smith attests in *We Have No Leaders*, "black leaders are integrated but their core community is segregated, impoverished and increasingly in the post-civil rights era marginalized, denigrated and criminalized" (279). Thus, while Jesse Jackson's bids for the Democratic nomination can be seen as the apex in the success of the Voting Rights Act, it also represents a moment when African American political thought became fully assimilated into the mainstream culture. The problem is that the assimilation was based on the individual acceptance of a select few African Americans, ignoring the structural conditions that disproportionately disenfranchised the majority of African Americans. Thus, as Smith notes, "In the post-civil rights era virtually all of the talent and resources of the leadership of black America has been devoted to integration or incorporation into the institutions of American society and polity" (278). Reflecting the comic critique that *Shuffle* seeks to illuminate, Charles goes a step further, suggesting that "since 'slavery days' black people have enslaved themselves in every three-card-monte movement that offered salvation or equality. No, you can't have both" (30). This failure of the black leadership has contributed to the nihilism that Cornel West claims threatens the psyche of young black America and that rap music, at its most incisive in the late 1980s and early 1990s, simultaneously reflects and holds at bay. Comic rage, through the adoption of the rhetoric of rap, can be seen as a logical complement to Gunnar's despair; it becomes a mode through which he can stave off nihilistic threat and expose the rage that permeates black culture in postindustrial, post-civil-rights urban America. Thus Gunnar's characteristic apathy, manifested in his desire to die, plays on the notion of existentialism and enhances the expression of rage that dominates his speech.

Yet while the rage in Gunnar's speech is apparent, an important comic inversion is taking place. While his speech signifies on King's quote, there is also a connection to Black Panther Party chairman Huey Newton's autobiography, *Revolutionary Suicide* (1973). As African Americans across the country start committing suicide after Gunnar's speech, Newton's proclamation of the specificity of his willingness to die for freedom has resonance. In the manifesto that opens his book, "Revolutionary Suicide: The Way of Liberation," Newton clarifies his position: "Revolutionary suicide does not mean that I and my comrades have a death wish; it means just the opposite. We have such a desire to live with hope and human dignity that existence without them is impossible" (3). Gunnar inverts these commitments through his post-civil-rights urban nihilism. Thus while King's and Newton's central idea of being willing to die for

African American freedom remains key to Gunnar's interpretation, he reverses the sentiment as encouragement for his own suicide. African Americans not only begin committing suicide but, perhaps out of their loyalty to Gunnar's status as a poet, leave "suicide poems."

Dexter Waverly, the first to commit suicide, leaves a poem titled "Death Poem for Gunnar Kaufman": "Abandoning all concern / my larynx bobs, / enlightenment is a bitch" (201). Even as Gunnar refuses to commit suicide until he is "good and goddamn ready" (202), African American suicides continue, culminating with the suicide of the increasingly unstable Scoby. Already moved by Gunnar's poetry to the point of weeping, and feeling the pressure placed on him by the fans' admiration, professors' sociological interest, and messianic worship, Scoby's response to Gunnar's speech solidifies his role as a character unable to establish an identity beyond the forces that have influence over his life. He is, like the tragic/heroic characters in the novels of the Wright school, unable to overcome the determinism fueled by white supremacist assault. Including a poem of his own in his suicide letter to Gunnar, Scoby attempts to discover the courage that has eluded him:

> I'm on my feet now, looking down into the cloudy quadrangle, my toes hanging ten into the void. I can feel hands on my back, gently pushing. It's funny I want to write a poem.
>
>   i step into the void
>   bravely,
>   aaa
>   aa
>   a
>   a
>   ahhhhh

Not bad for an amateur. (206)

Scoby's death is comparable to Tod Clifton's in Ellison's *Invisible Man*. In fact, Clifton is a character with significant parallels to Scoby. Like Clifton, Scoby is pulled in numerous directions, unable to establish fully a distinct identity or express uncensored rage constructively. The inability of both to negotiate the contradictions within themselves and the society that exploits them inevitably lead to self-destructive breakdowns. Scoby's increasingly bizarre behavior mirrors Clifton's dissatisfaction with the Brotherhood and eventual expulsion. Both have connections to

Charlie Parker and ideas of time. As mentioned in chapter 1, Clifton, who steps "outside of time," reflects the combination of comedy and rage that dominated Parker's jazz career. Scoby, in trying to explain to Gunnar the infiniteness of music, asserts, "Time is what makes music infinite. . . . For Parker, time was a bitch. He wouldn't play Dixie as no happy-go-lucky darkie anthem. He'd play it as a 'I'm mad and I *know* them cotton-picking niggers was mad,' piss-on-their-graves dirge" (204–5). While Clifton's selling of Sambo dolls and his eventual murder at the hands of the police are witnessed by the Invisible Man in almost surrealistic and ironic fashion, Scoby's suicide is complemented by the suicide note that mixes poetry and prose in the same style that permeates the novel.

With the death of Scoby, a distraught Gunnar is led back to Los Angeles, where he almost drowns himself. After this fails, Gunnar and Yoshiko come under constant surveillance, turning the police light that follows them everywhere at night into a communal open mic. In celebration of the two-year anniversary of Scoby's death, Gunnar solidifies his role as the African American messiah with a rousing poem called "Give Me Liberty or Give Me Crib Death" and a challenge to the American government to drop on Hillside the third atomic bomb that President Truman intended to drop during World War II. The response of America mirrors the reductio ad absurdum in George Schuyler's *Black No More*. While a "massive letter-writing campaign asking the government not to waste the uranium and to test the antiquated A-bomb by dropping it on 'those ungrateful passive-aggressive L.A. niggers'" is initiated, Hillside's response to Congress's demand that the neighborhood "rejoin the rest of America or celebrate Kwanzaa in hell" is to "paint white concentric circles on the roofs of the neighborhood, so that from the air Hillside looks like one big target" (224). The novel cements itself as a work of comic rage by using parody and irony to avoid being consumed by rage and violence while nonetheless challenging racist perceptions of race and identity. The painting of the roofs is the final act of defiance that places the American government in an undeniable checkmate: dropping the bomb would expose the existence of a third atomic bomb and manipulation of history, while not dropping it would eventually create a separate, distinct black nation.

Despite Gunnar's claim that "It's been a lovely five hundred years, but it's time to go" (225), the novel ends with Gunnar still alive, passing on the history of the Kaufman family to his daughter Naomi, beginning with the suicide of his father. The poem that Rolf Kaufman leaves highlights the discernible gap between the "dream" that post-civil-rights America uses to promote a "color-blind" society and the reality of white supremacy enacted on African Americans. The novel ends with Rolf's poem stating that he shares King's dream, "but when I wake up / I forget it and / remember I'm running late for work" (226). The poem exposes the incompatibility of the mainstream's assimilationist vision of a race-free society and the continued disenfranchisement of African Americans. Gunnar's own failure to die is the result of his immersion in family and African American cultural tradition. The telling and writing of his story, like the narration in Ellison's *Invisible Man*, or Amiri Baraka's book of poems *Preface to a Twenty Volume Suicide Note* (1961), or the Notorious B.I.G.'s rap album *Ready to Die* (1994), staves off nihilistic ideas of suicide through the alternating artistic expressions of despair, humor, and rage. B.I.G.'s album is particularly noteworthy here because of Beatty's connection to hip-hop, a genre in which the critical and popular success of *Ready to Die* established B.I.G. as one of the premier lyricists. In the final song of the album, "Suicidal Thoughts," B.I.G. not only contemplates suicide throughout but cathartically ends the single and the album with a gunshot to his own head. Although he returns in his second album, *Life After Death* (1997)—a signal that Notorious B.I.G.'s lyrical abilities are capable of defying death itself—Beatty spares his protagonist such an ending and rebirth, replacing the depression at the end of *Ready to Die* with humor. While humor is certainly a vital part of the *Ready to Die* album, Beatty's use of humor as the dominant tone throughout his novel tempers the rage that exists, while counteracting the despair that ultimately seems to overwhelm B.I.G.'s consciousness.

Conclusion: Beyond Literature

The similarities of *Shuffle* and *Ready to Die* are representative of comic rage's ability to cut across the landscape of African American cultural production. The development of comic rage in the post-civil-rights era was nurtured by the NBA's commitment to parodying blacks and whites and its inclusion of a range of artists as contributors to the NBA. The figures that guided and participated in the NBA reflected the panoply of approaches the NBA could employ, as well as their pervasiveness throughout black popular culture. Aside from the literary influences, Ellis's citation of rap artists, specifically Public Enemy, encouraged the linguistic versatility that rap music accumulates from African American vernacular and comedic tradition. The willingness of NBA artists to ridicule, parody, and signify as a way of critiquing white American and African American life is a definitive feature of comic rage. Not only is comic rage able to mature from its appearance during the Black Arts movement, but through the NBA's connection to African American cultural tradition, comic rage filters into African American movies and music. Beatty's own use of comic rage can be traced into the twenty-first century to HBO's recurring spoken-word program *Russell Simmons Presents Def Poetry* and Adam Mansbach's 2005 novel *Angry Black White Boy*. Similarly, as Euell notes, "Wolfe's razor-edged satire, which explores the sometimes painful contradictions of being black in America, has inspired a number of writers to expand on a theme he introduced—the ritual of assessing the value of the culture's daunting legacy of stereotypes and icons" (667). Just as *Day of Absence* influenced works like *The Colored Museum*, numerous plays that have followed Wolfe's, such as Matt Robinson's *The Confessions of Stepin Fetchit* (1993), question the simplistic stereotypes of African Americans. Also, the imprint of Wolfe's play acts as the core to the aptly named *Colored Contradictions: An Anthology of Contemporary African-American Plays* (1996), edited by Harry J. Elam and Robert Alexander. Including the previously mentioned Carlyle Brown play *The Little Tommy Parker Colored Minstrel Show* and Breena Clarke and Glenda Dickerson's *Re/membering Aunt Jemima: A Menstrual Show* (1996), the anthology is constructed of plays that further explore the lives of African Americans in their full intricacy.

As film has become an increasingly important form of African American expression, two of the most important figures in the NBA are Robert Townsend and Spike Lee. Coming on the heels of the mainstream popularity of Sidney Poitier and the economic and cultural impact of the Blaxploitation era, Townsend and Lee break new ground in depicting life in post-civil-rights America. Their works often use humor to examine and critique one-dimensional counter-representations meant to appeal to whites or hyperaggressive portraits influenced by the Black Power and Black Arts movements. Both men produce works in which their characters wrestle with the meaning of their cultural past in the present. Ellis's essay points out that "Mr. Wolfe's *Colored Museum* includes a sketch in which a pair of wigs—one Afro, one straightened—discuss the politics and love life of their owner; and in Mr. Townsend's *Hollywood Shuffle* his character defeats the villain Jheri Curl by withholding his curl activator until the man's greasy ringlets dry back up to their natural naps" (238). Townsend's film acts as a blueprint for many films that followed by evaluating problematic images of black life while exploring the responsibility of black artists in the midst of an incredibly rich period in African American cinema. In relating Spike Lee's declaration that "The number one problem with the old reactionary school was they cared too much about what white people think," Ellis seems to view it as laudable: "And it is precisely because Mr. Lee isn't afraid of what anyone else thinks that he dares to show his world warts and all in both his first film *She's Gotta Have It* and in this year's controversial musical *School Daze* that opened up, among other things, the previously taboo subject of intra-racial, skin-color prejudice" (237–38). Coming at the end of the twentieth century, Lee's film *Bamboozled* challenges the assumption that post-civil-rights America has produced more complex images by using the breakout success of a minstrel show to expose the continuum on which mainstream images of blackness remain dependent. Acting as a bookend to Townsend's *Hollywood Shuffle*, *Bamboozled* employs comic rage to chronicle the proliferation of racist stereotypes under the guise of racial authenticity.

☞ 5

Hollywood Shuffle and *Bamboozled*

Comic Rage, Black Film, and Popular Culture
at the End of the Century

In *Toms, Coons, Mulattoes, Mammies, and Bucks*, Donald Bogle argues,
"Spike Lee and [Robert] Townsend brought to the forefront a new movement of independent black filmmakers who had been around for a time,
some of them working on projects as far back as the late 1960s" (300).
Of course, unlike literature and drama and stand-up, black film does not
possess a long tradition, because of the problems of production, money,
and access. While many films have engaged questions of race, the films
with black directors, writers, and producers have been dishearteningly
few. During the Blaxploitation era, many of the films were either written or directed by whites even as they featured black actors. Lee and
Townsend are especially important, then, because of the control both
were able to exercise over their films, as both directors and writers. Both
artists rejected limitation to straight drama and strict realism in depicting the lives of black Americans and in indicting the continued presence
of white supremacist hegemony. Their use of humor expanded the possibilities for black filmmakers and for exploring black life in contemporary
America. As two of the examples of the NBA alongside George C. Wolfe,
Townsend and Lee produce work that "rejects previously held ideas on,
for example, essentialism and positive representation, fully understanding that there is neither a monolithic African-American culture nor a politically correct notion of blackness to represent" and that "argues for the
complex, multifaceted nature of African-American culture that moves

across race, class, and gender boundaries regardless of the contradictions incurred" (Boyd 157). Where Wolfe, Townsend, and Lee differ from their NBA colleagues is in the fury that accompanies their deployment of humor, parody, and satire. What I mean, in particular, is not simply that their characters are angry or that they make critiques about race, but that the works themselves stand as expressions of comic rage, in tone and plot and vision. The expressions of comic rage that we see in *The Colored Museum*, *Hollywood Shuffle* (1987), and *Bamboozled* (2000) are so pervasive that it becomes impossible to ignore their critique in favor of uncritical consumption.

Margolis rightly observes, "In the case of African American traditions of humor, the connection between genre and audience address is, arguably, particularly strong and inflected in specific ways" (52). Thus comic rage in literature and comedy albums can be extended farther than in other genres, allowing them to capitalize more fully on an intertextuality that signifies on previous works and racist stereotypes. Dramatic works and comedy concerts benefit from the live audience to create an intimate space where the performer's rage can be expressed more freely and the audience's recognition of the rage they share with the performer can be manifested without fear of that rage being considered pathological or irrational. Film, in which the image is imposed on the audience, can make clear its use of "self-directed stereotypes" for critique instead of promotion. The laughter of the audience operates similarly to that of the stand-up concert, but while stand-up frequently challenges its audience to consider old truths in new ways, film often takes popular characters and tropes and extends them to an absurd extreme that exposes their limitations. Both *Hollywood Shuffle* and *Bamboozled* use the latter approach.

In *Hollywood Shuffle*, the ambition of Bobby Taylor (Robert Townsend) to be an actor and to win a role in the film "Jivetime Jimmy's Revenge" forces Bobby, his friends, and his family to wrestle with popular representations of African Americans on television and in movies. Torn between his grandmother's clear distaste for negative images of African Americans and his other family members' desire for him to be successful, Bobby spends his time preparing for auditions and thinking about the changes his presumed success will bring in his life and those around him. As Bobby gets closer to his goal, he begins to understand the impact not only on his own life, in which he sees himself as a Hollywood star, but on his family, particularly his brother. Bobby responds to the frequent skepticism about his prospects and criticism of the film industry itself through the multiple vignettes that critique films from African American artists or from an industry that encourages images of African Americans who "talk jive" or "walk black." *Shuffle*, which was famously completed only because Robert Townsend maxed out all his credit cards, targets directly the post-civil-rights state of race and media and produces an unrelenting tone that often seems satirical but that rejects instruction and replaces it with militant critique. Additionally, Townsend's film attacks the popularity of Eddie Murphy—whose films were groundbreaking in the 1980s, to be sure, but also led white filmmakers and companies to view Murphy's brand of "wiseass" as the authentic black persona.

The distinction between traditional African American humor, traditional satire, and comic rage is crucial to this study. Works embodying comic rage are frequently misinterpreted and marginalized because they are considered failures as works of humor and satire. For example, critics assume, understandably, that Spike Lee's definition of satire at the beginning of *Bamboozled* refers to the film itself. I would suggest, however, that it refers to the attempt by Pierre Delacroix (played by Damon Wayans) to create an African American show so offensive that his boss will allow Delacroix (Dela for short) to produce instead the show about middle-class black America he wants. Perhaps if Lee had stuck solely to this story, alongside the ongoing critique of Delacroix's self-hatred and discomfort with any type of blackness beyond the upper-class, Ivy-league identity he has created for himself, then the reference to the film would hold up. Yet once Dela's show, *Mantan: The New Millennium Minstrel Show*, appears with such vivid ferocity, Dela and his assistant Sloan (Jada Pinkett Smith), along with the two main actors of the show, Manray/Mantan (Savion Glover) and Womack/Sleep 'n' Eat (Tommy Davidson), lose their critical perspective and become wrapped up in the runaway success of the show. From there, the film moves beyond the definition Dela provides at the beginning and produces a growing unease and anger at what the success of the show reveals about white racial anxiety, black self-hatred, and mainstream continued comfort with specific concepts of blackness. As the late twentieth and early twenty-first centuries witness an unprecedented expansion of African American films and shows, this chapter explores how Robert Townsend's *Hollywood Shuffle* and Spike Lee's *Bamboozled* humorously trace and critique the evolution of images of black life in popular media by exposing historic representations of African Americans on film and current manifestations of racist stereotypes. While most African-American-led films infuse a cultural specificity that implicitly critiques their absence from mainstream film, *Shuffle* and *Bamboozled* launch multiple explicit attacks on mainstream popular culture's simplistic, often one-dimensional, portrayals of black life that fail to critically examine the realignment of white supremacy at the end of the twentieth century.

Hollywood Shuffle

When I refer to "African American shows," I specifically mean films and television shows that are black controlled, with blacks making up the majority of the main cast and with blacks serving as creator/executive producer or writer/director. Additionally, this chapter will generally focus on works from the end of the 1970s through the early years of the twenty-first century. Chronicling the explosion of black films in the late 1980s and early 1990s, Todd Boyd rightly distinguishes these from the Blaxploitation era, pointing out how "audiences became increasingly aware of the multifaceted nature of the culture. Often neglected or totally denigrated, it is represented by the proliferation of images that affirm the dominant society's retrograde view of African Americans" (154–55). Perhaps as important, many of the works of the Blaxploitation era may have featured predominantly black casts, but they were frequently written and directed by whites and consistently abandoned the radical politics of early Blaxploitation films in favor of gratuitous scenes of sex and violence that reinforced notions of an authentic black coolness that many whites found desirable. Often these writers and directors, and the whites who made up the audiences of these films, failed to critically examine how their appropriation of black culture distorted mainstream perceptions of African Americans and impacted representations of African Americans in popular media and assumptions about African Americans that reinforced institutional racism in the last two decades of the twentieth century. Some works in the 1980s perpetuated the inherent problems of Blaxploitation films written and directed by whites, while works from a younger generation of African American filmmakers, like Robert Townsend and Spike Lee, rejected those representations in interviews and in their work.

While not as popular or well known now, *Hollywood Shuffle* was considered groundbreaking upon its arrival. Appearing between the end of the Blaxploitation era's guerrilla-style filmmaking and the independent filmmaking boom of the 1990s, it was noteworthy not only for its attack on stereotypes of blacks in cinema but for Townsend's ability to get the film made at all. As Todd Boyd recounts, Townsend "reportedly saved rejected film stock from the sets of previous movies in which he acted, and he used credit cards for cash purposes to get this film produced, financed, and released" (159). The urgency behind Townsend's filmmaking can be felt in its tone. *Hollywood Shuffle* is a film deeply invested in chronicling the cinematic images of the past and present, and it depicts their impact on the lived experiences of the African American community. A key sequence appears when, as Bogle contends, Townsend "does what can only be described as a brilliant impersonation of Stepin Fetchit: it is a parody and a homage to Fetchit. Townsend sees clearly the timing and skill that went into Fetchit's work" (300). The use of Stepin Fetchit becomes significant because, as constructed in the film, he does not fit on either side of the Hollywood racial dichotomy. His nuance, particularly his "timing and skill," couples with the humanity brought to the character to undermine the scripts he was given. However, Stepin Fetchit's depiction as one of the most recognizable figures of black inferiority in cinematic history makes him a less than ideal candidate for the important, but sometimes equally problematic, counter-representations of the 1960s and 1970s. The effort by writers like Mel Watkins to recover the actor who played him, Lincoln Perry, collapse our traditional discourse about race and cinema while affording *Shuffle* the opportunity to parody Stepin Fetchit to highlight Perry's lack of choice in film roles as opposed to the multiple choices that Bobby has. Like Ishmael Reed's reconfiguration of the Uncle Tom figure in *Flight to Canada*, Townsend interrogates our perception of Stepin Fetchit by moving away from the demonization of the actor, demonstrating the humanity he infused into a caricature, and focuses on the absence of opportunities for Perry to apply his clear talents. Townsend's reconsideration of Perry casts an even more critical light on Hollywood's racist stereotyping and the black community's failure to resist the images presented to them.

In its comic exploration of black images in film, *Shuffle* has much in common with Keenan Ivory Wayans's 1988 Blaxploitation send-up *I'm*

Gonna Git You Sucka. *Sucka* was written and directed by Wayans, who was also a cowriter on *Shuffle*. *Sucka* has become the more popular and iconic film, bolstered by the popularity of Wayans's 1990–94 television show *In Living Color* and the success of the other Wayans siblings. In "Stereotypical Strategies: Black Film Aesthetics, Spectator Positioning, and Self-Directed Stereotypes in *Hollywood Shuffle* and *I'm Gonna Git You Sucka*," Harriet Margolis points out that both films "rely heavily on the playful use of stereotypes, and formally both are episodic, frequently interrupting their narrative flow to present fantasies that their heroes (both played by the directors) have of themselves in alternative situations that comment on whatever situation they find themselves in within the film's diegetic world" (52). Yet there is a clear distinction between the two movies, specifically the presence of Townsend's vision. Wayans's use of parody fits within more traditional concepts of humor and satire that might suppress rage. In fact, the vignettes and daydreams that we see in *Shuffle* are similar to what we find in *In Living Color* and in Townsend's 1987 HBO stand-up special, *Robert Townsend and His Partners in Crime*. However, the overarching narrative that we find in *Shuffle*, Bobby's frustration with the tension between his desire to be a successful actor and the destructive impact of the limited representations of African Americans onscreen, provides the opportunities for Townsend's critique and rage to exist alongside the humor that permeates the film.

The tension between his grandmother's anger and the material success his family imagines for him exacerbates Bobby's ambivalence and provides the opportunity for the larger political commentary the film pursues. Bobby quits the film despite being given the key role, because he realizes that his decisions are having a direct impact on his brother Stevie. More important, Townsend's film does not encourage the return to a golden age of black cinema that one might see in a traditional satire. Indeed, the Blaxploitation era, which many romanticize as an ideal moment, gave rise to the "jive talk" that Bobby Taylor finds problematic as the only representation of African Americans on film and the "self-directed stereotypes" that we find in counter-representations that are often as simplistic as the racist stereotypes they attempt to refute.

Margolis defines self-directed stereotyping as "the deployment of stereotypes by the people being stereotyped in order to undermine those stereotypes by exposing their ridiculous underpinnings" (53). A traditional satire might use the stereotypes employed in both films to turn its audience to an idealized representation of blacks in Hollywood. Certainly Keenan Ivory Wayans does this in *Sucka*, which promotes a breed of black hero influenced by the Blaxploitation era but with a self-awareness that avoids caricature. By contrast, Lee's and Townsend's films avoid idealized portraits of black heroes and characters in favor of a larger critique about the structures that the characters must confront, navigate, and overcome (or fail to overcome). In Margolis's view, "The ways Townsend and Wayans use stereotypes, however, leave them vulnerable to charges of furthering, rather than destroying, those stereotypes. Townsend grounds his attack in a traditionally realist story; Wayans uses parody as his platform. In fact, although *Sucka* attacks the media's use of negative stereotypes of African Americans, that attack is not foregrounded, as it is in *Hollywood Shuffle*" (53). *Shuffle*, then, separates itself from *Sucka* by moving beyond satire's traditional, often insular, tendency to advocate for the return to an idealized past. For instance, *Sucka* retains the focus on individual desire and fulfillment, often at the expense of the African American community, found in other films featuring African Americans. *Shuffle* expands its lens to include the needs and desires of the larger community and assesses not just past but contemporaneous distortions of blackness.

Townsend's realism, matched by *Bamboozled*'s frequent and direct references to real-life figures and events, provides an ideal atmosphere for extended expressions of comic rage. Audiences are unable to dismiss these stories as mere entertainment. They depict post-civil-rights worlds of the black working and middle class that are easily recognizable. The characters attempt to navigate a post-integration world that claims a commitment to equality and multiculturalism, but in both films that world allows only stereotypical images of blacks to be produced. Margolis claims, "Townsend's more direct confrontation with the media's negative role in developing and maintaining harmful black stereotypes, his more direct expression of the personal anguish individual African Americans experience in the face of these stereotypes, and his incorporation of a disapproving observer's point of view result in a different audience address than that of *Sucka*" (54). Despite the film's clear indictment of the maintenance of racist stereotypes, Townsend does not absolve his characters of their responsibility. Not only is Townsend's protagonist well aware that auditioning for a stereotypical black role is a deliberate choice, but he also understands the consequences of his choice for his community and himself. While there are clearly external forces at work that have led him to seriously consider what he and the audience see as a degraded role, the film consistently reminds us that its protagonist possesses the agency to impact his fate. Here, then, Townsend's film critiques African Americans who, especially in the post-civil-rights moment, knowingly choose roles that reinforce racist stereotypes permeating the mainstream imagination. *Bamboozled* transforms *Shuffle*'s critique into an outright indictment by ridiculing African American actors who not only willingly embrace stereotypical roles but openly seek white approval to the point of being buffoonish.

Although Margolis points out, "Townsend attacks specific, individually expressed stereotypes more than the process of stereotyping itself," she sees this as less radical than *Sucka*'s critique of "the problem of stereotyping as process, a process presented by the media as a means of conceptualizing the world" (55). While Margolis's critique certainly has merit, particularly her contention that in *Sucka* "no point of view remains secure for viewer identification" (55), two elements of the film establish that *Sucka* is not, like *Shuffle*, a work of comic rage. The first is *Sucka*'s dependence on its audience's interpretation of the film as more than mere entertainment. The second is *Sucka*'s promotion of a new black male hero, a hero influenced primarily by the iconography of the Blaxploitation era, whose major achievement is the adoption of a traditional concept of manhood. Both elements fit more in the tradition of satire that works of comic rage seek to avoid. *Shuffle* differs in its direct confrontation of stereotypes of blacks in Hollywood, particularly in making its audience continually aware of its intent to critique as well as entertain. Rejecting the idealized role or identity on which many satires depend, *Shuffle* builds off of *Flight to Canada*'s contention that "Canada, like freedom, is a state of mind." Bobby Taylor frees himself to create his own expressive space, one that allows for his individuality while remaining "community-oriented" in the way that his grandmother advocates.

Bobby realizes that while the roles of Lear, Superman, and "Rambro" may not be "harmful, they are not necessarily appropriate roles for black actors to aspire to, at least not from the point of view of the community, with which he now identifies" (Margolis 58). Additionally, Bobby's choice returns us to the limited options of white-authored works on both sides of the color line. Such works, from big-budget blockbusters to Blaxploitation films, exclude the varied and complex depictions that we see throughout Townsend's film. The black-authored narratives we do see in *Shuffle* appear through the desires of Bobby's family. Yet instead of the single idealized narrative that might be favored in a satire, *Shuffle* provides two competing narratives that tug at Bobby. The first is his uncle's belief that he should not give up on his dreams, for he will feel regret later. The uncle's sacrifice of his own dreams drives his advice to Bobby and privileges individual desire over community uplift. By contrast, Bobby's grandmother encourages him to embrace the community's needs. Bobby's uncle makes a compelling case based on personal satisfaction, but it quickly becomes apparent that Bobby's only road to realizing his individual dreams runs through the degrading roles that, while allowing him to pursue materialist fantasies, reinforce black criminal fantasies that allow the mainstream to play on racial anxieties in the post-integration moment.

In fact, while *Sucka* embraces the Blaxploitation era, and at times its more celebrated figures, as the scene and the template through which it conceives black masculinity, *Shuffle* rejects the Blaxploitation era because the counter-representations it created are as simplistic as the racist images they seek to contradict. Margolis notes that the protagonist Jack Spade's main problem in *Sucka* is that "the old heroes have gone the way of yesteryear's Blaxploitation films" but "by film's end he has resurrected his old heroes, the ghetto villain pushing gold is dead, and the widow is Jack's own reward. Even his mother has been put in her place, back on the arm of John Slade (Bernie Casey), the Shaft-like hero of Jack's youth whom his mother used to date" (57). While *Sucka* makes important critiques of the hypermasculine, hypersexualized ideal of the Blaxploitation moment, *Shuffle* destabilizes the ideal at its root by forcing its audience to recall that many of the films that appeared then were written and directed by whites. We see this in "Bobby's first fantasy, about the Black Acting School, where whites with British accents teach blacks to talk and walk jive so they can play gang members and rapists in movies and on TV" (Margolis 56). Thus the romanticized conceptions of blackness that are vital to *Sucka's* world are viewed as another reductive stereotype conceived by whites that exclude more complex representations of the African American community.

In *Sucka*, Margolis points out, "For Jack, the hero's relation to his community involves separation, isolation, and distance. The hero acts alone, or perhaps with a team of other worthy heroes, for the benefit of the community" (59). In practice, the Blaxploitation hero exists apart from the community and within the American individualist tradition that often ignores the community and casts the hero as virtually super-human, without need of substantive relationships. The result, of course, is a well-defined, easily consumed character against the backdrop of a community that seems a single mass without effective strategies to ward off racist oppression, save the violent retribution/justice that the hero seeks. The singularity of the representation counteracts the often cowardly and powerless buffoon in previous depictions, but it also reiterates limited images of African Americans and reinforces the uniqueness of the individual instead of the potential of individual expression within the collective's expressive culture.

By contrast, in *Shuffle*, as Margolis argues, "the grandmother's point of view reflects that of the community, especially the family, superseding those of the individual. Whereas a figure representing the female and older segment of his family urges Bobby to embrace community values, his uncle, a member of the middle generation of his family who gave up his career dreams early in life, encourages him to pursue his dream for personal satisfaction" (58). Townsend's early rejection of the Blaxploitation iconography as an alternative eliminates the simplistic response to the passive, asexual, comic black figures that dominated mainstream American film throughout the early part of the twentieth century. Instead it is the image based on the grandmother's point of view that sits at the center of the film and rejects both stereotype and counter-representation. Both are revealed to be based on individualist, capitalist, white supremacist hegemony, excluding nuance and frequently marginalizing other, more complex voices. The contradictory advice that Bobby receives is clearly gendered: the uncle's belief that individual desire should take precedence fits squarely within a white Western masculine ideal that often romanticizes the individual at odds with his community, while the grandmother's belief demands an expansion of the community into a collective space that still allows for individual expression. So instead of shelving his acting ambitions and working at the post office, the film finds Bobby acting in commercials for the post office, merging his individual passion for acting with "respectable" work in order to benefit the community.

Donald Bogle suggests, "Uneven, more a series of clever skits than a fully developed film, *Hollywood Shuffle* was carried along by its young director's spirit and enthusiasm," yet surprisingly claims, "The film's greatest asset was Townsend, the actor. (He's a better actor than director.)" (300). Bogle seems to think that Townsend's talent as an actor helps compensate for weaknesses of Townsend the director, particularly in cohesive storytelling. However, I see Townsend's role as the director as vital to the very virtues that Bogle mentions. Throughout his career, Townsend, like Lee, has demanded the opportunity to shape the projects in which he participates. Whether as creator/writer, director, or executive producer, Townsend consistently seeks to set a clear and specific tone, one that is often openly political and distinctly black. For example, his 1995–99 television show *The Parent 'Hood* was very pointedly in the vein of middle-class black family comedies from the mid-1980s through the late 1990s. Showing a side of African American life that much of white America did not know existed, these shows attempted to push back against the emergence of "gangsta culture" in hip-hop and film. In *Hollywood Shuffle*, Townsend targets white executives and filmmakers, but perhaps more important, he critiques members of the black community who encourage or succumb to the influence of racist and limiting stereotypes. Townsend has been clear that shows and films featuring African Americans were "so small and so narrow" (Braxton) and, in the tradition of works of comic rage, he expands the possibilities and choices for African Americans internalizing the narrow collection of images they see. Accordingly, what Bogle sees as "spirit and enthusiasm" I see as comic rage tying the seemingly disparate parts of the film together. Townsend's role as director, then, becomes vital because he sets and maintains the tone that permeates the film and that moves beyond the parodic and satiric thrust it employs. Instead we see a film that engages overtly the impact of black stereotypes in film on the daily lives of underclass African Americans. In the process, Townsend examines a Hollywood corporate culture that constructs and sustains stereotypical images of blacks as well as the black community's internalization and manifestation of the messages they receive and perpetuate. Part of the struggle that Bobby faces in his desire to become a successful film star is the community's clear investment in Hollywood's production of blackness and their expectation that Bobby will become an important star in that tradition. Yet both Townsend and Bobby realize that the cycle these performances engender can contribute to racial profiling, job loss, and community destruction. Their ability to make these links creates a crisis in Bobby but provides an opportunity for the film to make numerous comic critiques.

In *Redefining Black Film* Mark A. Reid points out, "The narrative structure of *Hollywood Shuffle* is a collection of stereotyped experiences that black performers encounter in Hollywood. The purpose of the narrative is to ridicule both whites and blacks who produce, perform, and direct racially tendentious films" (40). Reid believes that *Hollywood Shuffle* fits within "racial essentialist narratives against which minstrel forms are impotent in their rebellions" (43) and cautions against the limitations of black counter-representations. Yet *Shuffle* indicts its audience, particularly those who attempt to avoid his critiques of the impact of media representations on everyday life. The film creates an atmosphere where Bobby's professional choice has a direct effect not only on himself but on the community at large. Townsend places Bobby's decisions squarely within the tradition of the race man who sees himself as representative of the masses of African Americans who are often rendered voiceless except through the successes and advocacy of the few individuals who gain access to mainstream spaces and audiences. The stereotypes that we do see in *Shuffle* must be viewed through the atmosphere they create, one that Bobby fears he will replicate should he take the role being offered him. The obvious manifestation of mainstream stereotypes of minorities, women, and homosexuals in his real life makes Bobby's attempts to separate the fictional world from the real-world consequences untenable.

The role of the gang member is not replaced by a nationalistic counter-representation after Bobby rejects it. While there is a desire for middle-class respectability that permeates Bobby's and the grandmother's rhetoric, that presence actually contributes to the collapse of the simplistic dichotomy that has frequently been part of our racial discourse. Margolis claims *Sucka* is the "more politically effective film" (63), and as a Menippean satire, *Sucka* stands proudly in the African American satirical tradition that is often more radical than more traditional satires. Margolis views *Shuffle* as a film that simply replaces negative images with positive ones. Yet *Shuffle* does not simply replace; it redefines. The film rejects the counter-representations that emerged during the Blaxploitation era and casts the success that Bobby Taylor seeks as a hybrid of his own desire for individual expression and an abiding interest in community uplift. More important, the film views its site of resistance as much in terms of consciousness as in terms of what job Bobby takes. Thus the markers of manhood and heroism upon which *Sucka* depends are unnecessary in *Shuffle*, where they are secondary to Bobby's emergent consciousness and embrace of community. *Shuffle* thus distinguishes itself from the parodic tone that we see many NBA artists adopt in order to take a more comprehensive view of white supremacy in media and reality in the post-civil-rights era. The film carves out a space for the expression for comic rage in film and on television that realigns our perceptions of old stereotypes while critiquing the attempt to create and solidify new ones. The groundwork in Townsend's film allows for an even more overtly furious work, by a director whose politics and rage leave little doubt about the film's purpose and tone.

All the Rage: *Bamboozled* and the End of Satire

Bamboozled begins with a definition of satire. The natural response, of course, has been to categorize and judge the film on these terms. Judged by the criteria of satire, most critics are content to see *Bamboozled* ultimately as a failure. However, such a limited evaluation leaves it open to gross misinterpretation. What reviews often point out is the seemingly didactic tone the latter part of the film takes. Even works that more closely link *Bamboozled* to comic rage, like Phil Chidester and Jamel Santa Cruze Bell's article "'Say the Right Thing': Spike Lee, *Bamboozled*, and the Future of Satire in a Postmodern World," rely on satire as an explanation for the elements in the film that defy the traditional satirical formula: "By openly defining his work as a satire, Lee may actually be providing his own commentary on the film rather than simply explaining the narrative direction it is about to take" (203). The plot of *Bamboozled* would seem to suggest that the definition at the beginning of the film applies to the show that Pierre Delacroix creates. Like the traditional satire, *Mantan* emerges out of Delacroix's anger at Dunwitty's ideas for more "respectable" middle-class black shows. Dela attempts to expose Dunwitty's assumptions about blackness by uncovering his coded language and linking it to the noxious tradition of the minstrel show. However, Lee's interest quickly expands beyond the minstrel show, similarly expanding the film beyond traditional notions of satire.

Cynthia Willett contends that if *Bamboozled*, "through its independent production, achieves what Delacroix's strategy of working for the network fails to do, this is because the film, unlike the projected minstrel show, stems from motivations and causes that are not fully reactive, not, that is, just dark ironic satire" (89). It is, in fact, the attempt to fit the film within the confines of satire that *Bamboozled* often resists. *Bamboozled* does not function only as Lee's indictment of popular culture's distortion of black life and culture. The film becomes a proactive effort in exploring the full complexity of contemporary black life. So, the film does not merely present the minstrel show as a counter to racist stereotypes, perhaps out of the fear of merely contributing to the reinforcement of those stereotypes, but it presents a multitude of black experiences that wrestle with new, coded versions of old stereotypes cloaked in a rhetoric of color blindness. I agree with Chidester and Bell that the first half of the film might certainly qualify, particularly as Delacroix's satirical "joke" on his boss becomes a joke on Dela and a larger commentary on the entertainment industry. The second half of the film erupts as the fury underneath the characters' multiple masks begins to seep through. The show's success—and its meaning—creates a crisis for Delacroix, Mantan, Sleep 'n' Eat, and Sloan that either leads them to important expressions of rage or exposes the rage they have been trying to cloak. In particular we see Mantan and Sleep 'n' Eat become capable of articulating their rage as they become aware of the forces exploiting and imposing upon them.

The humor the film elicits, specifically from the success of *Mantan: The New Millennium Minstrel Show*, emerges from Lee's fury at representations of African Americans in television and film. The seemingly cathartic laughter of the whites who embrace the show—eventually donning blackface in the audience—is meant to produce a profound anger at the similarly destructive images of African Americans that are presented to and eagerly consumed by contemporary white audiences. Delacroix's original pitch is for a show he hopes will fill the absence of shows like Cosby's with majority black casts that might provide a variety of representations of black life. Two of the most controversial shows that Lee targets—mentioning *Homeboys in Outer Space* and *The Secret Diary of Desmond Pfeiffer* by name in the film, for example—embody television's inability to conceive of a distinct African American experience beyond simplistic stereotypes. Very rarely complex and never dramatic, these shows often seemed to tout themselves as authentic black behavior, readily accepted, celebrated, and consumed by whites. *Bamboozled* attacks the contemporary belief that some subjects have been depoliticized as the markers of racial reconciliation. This mainstream belief ignores hegemonic oppression rooted in maintaining white privilege through the promotion of the absence of race or the ability of whites to define the markers of blackness. The only African American in his division, Delacroix attempts to create another *Cosby Show* but is rejected by his white boss. The boss, Thomas Dunwitty (Michael Rapaport), believes that having an African American wife and two biracial children absolves him of responsibility in the perniciousness of blackface minstrelsy, the history of "nigger," and "keeping it real," which he sees as being authentically black. Dunwitty fails to realize that his sense of the "real" remains rooted in a stereotypical image of blackness that views blacks as pathological objects that reaffirm the racial hierarchy. Dunwitty's performance of blackness, then, continues to marginalize African Americans and privilege whites. The blackface the whites don not only recalls the blackface minstrel shows of the nineteenth and twentieth centuries but encourages a critique of the continuing white exploitation and appropriation of the perceived black experience.

In the late 1990s and the early twenty-first century, Lee consistently cast himself as the marginalized voice willing to expose the continued presence and manifestation of white supremacist hegemony. In *He Got Game* (1998) Lee takes on the exploitation of African Americans playing college basketball, and the controversial *She Hate Me* (2004) attempts to address a corporate culture that manipulates consumers and discredits whistleblowers. Additionally, Lee frequently criticized Quentin Tarantino, on whom the Dunwitty character seems based, for his controversial portraits of black characters. *Bamboozled*'s assault on network television and media continues in Lee's tradition of telling the uncomfortable truth of the often simplistic representations of African Americans in a predominantly white network, shaped by predominantly white writers, catering to predominantly white audiences. The film dramatizes Lee's critique of a supposedly "color-blind" entertainment world when we see Delacroix as the sole African American writer on a team attempting to write dialogue for African Americans. The ideas the writers toss around become increasingly disturbing for Dela and Sloan as the writers consistently fail to examine the satirical intent of the show or their own racist attitudes. The film makes clear that the writers would not consider themselves racist, because they are working on a show starring African Americans—an attitude shared by many whites in an era when popular black figures in sports, music, and entertainment are embraced by whites as well as blacks. Obvious moments like Dunwitty's outburst to Delacroix and the all-white writers room produce a laughter of recognition from black audiences at the echoes of white racist construction of black identity through white control of African American representation in popular media. Here, then, comedy does not suppress rage but activates it and produces a space for it to be constructively and effectively expressed. Michael Epp's contention that the film "rejects satire as a cynical excuse for [racist stereotypes'] repetition" (25) negates satire as a haven that would excuse the continued dissemination of minstrelsy as an acceptable form of entertainment. What it reveals for Lee's film is that *Bamboozled* is an essentially dramatic—not satirical—critique. Humor then merely becomes the lens through which that critique is clearly realized. In Lee's case humor buffers the rage that often (allegedly) overwhelms his films and marginalizes his critiques.

Beretta Smith-Shomade contends that at the "nexus of entertainment and authenticity . . . *Bamboozled* wages war on television and related media conglomerates" (235). Lee's activation of his audience's rage separates *Bamboozled* from Chidester and Bell's postmodern satire, which seeks to promote individual behavior and responsibility. Chidester and Bell ask us to consider *Bamboozled* not so much as a satire but as a "foundation for an even more complicated and demanding cinematic work: namely, a satirical take on satire itself" (204). Comic rage seeks to galvanize the community not by demanding allegiance to an authentic black experience and ideology but by critiquing racist representations and myopic counter-representations. The film creates space for a variety of images and ideologies to exist and push back against the external forces that surround him.

The tone of *Bamboozled* acts as the vehicle through which Lee delivers his critique not merely of representations of African Americans in television and film, but of African Americans' participation in their narrow and reductive depictions. As Ray Black points out, "Delacroix and his creation become the object of the film's satire, rather than the subject delivering his critique of race and society" (19). Indeed, by making Delacroix the target of the film's critique, *Bamboozled* avoids the trap of promoting minstrelsy even as it critiques minstrelsy. In the mainstream narrative of the post-civil-rights world, Delacroix might be a celebrated figure, someone whose success in a predominantly white space would be hailed as the manifestation of a more inclusive America. That Delacroix feels forced to turn to minstrelsy to make a statement about the limited images of African Americans speaks to the failure of the entertainment industry to address larger institutional problems.

The ineffectiveness of direct protest or action leaves only the satirical for Delacroix to use. The minstrel show itself, then, becomes a satirical comment on Dunwitty's racism and the de facto minstrel state of television and film. However, as Jamie Barlowe contends, "The enthusiastic re-embracing of blackface by African Americans" that we see in the film "reveals painfully the continuing problem of mimicry of the white colonizer by the formerly colonized. In the film, mimicry is depicted primarily through the internalization of self-commodification among African Americans as a consequence of capitalist desire and as an example of neo-colonialism" (9). Delacroix's loss of control, and eventual exploitation, of the show's success reveals the dangers of using inflammatory stereotypes to critique our embrace of those stereotypes. The appropriation of blackface minstrelsy, to either critique or engage the taboo, fails to recognize the continued presence of older racist stereotypes—and the public's willingness to accept them. Additionally, it ignores the connections between the literal examples of blackface, themselves incomplete, and the more metaphorical ones being perpetuated through media representations. Lee, by contrast, extends in *Bamboozled* a project he has continually pursued in his films: portraying the full and complex lives of African Americans. While showing how popular culture reduces black lives to one-dimensional caricatures and eliminates the choices blacks have for self-expression, the film avoids falling victim to a promotion of minstrelsy by refusing to let anyone in the audience escape unscathed or, more specifically, without bearing witness to the damage that the presence of blackface minstrelsy causes.

By expanding the scope of the film beyond the minstrel show to leave no one untouched, Lee provides a fuller picture of an America coming apart at the seams because of its contradictions about race. When we see Delacroix's white boss claiming to be "blacker" than Delacroix and claiming the right to spew "nigger" repeatedly, Delacroix's docile response intensifies the audience's rage at his offensiveness. The discomfort, and then anger, of Manray/Mantan and Womack/Sleep 'n' Eat mirrors the reactions of the movie's audience and becomes increasingly visceral as it leads to the destruction of their friendship. The detachment that is afforded characters and audiences with the lighter tone of Horatian or the protective sarcasm of Juvenalian satire collapses under the film's refusal to stay objective or hide its anger at specific real-life targets. I agree with Stanley Kauffmann that many "have called it satire, but I think this is mistaken. It is a long ironic outburst of anger, anger that *derives* from satire" (32). Once *Mantan* becomes a critical and popular darling, the initially horrified Delacroix celebrates the awards he receives by doing a back flip and attempting to give his award to the actor Matthew Modine, although they have never met. Delacroix's action recalls, purposely and at times precisely, the celebration of actors Cuba Gooding Jr. and Ving Rhames when, after winning an Oscar and a Golden Globe respectively, they seemed more interested in seeking (shucking and jiving for) mainstream acceptance than in understanding the institutional inequities that made their successes remarkable rather than routine.

Delacroix's story embodies the larger contemporary story of African Americans in an allegedly post-racial world where prejudices are exposed, but, as Kauffmann believes, "this enlightened exposure of old prejudice is fundamentally just another way to exploit them" (32). So instances of color-blind casting and the success of individual shows or artists mask the continued institutional exclusion of African Americans. The few successful African Americans remain beholden to a white power structure that limits the number of African-American-controlled films and African American television shows, particularly dramas. Dela's—and Gooding's and Rhames's—overreaction to their awards is viewed with disdain because they are attempting to ingratiate themselves with a system that limits their opportunities to play or produce complex, distinctly black characters. We see a Delacroix who, according to Beretta Smith-Shomade, is "radicalized enough to create a coon show but too committed to living out his American dream to quit" (235). The film's white characters attempt to perform blackness in much the same way that whites during the height of minstrelsy adopted blackface. They invoke their privilege to shift across the color line without consequences to the racial hierarchy, and their use of the phrase "I'se a nigger" exposes their relief over fears of being marginalized in a show that features an all-black cast.

Of course, the most important expression of rage in *Bamboozled* is the blackface itself, specifically because of the rage it automatically elicits from the film's audience. Smith-Shomade points out, "The past's authentication of minstrelsy and blackface (already false constructions) returns according to Lee in contemporary television" (241). Lee uses the visceral nature of blackface to highlight the continued misrepresentation of African Americans in popular culture. Instead of returning to stereotypical counter-representations of African Americans as the ideal—as we frequently see in satire—or promoting the images "in the name of progress," as Smith-Shomade contends, the film rejects the claims of progress by revealing the almost primal dependence the mainstream has on seeing stereotypical images of African Americans. The image of the black comic-criminal sits at the center of the construction of white American identity as well as American national policy and culture. As Delacroix's assistant Sloan details the application of blackface, the disturbing sight of the finished product seeks outrage from the film's audience as opposed to the amusement of seeing Robert Downey Jr. don blackface in the film *Tropic Thunder*'s satirical treatment of a white actor's hubris. *Bamboozled* continues to evoke anger when, with the show's runaway success, the mostly white studio audiences begin to wear blackface and to proclaim themselves "niggers." The blackface acts as the most obvious marker of the film's comic rage, in much the same way whiteface operated in *Day of Absence*. Lee's use of blackface goes beyond the vignettes that Townsend uses, becoming the organizing symbol on which the film's anger centers. As such, blackface ties together the disparate stories of the characters, which range from the dramatic attempts by Manray and Womack to survive to the absurd attempts by Sloan's brother, Big Blak Afrika, to perform a radical black nationalism. The history of blackface, which Lee presents in a devastatingly effective montage of film and television clips at the end of *Bamboozled*, keeps the rage of the film at the forefront of its narrative, as the weight of that history on the lives of the characters causes each of them to slowly unravel.

I say "unravel" because underneath the primary narrative of the film sits the theme of reinvention. Obviously Manray and Womack reinvent themselves from the street act at the beginning of the film to the minstrel show performers Mantan and Sleep 'n' Eat, both on the show and off. However, the film presents them as perhaps the most sympathetic characters, certainly more so than the actors Lee uses the film to criticize. In interviews, Lee has claimed that much of the venom he unleashes is for actors who have multiple options. By contrast, Manray and Womack represent entertainers in the early twentieth century who had no options other than blackface and minstrel-show characters. Lee's sympathy echoes Townsend's reconsideration of Lincoln Perry in *Hollywood*

Shuffle, which highlights Perry's talent while indicting his lack of choices. Similarly, Manray and Womack could easily be cast as Uncle Tom figures, but the film views them as pawns being manipulated because they have no other options as performers beyond working for change on the street. The education of the two men and their increasing discomfort and rage at what the success of the show means form the backbone of Lee's critique.

In "Spike Lee's Revolutionary Broadside" Saul Landau rightly points out, "The driving force of Lee's story is contemporary, untamed capitalism in its mad race for profits or, in media jargon, ratings," and the minstrel show acts as a product "so outrageous that the manipulative media can convince audiences to turn it into a fad" (11). Womack expresses his dissatisfaction almost immediately, while Manray simply wants to perform, entertain, and profit. Manray in particular serves himself up as the perfect object upon which Landau's "savage capitalism" feasts. His willingness to participate in the show so long as the "hoofing is real" ignores any critical consciousness about his artistic choices as well as Dela's larger critique of the entertainment industry. Sloan's, and by extension the film's, effort to educate Manray about the context of blackface minstrelsy resists the blind internalizing of racist ideologies and images. Her narration of the application of the blackface does not simply augment the physical transformation the men undergo; it chronicles the emergent consciousness, pain, and rage that sits underneath. Also, her voice-over mirrors the sense of fury, despair, and eroded hope the film's audience feels as the show exposes the racist sentiments of the industry and the public.

As part of the "untamed capitalism" that surrounds the show, Lee takes aim at the advertisers who support it. Despite multiple protests of *Mantan* by Al Sharpton and the NAACP, sponsors flock to the show. The film depicts companies clearly valuing profit over the effects of offensive stereotypes. It rejects the narrative of corporate America embracing diversity, whether in its hiring or in its marketing. The movie draws clear connections between the racist stereotypes in the show that the white audiences embrace and the racist notions of blackness animating the commercials for the products being sold, from the outlandish alcohol Da Bomb, an exaggerated take on the forty-ounce beer often associated with inner-city blacks, to the exploiting of a materialist culture that targets popular notions of hip-hop youth. Barlowe points to "white fashion designers, particularly Tommy Hilfiger, who, while also fetishizing difference and promoting neo-colonialism, grow increasingly wealthy and powerful by commodifying and consuming African Americans by producing consumer desire for the products and productions" (10). Thus in *Bamboozled* one of the chief advertisers supporting the minstrel show is Hilnigger clothes, a savage comic attack on Tommy Hilfiger who, along with Ralph Lauren, famously confessed that he did not make his clothes for an "urban" audience, even as both designers exploited their prestige in the world of hip-hop and black America. In the Hilnigger commercials, the older white male stand-in clearly mocks his black consumers because he has no investment in the images they produce and happily benefits from the hypermaterialism that has elevated him to elite status. Smith-Shomade contends, "While Lee attacks the raiding of black culture by whites and others in many parts of the film, this example connects the paradoxical nature of black success, commercialism, and racist/sexist thought, most clearly" (234). As with *Flight to Canada*'s Robin and Quickskill, Manray and Womack may initially seem like Uncle Tom figures, but Lee, like Reed, complicates our assumptions by challenging us to consider that those figures assumed to be Uncle Toms are often catalysts for the most radical change. However, Lee does present Uncle Tom figures who willingly exploit themselves to reinforce the racist stereotypes the mainstream clamors for with the success of *Mantan*. Lee's film takes the desire for white mainstream acceptance to its absurd and logical conclusion as other members of the show such as Honeycutt (Thomas Byrd Jefferson) pursue financial gain and popular fame by adopting their minstrel personas as their authentic selves.

Lee frequently undermines his characters' attempts at reinvention and the ideologies that they adopt as part of their performance. So while Manray and Womack take an apolitical stance on the minstrel show as part of their role as celebrities and artists, their performance collapses under the weight of blackface's history and their emergent consciousness. Similarly, the self-proclaimed radical black nationalist/hip-hop group the Mau Maus initially appear as a counter to the assimilationist politics of Dela and Manray. The leader of the group, Big Blak Afrika (Mos Def), is Sloan's brother Julius Hopkins, which leads to a bizarre audition for *Mantan*. Julius provides a stark contrast to his sister's relationship to white corporate culture, but his critique of her and her choices rings hollow not only because we discover that the two come from black middle-class roots but because Julius's work as an artist is nonsensical. Although making references to Kenyan revolutionaries, socially conscious rappers, and Frantz Fanon, the Mau Maus merely appropriate the signposts of nationalist fervor. As Smith-Shomade contends, the "Mau Maus know some of the lingo and the rhetoric of revolution but virtually nothing of the substance. This assertion bears itself out in the actions they take in the latter part of the film" (238). The film rejects the Mau Maus' attempt at the type of counter-representation that we have seen at other moments, particularly during the Black Arts movement and the Blaxploitation era. Indeed, the presence in the Mau Maus of a lone white member is at odds with the blacks-only sentiment of the late 1960s and 1970s. Also, the members' adoption of such language and behavior clearly mocks the white adoption of hip-hop culture that was rampant throughout the 1980s and 1990s and was assumed to be authentic blackness. Willett rightly argues, "The uneducated revolutionaries caught in the past do not challenge stereotypical blackness; in their vanity and ignorance, they just repeat it. The once earnest dream of a nationalistic revolution has become, in the age of the network, embarrassing" (87). Like the works of comic rage that previous chapters have examined, *Bamboozled* does not promote simplistic counter-representations; rather, Lee often critiques them as harshly as he does the traditional and contemporaneous racist stereotypes.

Julius's attempt to reinvent himself as Big Blak Afrika, a name that itself embodies the absurdity of his effort, mirrors Delacroix's own attempts. When Dela visits a comedy club, we discover not only that his father, Junebug (Paul Mooney), is a comic who openly confronts racist oppression but that he frequently ridicules his son's bourgeois, Ivy League persona, continuing to call him by his actual name, Peerless Dothan. With an unfiltered, sometimes blasphemous comedy that toys with stereotypes of African American humor, Junebug provides a fuller picture of the beauty and ugliness of black life, while Delacroix wants to promote middle-class images that ignore any hints of traditional racist stereotypes. Yet trading one one-dimensional representation for another renders Delacroix unable to engage any complex identity that could withstand the external and internal forces that threaten his status and success at the network. Cynthia Willett points out that "Delacroix is also a puppet, doomed as are the other types of inauthentic souls to being bamboozled out of a true self," and that "the more Delacroix clings to the romance of the self, the more he exemplifies the flight of inauthenticity" (86). The film castigates both figures for basing their attempts at reinvention on perceptions of the African American lower and middle class instead of their actual existence. Indeed, a more accurate performance of the personas they adopt would occur if Julius examined the early life of Dela and if Dela researched the particulars of Julius and Sloan's middle-class life.

Lee's purposeful casting of the rapper Mos Def and the comic Paul Mooney amplifies the film's mix of humor and militancy because of the two men's use of humor in their incisive and unyielding critiques of white supremacy in hip-hop and stand-up respectively. Mos Def has frequently been cited as one of the most "conscious" rappers, one who often sacrificed more pop-friendly status for creative diversity. Whether singing or rapping, as part of a group or a solo project, Mos Def's work conveys a critical understanding of history and context that neither his character nor the Mau Maus ever even approach. His willingness to participate in spoofing faux-revolutionary groups separates him from such hip-hip artists while also signaling the need for audiences to view artists more critically. As Delacroix's father, Mooney exposes the self that Dela attempts to escape. Working on the Chitlin' Circuit, Junebug's act is anything but made for TV and is destined to be marginalized by the mainstream in which Delacroix seeks acceptance. The father mirrors the career of Mooney himself, who was a longtime writer for Richard Pryor and a supporting player on *Chappelle's Show*. In the 2012 film *The Godfather of Comedy*, Mooney launches an aggressive assault on subjects on both sides of the color line, ranging from an unyielding defense of President Obama's election to Rihanna and Chris Brown to race and Elizabeth Taylor. Mooney has frequently refused to accept roles he considered buffoonish, and he has rarely performed acts that reached the mainstream appeal of comedy concerts from Pryor, Rock, or Chappelle, artists who acknowledge Mooney as an influence. Mooney's brand of comic rage drives the film, particularly its unwillingness to subscribe to traditional or mainstream forms or expectations.

In Richard Corliss's review of the film, "The Shame of a Nation," he charges that *Bamboozled* "has big third-act problems when the caricatures are meant to morph into poignant humans. Then everyone pulls guns out. Insanity!" (108). Corliss expects that after Lee's point has been sufficiently made, he will pull back for a more moderate ending, along the lines of an intellectual plea for reform. In its shift from an overtly comic tone in order to drive home its more dramatic point, Corliss and other critics believe, *Bamboozled* gets lost underneath Lee's confrontational tone. This critique follows a comfortable, marginalizing narrative, one that charges that Lee's politics and often sensationalist style undermine his artistry and box-office appeal. This charge consistently surrounds *Do the Right Thing* (1989), his most celebrated and controversial film, in which the boiling fury that permeates the characters' relationships and language on the hottest day of the year in Brooklyn finally spills over into riot.

Viewing Lee as a one-dimensional artist who would sacrifice aesthetic quality for political force accepts a false dichotomy between art and politics and assumes that the world and subject matter of the African American filmmaker are incredibly small. In fact, Lee films like *25th Hour* (2002), starring Edward Norton, and *Inside Man* (2006), with Denzel Washington and Clive Owen, are among his most financially successful, even as they contain clear political critiques. While many people were unaware that Lee directed these films, his work with casts that were not predominantly black reveals a flexibility that refutes our unwillingness to view him as anything other than the "angry black director." In two documentaries, the Oscar-nominated *Four Little Girls* (1997) and the critically acclaimed *When the Levees Broke* (2006), Lee respectively chronicles the bombing of a Birmingham church and the tragedies during and after Hurricane Katrina, without the dramatic flourishes that have dogged him for years. His most consistent elements have been the visceral emotional tone of his films, a deep love of jazz and hip-hop, and a black nationalist political consciousness most clearly seen in his reverence for Malcolm X and culminating in his 1992 film of the same name and an Oscar nomination for Denzel Washington. Jamie Barlowe points out, "Ironically revealing that satire is . . . misread by the American public as well as exposing and defamiliarizing the myriad allegorical, fetishized stereotypes that have been the very staples of the American entertainment and advertising industries, *Bamboozled*'s narrative portion ends, like Lee's film *Do the Right Thing*, not in peace and harmony, but in violence" (12). The rage that fuels *Do the Right Thing* also permeates *Bamboozled*. Yet the humor that sits alongside that rage produces a more imaginative expression that makes it less controversial than *Do the Right Thing* and, perhaps more important, avoids the attempts to marginalize

Lee's clear anger at the state of popular culture's treatment of African Americans. The film's visceral humor appeals to a black audience who will recognize Lee's anger and appreciate his ability to articulate it, because they share his frustration.

As Richard Corliss notes, Lee "condemns whites for manufacturing the old image of the shiftless, larcenous Negro and for still seeing blacks through that warped prism. He also chastises blacks for inhabiting restrictive new and polar-opposite categories: the gangsta and the Buppie" (108). Like other works of comic rage, *Bamboozled* skewers both sides of the color line. So instead of serving up the satirical return to the idealized black elite that Dela privileges, as Corliss expects, Lee goes in the opposite direction, opting to reveal how the African American elite's separation from the working class—and in general from black cultural tradition—leaves them with no outlet to effectively express their rage. The gap between the emerging black middle class and the marginalized and scapegoated black underclass problematizes the attempt to define and revise authentic blackness and, as significant, leaves the two groups isolated from each other and vulnerable to updated hegemonic oppression that cloaks itself in post-civil-rights acceptance. In his critique of African Americans, Lee does not seek out a "nebulous black authenticity" as Smith-Shomade contends. In fact, all those who pursue limited representation of blackness, whether in their own lives or at the service of others' entertainment, fail miserably.

In their creation of virtually new identities, Delacroix and Big Blak subscribe to incomplete notions of blackness that ignore the realities of the pasts they both try to shed. Delacroix's attempt to create an identity separate from his father's finds him virtually rootless. Mantan and Sleep 'n' Eat make the more pragmatic decision to star in the minstrel show to escape poverty. Yet both come to realize that they are being consumed within the mainstream's myopic view of the minstrel show as authentic black entertainment. Distaste at performing in *Mantan* eventually leads Womack not only to leave the show but to end his friendship with Manray, who retains an apolitical commitment to the performances. Sloan, who sits at the intersection of the male characters' identity crises, remains caught between her onetime lover Dela's submission to the role of what Cynthia Willet calls "the grateful Negro" and her brother Julius's absurdly grand black nationalist dreams. While she does not seek her own reinvention, through her relationship with Manray she attempts to raise his consciousness about the problematic use of blackface and his responsibility as a black artist to challenge the racist stereotypes that the show reinforces. Sloan's attempts are effective, both for Manray and for the film's audience, but *Bamboozled*'s inevitable descent into violence demands that its audience face the literal and symbolic wreckage caused by their dependence on the stereotypical images fostered by blackface minstrelsy and its antecedents.

A succession of attempts at transforming rage into cogent critique go wildly awry: the Mau Maus kidnap Manray and kill him online for the world to see, Sloan shoots Delacroix after the deaths of Manray and her brother Big Blak Afrika, and the NYPD murder the black members of the Mau Maus in a hail of bullets that miraculously misses their one white member, who screams, "I'm black!" as he is being taken into custody. Manray's capture by the Mau Maus and the ensuing violence provide an example of the unchecked rage that many poor black youth experienced at the end of the twentieth century—and still do—because of the absence of any effective outlets for expression. But just as Delacroix becomes the object of the film's comic critique, so do the Mau Maus become objects of the film's rage. As Stuart Klawans in "Amos, Andy, 'n' You" puts it, "The Mau Maus conform to the most noxious stereotypes—they're unlettered, inarticulate, unemployed, slovenly and very fond of malt liquor—so of course they declare war on the minstrel show for perpetuating such images" (34). They are revolutionary without critical consciousness and, as such, they appropriate violence as part of an authentic revolutionary response. The violence, then, does not become the film's solution to retrograde stereotypes but a critique of the simplistic response that acts as myopically as the initial stereotype. The film's "third act" becomes an exploration of the uncritical rage that emerges when no effort to articulate that rage is made or no outlets for constructive expression exist. The absurd and reckless violence becomes a byproduct of that rage uncontrollably spilling out of its characters. We have seen similar acts of violence in the protest fiction of the 1940s and 1950s. Instead of complex, multilayered images, *Mantan* amplifies the comic-criminal stereotype that took hold at the end of the nineteenth century and that devalues black life. Thus the survival of the lone white Mau Mau reveals that, despite his claims of blackness, the police still value his whiteness while reducing the others to subhuman threats whose killing seems justified. When Sloan, distraught over the deaths of both Manray and Big Blak, shoots Dela, we see the cost of his embrace of the show's popularity and his willingness to ignore his initial understanding of its offensiveness. Although Sloan rightfully acts as the agent through which Dela's comeuppance is delivered, her own complicity in the show scars her. The loss of Mantan and Big Blak is impossible to dismiss, and the sentimentalist tone that satires often take is impossible as well.

I agree with Chidester, Campbell, and Bell in "'Black Is Blak': *Bamboozled* and the Crisis of a Postmodern Racial Identity" that "In the end, *Bamboozled*'s message is far too complex to be confined within the generic expectations of satire. Lee himself alludes to his conclusion by opening the film with voice-over definitions of both satire and irony—as if to suggest that the work is an ironic comment on itself as a satiric film" (290). In a traditional satire Manray's speech would form the culmination of the author's critique. Yet instead of the mere lesson that can be easily dismissed or absorbed, Lee's film allows its rage to spill over as a demonstration of the material consequences of the destructive images that frame our racial discourse and identity formation. Dela's death would seem to conform to the traditional notions of the protest novel in which unchecked rage and violence end in the destruction of the main characters. However, like Ralph Ellison's *Invisible Man*, where the narrator's killing of Ras and his flight underground are not the ending of the novel, Dela's narration—"Goodbye, cousins, and please tune in next week for *The Best of Mantan: The New Millennium Minstrel Show!*"—informs us that the show will continue without him. His intent becomes to raise our awareness of the persistence of the racist stereotypes the show has perpetuated. His reference to his audience as his "cousins" resembles the narrator's final words in *Invisible Man*: "Who knows but that, on the lower frequencies, I speak for you?" Both moments seek to engage their audiences and to enlist them in the larger resistance to white supremacist hegemony. While Ellison's narrator prepares us for his eventual return to the surface, Dela's dying comments are followed by a history of blackface in American popular culture meant to be a final instance of rage that becomes a clarion call to openly oppose explicit and implicit representations of minstrelsy.

Conclusion

"But then," Willett asks, "is authentic revolt possible in an age not of revolution, but of satire?" (87). I see the montage at the end of the film as the moment when Lee demands that we face the size and scope of the history of blackface minstrelsy. Seeing the pervasiveness of blackface minstrelsy throughout one of the most popular mediums not only brings home the point Lee hammers, but it simultaneously horrifies its white audience and enrages its black audience. As Chidester and Bell suggest, Lee forces us to see the images "as a single contemporary depiction, and to consider how those images not made present in the montage—snippets from hip-hop videos, scenes from modern buddy films, etc.—would themselves fit seamlessly within this collage" (209). In his quest to make clear the pervasiveness of white supremacy and indict African Americans' participation in the modern minstrel show, "Lee has discovered a means of turning postmodernism's fascination with the image as image into a potent satirical tool—a means of encouraging audiences to recognize and consider the meanings that cannot help but accrue to the patterns of images that collect around any given social circumstance or ideal" (209). In the tradition of comedy's "third eye," the film forecasts several incidents on college campuses that have found white students dressing in blackface at Halloween parties without any appreciation for the controversy that ensues. While such incidents are often dismissed as isolated occasions, the film's montage presents a cascade of images that make the larger meaning inescapable.

Chidester and Bell argue, "For Lee, the postmodern necessity of treating images as discrete entities, shorn of any shared meaning, hardly prevents the artist from infusing his or her visuals with true persuasive force. In fact, the filmmaker seems to have discovered that, by piecing together entire collections of images, the artist can suggest a certain narrative visual logic, a history that is founded not in material fact, but in the invitation to read a series of visuals as a related whole" (208). The film's collection of images at the end attempts to elicit a visceral response, not simply for the reason that Chidester and Bell lay out, but because humor becomes the dominant vehicle through which the racist images are delivered. An audience's willingness to internalize humor uncritically makes it a more effective way to reinforce the racist stereotypes seen in other spaces of society. The anger Lee's film seeks to create in its audience comes from the knowledge that such images have been at the center of our concepts about race and the formation of national and cultural identities. Lee's counter to the use of humor as a delivery system for racist stereotypes is the use of humor as a way to reject those stereotypes and collapse the byproducts and dichotomies that emerge as a result. The film uses humor's ability to move beyond debates that have grown stagnant or simplistic to attack core arguments about the roots of white supremacy. The avalanche of images exposes a pervasiveness that informs these questions of authenticity, privilege, and hegemony. It bookends the fury it has incited throughout the film.

Cynthia Willett believes that a "call for authenticity appears through the character of the old comedian, who prefers his smaller audiences over the lure of Hollywood. Spike Lee no doubt aligns *Bamboozled* in a similar tradition of film, one that includes Robert Townsend's 1987 satire *Hollywood Shuffle*" (88). Here we see a theme that not only connects *Hollywood Shuffle* and *Bamboozled* but permeates many of the works of comic rage produced over the last forty years. As the question of authenticity has become an important one for post-civil-rights black authors, works of comic rage serve increasingly as a site through which old images can be reexamined and new, "better" ones can be interrogated.

Harriet Margolis submits that, "despite the diversity of personalities, genres, styles, and political commitments involved, there must be some value in evaluating films by black filmmakers in terms of a black aesthetic. The relation to imagery, conditioned by past representations of blacks, is the obvious starting point. That past history is characterized by offensive stereotyping" (52). Too many films, rather than seeing those past representations as a "starting point," end their exploration in the past or idealize the past in ways that ignore how racist stereotypes have evolved in the post-civil-rights moment. *Shuffle* and *Bamboozled* expose how the continued legacy of white supremacy has roots in the past, while complicating the representation/counter-representation dichotomy that reinforces white supremacist hierarchy and reduces African Americans to politicized abstractions. While some dramatic works use the discussion of authenticity to reject an African American identity deeply attuned to and engaged with questions of race and racism, works of comic rage explore the shifting rhetoric that blames personal choices and behaviors for the inequities between blacks and whites as opposed to blaming the continued presence of racial hierarchies. *Hollywood Shuffle* and *Bamboozled* demonstrate how personal relationships and ideas about race are impacted by simplistic and problematic images continually shaped by racist assumptions based on old stereotypes. If there is a black authenticity that Lee pursues, it is a stark and furious portrait of a present still deeply influenced by the past.

Lee turns again to humor as director of the 2000 stand-up comedy concert *The Kings of Comedy*, featuring Steve Harvey, D. L. Hughley, Cedric the Entertainer, and Bernie Mac. Like Townsend, Lee finds stand-up an important medium for illustrating the fullness of black life. They share with Trey Ellis an understanding of the growing importance of humor in multiple genres. While Townsend pursued his own style during his career as a stand-up and Lee used *Kings* to present a range of differing styles, Ellis turned to Eddie Murphy as a critical figure in part because of his work in television, film, and stand-up. For our exploration of comic rage, however, I am interested in Ellis's claim that one of the key influences for the New Black Aesthetic was "Richard Pryor with his molten parodies of black life on his early albums and short-lived television show" (237). Just as stand-up comedy, through the figure of Dick Gregory, helped construct the template from which comic rage arose, so too do stand-up comedians Richard Pryor and Chris Rock come to embody the appearance and maturation of comic rage in their stage acts. Pryor, who stands as the most influential figure in African American comedic tradition in the last half century, transformed his personal tragedies into comic catharsis. Whether those tragedies involved his encounters with the police, his continual drug use, or his multiple sclerosis, Pryor was able to funnel the evident pain and rage into the creation of a space where the complex issues of race, love, and self-destruction could be engaged through the healing power of laughter. Influenced by both Ishmael Reed and Huey Newton during his transition from Cosby-wannabe and emerging from the militancy of the Black Arts and Black Power movements, Pryor nonetheless foreshadowed the New Black Aesthetic through the presentation of African American characters, like the infamous Mudbone, who often contradicted the counterimages that many African Americans sought to produce.

If Pryor can be thought of as an important influence on the New Black Aesthetic, then Chris Rock must be seen as a product of the NBA. Rock's multimedia assault, through his presence on stage, television, and comedy albums, reflects the NBA's and comic rage's impulse to permeate a variety of forms with African American cultural expression. Perhaps the closest personification of comic rage as of this writing, Rock fuses hilarious observations with fierce critiques that spare no person, subject, or race. Like Spike Lee's *Bamboozled* or Aaron McGruder's comic strip *The Boondocks*, Rock expresses an unparalleled militancy through a humor that, because of its investment in African American comedic and vernacular tradition, cannot easily be dismissed as mere entertainment.

6

Direct from a Never Scared Bicentennial Nigger

Comic Rage in the Work of Richard Pryor,
Whoopi Goldberg, and Chris Rock

There's not a white person in here that would trade places with me,
and I'm rich!

Chris Rock, *Bigger and Blacker*

If Richard Pryor's 1976 comedy album *Bicentennial Nigger* seems dated today, it is only because subsequent comics have so extensively stolen from Pryor's routines. As Glenda Carpio says, in *Bicentennial Nigger* "Pryor highlights his country's founding contradiction: its profession of democratic principles despite its history of racial oppression" (72). While Carpio focuses on the final track of the album, I view the other tracks as explicit demonstrations of the byproducts that emanate from that "founding contradiction" and that inform Pryor's observations on the differences between black and white women or popular images from Hollywood. Among the comics fulfilling Pryor's legacy, then, we see certain figures whose work does not suffer from abjection, but becomes the abject. Although marginalized by mainstream notions of comedy, their constant return to the center of the American cultural landscape—consistently and hilariously re-visioning—breaks down the dichotomy that we find in the African American literary movements that privilege a more somber, realistic tone and in the reconfigured racist representations that continue to influence the popular imagination.

Numerous comics have claimed Pryor as a vital influence on their comedy, from Eddie Murphy to Sarah Silverman. In particular, artists took Pryor's usage of characters and mimicry and expanded those ideas to encompass the entirety of their live performances. To trace the depth of Pryor's influence, it is crucial to distinguish between comics who offer only gratuitous cursing or generic discussion of race to achieve mainstream success and artists who dare to take the comic risks that Pryor dared to take.

An important example is Whoopi Goldberg, whose self-titled one-woman Broadway show recorded in 1985 as *Direct from Broadway* examines the intersection of race, class, and gender through a variety of different characters, particularly Whoopi's alter ego, the furiously funny PhD junkie Fontaine. Goldberg pulls from the tradition of Moms Mabley in disrupting not only the male perspective that dominates stand-up comedy but the gendered and racial privilege that often permeates the literary representation and counter-representation we have seen throughout the twentieth century. Crossing race, gender, class, and sex lines, Goldberg's characters are equally livid and funny, naïve and knowing, tragic and uplifting. The roles in which we find her throughout the 1980s and into the 1990s—culminating in a Best Supporting Actress Academy Award for the 1990 film *Ghost*—are rooted in her ability to collapse boundaries and transcend convention. Goldberg has famously cited Pryor as the main influence on her work, but in this chapter I explore the ways in which she expands on the foundation laid by Pryor by pulling from a greatly underappreciated black female comic tradition.

In looking at the generation after Goldberg, the comic I see fulfilling Pryor's legacy of comic confrontation is Chris Rock. Though Rock moves beyond observations on the differences between blacks and whites toward an engagement of national racial and political issues, he, like Pryor, centralizes African American perspective to confront his audiences with the continued presence of white supremacy in the post-civil-rights era. It becomes apparent that stand-up comics like Rock, who can serve as sole writer, producer, and star, are the artists most capable of exercising the type of substantial control that literary authors do in extended expressions of comic rage. While his Emmy-winning 1996 stand-up comedy special *Bring the Pain* continues to be Rock's breakthrough work, I focus on his 2004 comedy album *Never Scared* because it directly exposes hypocrisies and contradictions in post-9/11 America. Although critical voices were silenced or branded unpatriotic during this time, Rock's voice remains unapologetically defiant. While the live performance of stand-up allows the African American oral tradition to be fully realized, from improvisation to call-and-response, the process of producing novels and plays provides the opportunity for revision that can more clearly focus the author's racial analysis. In addition to Goldberg's stage show, in which she disappears into multiple characters, this chapter focuses on African American comedy albums, because they merge live performance and revision to maximize the expression of comic rage. Comedy albums often combine the two techniques, using moments from the artist's live performance—even several different performances—as well as skits or riffs that supplement a specific routine. As comedy albums are one of the most effective avenues for the expression of comic rage, in this chapter I examine, along with the filmed version of Goldberg's show, *Direct from Broadway*, Richard Pryor's *Bicentennial Nigger* and Chris Rock's *Never Scared* because they comically confront America at a moment when the country's celebration of its own myth threatens to silence their volatile pop-cultural mixture of comic rage.

Happy Birthday America! Critiquing Nationalism in Richard Pryor's *Bicentennial Nigger*

Pryor's road to comic rage began in the 1950s and 1960s when African American comics like Nipsey Russell and Dick Gregory presented images of African Americans that rejected stereotypes made famous by blackface minstrelsy. According to Christine Acham, racial critiques were initially "evidenced within hidden transcripts—themes, humor, and ideas that could be understood in ways unique to an African American audience. However, as the era progressed, black critical thought within popular culture became more vocalized" (152). Pryor's presentation of uncensored African American street humor/commentary, especially in front of integrated audiences, was unprecedented. According to Watkins, "with the possible exception of Flip Wilson, Pryor's disclosure of previously closely guarded comic referents, racially based attitudes, and cultural eccentricities that were often 'embarrassments to the black middle class and stereotypes in the minds of most whites' was untried on the mainstream stage" (544). In routines like "Drunk and Wino," or "Wino and Junkie" as Carpio calls it, Pryor "in *Live and Smokin'* (1971) combines the power of humor as cathartic release and politically incisive mode of critique with deep pathos" (11). Those featuring perhaps his most famous character, Mudbone, likewise revealed underclass black life in a way that was virtually unknown to whites and deeply uncomfortable to the African American elite. As Pryor demonstrates the humanity of these characters, he fearlessly critiques society and hauntingly explores all of our vulnerabilities.

Pryor's refusal to change his act in front of white audiences, specifically the rage that permeates African American expressions from music to literature to political ideology, was groundbreaking. Although most point to albums like *That Nigger's Crazy* (1974) or stand-up work like *Richard Pryor, Live in Concert* (1979) when discussing Pryor, I examine *Bicentennial Nigger*, the album that Pryor in his memoir *Pryor Convictions, and Other Life Sentences* calls "my fourth and most political album" (148). *Bicentennial Nigger* appeared during a yearlong celebration of the American Dream, with the nation eager to move beyond the tumult of Watergate and Vietnam. Yet the bicentennial also was a time when many began to express hostility to the gains African Americans were making as a result of the civil rights movement. Bambi Haggins suggests, "The risks that Pryor took in his comedy seemed driven by the desire to articulate multiple forms of blackness—black voices—that had not previously been heard" (51). If *Live in Concert* is Pryor at his very best—and the greatest comedy concert ever, according to some—then *Bicentennial Nigger* is a fitting precursor. The album contrasts markedly with contemporaneous films like *Rocky* that promoted the bicentennial's refocus on the American Dream by updating the Horatio Alger myth and ignoring the racial, gendered, and class forces that prevented many in America from reaching that dream. As Daniel J. Leab in "The Blue Collar Ethnic in Bicentennial America: *Rocky* (1976)" argues, "*Rocky* captured the mood of bicentennial America, a mood which saw the reaffirmation of many traditional values, including racial prejudices that seemed rejuvenated by the economic and social pressures of the 1970s" (269). Looking at a very different America from the one caught up in two-hundredth-anniversary celebrations, *Bicentennial Nigger* sees a country still struggling to live up to its most basic democratic principles. In addition to contesting America's promotion of its exceptionalism during 1976, the album was released the same year as Richard Pryor's first pairing with Gene Wilder, in *Silver Streak*. The movie established the two as one of the funniest comic duos in the last quarter of the twentieth century. The movie's most memorable scene, in which Pryor applies blackface to Wilder in the bathroom and coaches him in "acting black," subversively reflects the more overt comic confrontations that are consistently present in *Bicentennial Nigger*. I mention these works because they reveal the narratives to which comic rage responds and, in the case of *Silver Streak* and the next Pryor-Wilder film, *Stir Crazy* (1980), the contrast between works that privilege the voice of the author (comedy concerts and albums) and those filtered through the multiple interests of producers, directors, and studios.

The third album to earn Pryor a Grammy for Best Comedy Recording, *Bicentennial* was also a popular success, eventually going platinum. The opening routine, "Hillbilly," finds a rural white man proclaiming that America is a "Goddamn great place to live!" and responds to those who might criticize it for racist oppression by suggesting they "Love it or Leave it goddamn it!" Citing the taming of the Native Americans and the cleaning up of the "buffalo shit" as accomplishments of the colonists, the hillbilly is eerily similar to the figures of "redneck culture" that white comics like Jeff Foxworthy and Larry the Cable Guy have made a vital part of their popular comedy routines. While the Foxworthy and Cable Guy characters present no overt racial critique, Pryor's hillbilly embodies the spirit of Western colonialism that views its presence as central to bringing civilization to native inhabitants. The hillbilly's unforgiving invocation of white privilege reflects Leab's claim that working-class white ethnic groups tended to "bitterly resent" the attempts to provide equal opportunities for African Americans because they felt that their rights had been sacrificed (270). It was this feeling that initiated a huge political shift by many whites, particularly in the South, to the Republican Party. Beginning with George Wallace's rupture of the Democratic Party through his presidential campaigns in the 1960s, the shift was well under way by 1976, solidified by Richard Nixon's "southern strategy" in his own campaigns in 1968 and 1972.

Pryor's commentary culminates on the first side of the album with the hilarious and ferocious "Bicentennial Prayer." Pryor mimics a black preacher, a character that Pryor portrays in previous albums, who is also equal parts con man and ringmaster. In addition to a pitch-perfect representation of a black church service, Pryor masterfully imitates the oral rhythm of African American sermonic and religious tradition. To be sure, Pryor's initial presentations of black ministers were not well received by the African American elite, because they confirmed stereotypes of African Americans as both comic and criminal. Yet the presentation of the

black minister is an example of the effectiveness of comic rage in critiquing both blacks and whites. Pryor's mimicry of the minister signifies on
a figure that, in the black community, represented educational accomplishment, middle-class status, and moral and sociopolitical authority.
Mel Watkins notes that Pryor's initial audience was made up of younger
African Americans, "who were increasingly rejecting the traditional black
middle-class tactic of de-emphasizing cultural differences between the
races and embracing the Black Power stratagem, which, besides its political agenda, encouraged an assertive flaunting of ethnic behavior that had
been disapprovingly associated with black masses and self-consciously
suppressed" (545). Moreover, Pryor explodes mainstream America's view
of itself on the world stage. As the audience applauds, Pryor begins,
"We are gathered here today to celebrate this year of bicentenniality,"
and quickly moves to his racial critique with "in the hope of celebrating
two hundred years of white folks kicking ass." Pryor's reference here to
America's history of racial violence against African Americans could, in
fact, be extended to encompass white American violence on people of
color both domestically and internationally from the Native Americans
to the Vietnamese. However, instead of expressing a tragic defeatism,
Pryor aggressively demands answers: "we offer this prayer and the prayer
is . . . How long will this bullshit go on? How long?! How long?! That is
the eternal question." Although the routine elicits the round of laughs it
was meant to, the rage that the prayer conveys is equally present. Pryor's
work expresses a clear frustration with contemporaneous racism while
resisting simplistic counter-representations of African Americans that
appeal to a white bourgeois system of values and ideologies.

   In "Mudbone Goes to Hollywood" Pryor resurrects one of his most
long-standing characters and juxtaposes his clear-eyed working-class
perspective against the absurdity and elitism of a Hollywood that seems
separate from the rest of America, even as it reinscribes many of the
same racial hierarchies and stereotypes we might see in "Hillbilly." Haggins reports, "In many ways Pryor's comic personae existed in this intersection of contemporary black comic sensibility and folk humor as exemplified by the Pryor character with the greatest longevity, Mudbone.
Through this sly, meandering country philosopher['s] . . . voice (equal
parts Mississippi Delta blues singer and early Chitlin' Circuit storyteller),
the comic embodied the black folk construction of the trickster that also
resonated within the street humor of urban black America" (53–54).

Pryor's use of Mudbone allows him to build off previous iterations of comic folk wisdom within the African American comedic tradition, such as Langston Hughes's Jesse B. Semple, while capturing the contemporaneous angst, despair, and urgency in the perspectives of African Americans in the city. With full access to the array of styles and perspectives found in African American humor, Pryor builds a bridge between generations while creating a comic performance unlike any that preceded it. Pryor's multiple character sketches disrupt the traditional cohesive stand-up performance that relied on the consistent voice of the comic shifting seamlessly from one topic to the next. Pryor's routines launch multiple attacks on a number of topics, all articulating the pervasiveness of white supremacy. His uncensored sketches paved the way for comics like Eddie Murphy, Martin Lawrence, and Dave Chappelle, whose appearances on television or in films feature them playing multiple characters. However, Pryor's use of those sketches in stand-up avoided the consistent struggles with censors or the limitation to less politically volatile topics that bedeviled *The Redd Foxx Show*, Pryor's own four-episode NBC show, and most recently the critical and popular darling *Chappelle's Show*.

In the title track that concludes the album, Pryor sardonically presents a "Bicentennial nigger" happily chronicling the history of racial violence and oppression:

They'll have some nigger two hundred years old in blackface. Stars and stripes on his forehead. Little eyes and lips just jiving. And he'll have that lovely-white-folks expression on his face. But he's happy. He's happy 'cause he's been two hundred years. He'll say, "I'm just so thrilled to be here. Over here in America. I'm so glad y'all took me out of my home. I used to live to be a hundred fifty. Now I die of high blood pressure by the time I'm fifty-two. That thrills me to death. I'm just so pleased America's going to last. They brought me over here in a boat. There was four hundred of us come over here. Three hundred sixty of us died on the way over here. I love that. That just thrills me so. I don't know, you white folks are so good to us. Got over here and another twenty of us died from disease. Ah, but you didn't have no doctors to take care of us. I'm so sorry you didn't. Upset y'all, too, didn't it? Then you split us all up, yes sir. Took my mama over that way. My wife that way. Took my kids over yonder. I'm just so happy.

I don't know what to do. I don't know what to do if I get two hundred more years of this. Lord have mercy. I don't know where my own mama is now. She up yonder, in that big white boat in the sky. Y'all probably done forgot about it. But I ain't gonna never forget."

The presence of an African American in blackface more aggressively recalls the history of blackface minstrelsy than Pryor's bathroom scene with Wilder. Like "Bicentennial Prayer," this track centralizes African American perspective in viewing the United States' two centuries of existence. The narrator chronicles a history that contains psychic and physical violence and the devaluing of black life. Ending with "Y'all probably done forgot about it. But I ain't gonna never forget," the routine assures the audience that attempts at erasure will prove futile. Reminiscent of Frederick Douglass's "What to the Slave Is the Fourth of July?" that was mentioned in the introduction, Pryor's closing section abandons the traditional forms and tones of black racial discourse. In the place of history or anti-lynching campaigns, Pryor ridicules America's celebration of its bicentennial with an explicit description of the horrors of slavery, one made more forceful through adoption of a subservient and thankful tone that lambastes the expectation that African Americans should be thankful for their treatment. In *Laughing Fit to Kill* Glenda Carpio sees Pryor's final track as "darkly satirical, even bitter. His laughter, mechanized and obviously constructed, is piercingly ironic, since far from expressing gaiety, it is from the start a laughter that kills" (76). Pryor's act demands recognition from its audience of his rage at slavery and at the attempt to ignore the continuing impact of white supremacy on the lives of African Americans, even at the nation's anniversary and moment of celebration and reflection. Through the figure of an African American whose past becomes insignificant in the face of his happiness to be in America, Pryor uses comedy to prevent the unmistakable rage from becoming destructive to the routine itself. Here, then, comic rage rejects the attempted erasure of America's racial history through the bicentennial's attempt to renew America's vision of itself.

A Man's World? Whoopi Goldberg and Black Female Comic Rage

Studies of Pryor's descendants have gravitated toward other male comics and often ignore his impact on female comics. As a result, expressions of comic rage can seem limited to African American men. Yet as we move from moments in the slave narrative of Harriet Jacobs to stand-up performances of Moms Mabley, we see a clear presence of comic rage in the work of women. To be sure, Zora Neale Hurston used humor to demonstrate the vitality of African American communities in the rural south, and we see authors like Ntozake Shange, Alice Walker, and Terry McMillan using humor as a way women collectively resist despair at racist and patriarchal oppression. Of importance to this chapter is Fran Ross's 1974 novel *Oreo*, which tells the story of an African American woman who attempts to find her Jewish father while navigating the constraints of gender and ethnicity. The novel is notable not only because of its willingness to launch into the complex minefield of black-Jewish relations but because she does so in the vernaculars of both cultures. Like many writers, such as Reed and Clarence Major, Ross challenges the traditional novel structure with a picaresque story that has echoes of *Invisible Man* and an embrace of oral culture that has been a hallmark of many of the works in this study. Mixing the tragic mulatto, the picaresque, and the Greek myth of Theseus, Ross's novel fits squarely in the development of comic rage despite appearing at the height of the Black Arts movement and the rise of black female authors. The novel sits at a crossroads between the tradition of black female humor that we can trace to Hurston in the early twentieth century and the expressions of comic rage we see emerging in the 1960s and 1970s. Ross's connection to Pryor, for whom she wrote material, solidifies her relationship to comic rage and helps draw connections between literature and stand-up in the works of and performances by black women. Finally, Ross's connection to Pryor extends the presence of Pryor's humor at the intersection of literature and stand-up, one that we see not only in his relationship with Ishmael Reed and the Black Arts movement but through one of his most significant comedic descendants, Whoopi Goldberg.

When Goldberg announced in 2007 that she was retiring from acting because she was no longer sent scripts and because there was "no room right now in the marketplace of cinema" for her, she not only expressed a pervasive frustration for women of a certain age in Hollywood—and black women generally—but reflected a parallel confusion and discomfort with women in a market that maintains the realm of comedy as a distinctly male space. Even though the woman born Caryn Johnson has been more successful crossing over into film and television than predecessors like Moms Mabley or Pearl Bailey, her career has been marked by a dearth of vehicles to showcase the full range of her abilities. Those that have come closest—*The Color Purple* (1985, Oscar nomination), *Ghost* (1990, Oscar), and *Sister Act* (1992, box office success)—have discovered ways to display Goldberg's mix of charisma, sass, humor, and fury. Her versatility has made her one of the few performers to win the EGOT: an Emmy, Grammy, Oscar, and Tony. Yet Goldberg continues to be underappreciated, in large part because her less celebrated films have found her cast in updated mammy/buddy roles or in fast-talking, street-smart roles that attempt a female take on Eddie Murphy's *Beverly Hills Cop* persona. Only since 2007, when she began hosting the daytime television show *The View*, have audiences come to see and appreciate a virtually uncensored Whoopi who seamlessly moves from probing interviews of current luminaries in politics and the arts to cracking wise about celebrity gossip.

I submit that Goldberg's use of comic rage—and the difficulty of mainstream popular culture in placing her—qualifies her as an "unruly woman." Like the women that Kathleen Rowe studies in *The Unruly Woman: Gender and the Genres of Laughter* (1995), Goldberg rejects "the conventions of both popular culture and high art [that] represent women as objects rather than subjects of laughter" (3). However, unlike such women as comedian Roseanne Barr, who must face the hostile response to their unruliness alone, Goldberg uses the multivocality of black female communities to create a multitude of comic interpretations to combat the charges of grotesque and hysteric that frequently accompany unruly comic female personas. While those personas, according to Rowe, exist in the world of "comedy and the carnivalesque" where "the ordinary world can be stood on its head" (11), they are frequently marginalized because they fail to find multiple ways to sustain their critique. Goldberg with her frequent transformations in her comedy sketches, her genre bending, her continual visibility, has remained able to inject her expressions of rage into the mainstream popular culture. The resulting confusion over where to situate Goldberg is not surprising, given that Goldberg has frequently and publicly rejected attempts at categorization. Since her act roots itself in multiple female perspectives and voices that build on the emergence of black female voices throughout the 1970s, it was no surprise that Goldberg appeared in the film versions of *The Color Purple* and *for colored girls who have considered suicide/when the rainbow is enuf,* works that embrace a polyphonic approach in the creation of a black female community.

Goldberg's act creates characters who are "subjects of a laughter that expresses anger, resistance, solidarity, and joy—or those which show women using in disruptive, challenging ways the spectacle already invested in them as objects of a masculine gaze" (Rowe 5). In *Direct from Broadway,* the cinematic version of Goldberg's Grammy-winning stage show—originally called *The Spook Show*—we see her building on the work of Richard Pryor and Moms Mabley in order to present an "unruly woman" not only capable of challenging narrow perceptions of gender in the popular imagination but willing to speak openly about questions of race, nation, and history. Goldberg disrupts the reductive view of black women that casts them as either asexual mammies or oversexed Sapphires. As the "unruly woman," Goldberg stands as "a special kind of excess differing from that of the femme fatale (the daughters of Eve and Helen) or the madonna (the daughters of Mary), whose laughter, if it ever occurred, no longer rings in the myths still circulating around them" (Rowe 10). The story of the Old Raisin, told by Goldberg's Jamaican Woman character, mirrors Mabley's discussion of female sexuality that inverts the male-subject/female-object dynamic that remains a central tenet of stand-up comedy. Goldberg extends her commentary to include the racially volatile dichotomy of the white male sexual subject and the black female exoticized object. The Jamaican Woman not only prioritizes her sexual desire, a desire we frequently ignore when discussing older women generally, but she also rejects the mammy figure that Mabley appropriated and destabilizes our assumptions surrounding the generally taboo subject of white male/black female marriages.

Goldberg's act "crosses the boundaries of a variety of social practices and aesthetic forms, appearing most vividly in the genres of laughter"; her characters, whether successful or not, consistently fit the mold of the unruly woman who is often considered "too fat, too funny, too noisy, too old, too rebellious" but ultimately "unsettles social hierarchy" (Rowe 19). Of course, Goldberg's expression of comic rage centers on the critical eye and the furious voice of Fontaine. The targets of her anger range from a man who opposes abortion with no regard for the rights of women to her inability to find a job despite a PhD in English. Fontaine's incisive commentary on politics in America, especially in the middle of the 1980s, virtually necessitated a show focused exclusively on her. In *Fontaine: Why*

Am I Straight? in 1988, Goldberg's character ups the confrontational ante, launching a fiery attack on Nancy Reagan's "Just Say No" slogan. Despite her education, Fontaine speaks with the plainspokenness of Pryor's Mudbone. In her 2005 show, which celebrates the twentieth anniversary of *Direct from Broadway*, Fontaine expands her critique to include 9/11, George W. Bush, and the Iraq War.

Rowe argues, "To deny women active participation in the mechanisms of the joke as well as in those of spectatorship is to replicate our culture's historical denial of women's anger as an available and legitimate response to the injustices they experience" (7). Fontaine's rage emerges unapologetically from a range of issues both personal and political. Fontaine seizes her right to be hostile without seeming hysterical, and she revels in her rage. However, Goldberg refuses to allow Fontaine to be consumed by her anger, and the final piece of Fontaine's act in Goldberg's original and twentieth-anniversary shows culminates with her trip to visit Anne Frank's house in Amsterdam, and Frank's challenge to believe that people are "good at heart" balances Fontaine's rage and takes the place of humor in preventing her rage from becoming pathological.

Although Fontaine serves as a primary vehicle for comic rage, Goldberg's other characters openly critique the racial and gendered hierarchy that marginalize black women. Goldberg's act demonstrates the pervasiveness of white supremacist patriarchy by producing poignant moments that reveal the tragic consequences of hegemonic oppression and often garner outrage from her audience. The most obvious, and perhaps tragic, are the two girls that Goldberg enacts. The first, Valley Girl, is a thirteen-year-old who begins by talking about her life surfing at the beach and slowly reveals that she is pregnant. After failing to get rid of the baby by drinking too much and jumping up and down on her friend's bed, the girl uses a coat hanger to abort the baby. The abortion is botched and the girl left barren. Goldberg's performance transfers attention away from the audience's feelings about abortion to the revelation that the girl is isolated from her family and is forced to rely on the knowledge of a friend as uninformed as she. The visceral nature of Valley Girl's experience makes the relevance of *Roe v. Wade* and the continuing debate over abortion abundantly clear.

Less controversial but perhaps more poignant is Whoopi's performance as a six-year-old black girl who holds a shirt over her head pretending to have the blond hair she desperately wants. The sketch explicitly assails the establishment of white femininity as the standard of beauty; the markers of white female beauty, aside from size, are, of course, blue eyes and blond hair, and Goldberg's girl instantly casts a light on the damage to the psyche of the majority of women whose looks lie outside the normative expectations of female beauty. As Sara Dunne in "Women as Children in American Comedy: Baby Snooks' Daughters" puts it, "Goldberg's persona indulges in fantasies which have been fueled by television and television advertising, but her race presents some special problems. Goldberg's child wants to grow up to look like Barbie and live at the beach with Ken, Barbie, Malibu Barbie and Skipper—all white role models" (33). The young girl's desire for "long, luxurious blond hair" recalls Toni Morrison's 1970 debut novel, *The Bluest Eye*, in which a young girl named Pecola Breedlove yearns to be like Shirley Temple and, more important, to have blue eyes. In each case the desire to attain what seems virtually unattainable gives the work its sense of tragedy while simultaneously injecting its audience/readers with a rage that emerges from their understanding that Pecola's and the young girl's longing is part of the larger society's devaluing of blackness. The comic rage that fuels these works reveals the instability of whiteness by exposing the inability, not just of African Americans but of many whites as well, to achieve normative beauty. Morrison is also important here because, while she has not explicitly stated that her works purposely adopted a comic tone, some critics have suggested that humor plays a larger role than one might initially think. Rita Bergenholtz has challenged us to see that Morrison's next work, the 1973 novel *Sula*, can be viewed as a satire on binary thinking, while Darryl Dickson-Carr believes that her 1992 novel *Jazz* satirizes African American narratives of victimhood in "an ironic allegory whose significance extends beyond a single epoch, signifying upon some sixty years of (African) American history" (183).

As Dunne relates, "Goldberg's little girl eventually becomes reconciled to her own hair and comes to accept her appearance, even though she doesn't look like any of the people she sees on television" (33). When the little girl rips the shirt off the top of her head at the end of the sketch, she seems to embrace the reality of her difference and leaves the audience hoping that she will come to love that difference. Goldberg's show concludes, however, with a character that reminds us of the significant role abjection plays in expressions of comic rage. Goldberg performs as a disabled female who demands, simply, to be seen. While the disabled have consistently been a group marginalized in literature, Goldberg comes close to making her character even more difficult to view. Physically disabled and afflicted with a speech impediment, Goldberg's character initially verges on the grotesque. Instead, the sympathy she generates negates the audience's initial discomfort at seeing her and difficulty in listening to her. As she describes her frustration with the people around her, we are reminded of the standard of beauty with which Goldberg's little girl has already become enamored. Here, however, we see a woman who has been more clearly rendered abject and who, through the recognition of her own beauty, has begun the process of return from the margin. Goldberg's transformation into the straight-standing, clear-talking "swan" that her character recognizes in herself rejects the imposition of external constructions. Finding a man who loves her and eventually marries her becomes secondary, for when Goldberg transforms back into the woman we see at the beginning of the sketch, her character's unique beauty and spirit have become unmistakable and destabilized our initial perceptions, completing the process characteristic of all the works of comic rage we see in this study, specifically the return of the abjected in order to break down mainstream assumptions and constructions that have previously marginalized groups and works. Goldberg's ability to remain a visible presence while other unruly women have faded speaks to the potential of comic rage as an intermittent but sustainable expression in mainstream popular culture.

Bigger and Blacker: Chris Rock's America at the Millennium

If the image of Richard Pryor begins this book and underscores the often symbiotic relationship between African American vernacular tradition and African American literature through which comic rage emerges, then a comic who follows and expands on Pryor's thematic palette should end this project. Although Eddie Murphy seems a natural choice, given his more obvious connection to and affinity for Pryor, his case is a typical example of the difference between traditional African American humor and comic rage, and of the importance of stand-up as a more accurate parallel to literature than are movies and television. Murphy's ability to cross over into the mainstream can be attributed, according to Mel Watkins, mainly to his "boyish charm and audacious approach," even though in his stand-up concerts and movies "he sometimes teetered on the brink of excess—stentorian and superficial profanity, crass indulgence in bravado, homophobia and sexism" (564–65). His stand-up often pulled from Pryor's routines, while his "bravado" and raunchier material recalled the days of Rudy Ray Moore (a.k.a. Dolemite), the underground comedian whose humor was so profane that even Pryor's success could not gain him a mainstream audience. Trey Ellis's inclusion of Murphy as an example of the New Black Aesthetic is due in large part to the impressiveness of his parodies. Yet while his work has demonstrated a comic defiance, it has not always produced a comic critique. In his response to Ellis's New Black Aesthetic, Eric Lott posits that "some of the art Ellis praises is marked not by its 'disturbatory' daring so much as by its timidity, including the extraordinary lameness of Eddie Murphy (whose 'raw' is only half-cocked)" (245). Lott is clearly making a reference to the much-lauded 1987 stand-up concert *Eddie Murphy Raw*, which is often pointed to as proof that Murphy is the rightful heir to the throne of Pryor. Yet while Murphy's comments on his ex-wife and alcoholic father remind audiences of the dark personal stories that Pryor turned into comic legend, he often misses the opportunity to expand Pryor's commentary on race relations. What remains is a repackaging of the Pryor material to fit the cocksure, often empty, hypernationalism of the 1980s. To be sure, Murphy's parodies and his freakishly accurate mimicry are popular and artistically memorable. During his stint on *Saturday Night Live* and in movies like *Coming to America* (1988), *The Nutty Professor* (1996), and *The Nutty Professor II: The Klumps* (2000), Murphy's work as multiple characters is comically inspired. His lack of rage—his rawness seems to apply only to sex—highlights an important distinction between stand-up and other popular mediums in their capacity for extended expressions of comic rage. In movies and television, control rests not with the artists but with those around them: movies inevitably conform to the vision of the director, who, along with the editor, decides which scenes are to be included and how they are to be played. Likewise, television remains a producer's medium, with the networks, censors, and advertisers determining the tone of a show and its content. Pryor's own movie choices and failed television show are clear examples of the artist's lack of control in these pop cultural forms.

The comic I see as taking up Pryor's legacy of comic rage, then, is Chris Rock. In contrast to the "timidity" that Lott attributes to Murphy, Watkins argues that "fearlessness—the courage to pioneer territory that most wits, or even politicians and pundits, diligently avoid—is the element that perhaps most distinguishes Rock's humor" (580). Like Pryor, Rock is influenced by the African American sociopolitical ideology of his times. We see Pryor's use of comic rage impacted by the Black Power and Black Arts movements in his embrace of the African American underclass. Implicit in his routines is a rejection of black middle-class values and behaviors that subscribe to an ethic of assimilation, particularly one resulting in individual benefit. Pryor's expression of comic rage reshaped stand-up through a focus on characters and topics that often superseded a more formulaic narrative. Like the poetry of Baraka and Sonia Sanchez or the novels of Reed, Pryor's comic rage adopted the Black Arts movement's employment of black speech and experimentation with form to challenge traditional ideas of American humor. While Pryor is certainly not considered a black nationalist by any stretch, it is clear that the Black Power and Black Arts movements' confrontation of white society informed Pryor's act.

Similarly, says Mel Watkins, "Chris Rock has taken the clamorous hip-hop style—too often associated with grandiose posturing and bullheaded allegiance to everything currently designated as black—and reshaped it to fit a grander concept of comedy" (581). Rock not only takes on issues specific to post-civil-rights America through comic reversals or frank confrontation, he places those issues within a historical context that highlights the continued impact of white supremacist hegemony in American culture. Unlike Murphy and Chappelle, Rock's rage is ever present, whether aimed at blacks, whites, the government, or celebrities. As in the best of hip-hop, underneath Rock's energetic, blunt tone is a finely tuned critique of America that centralizes working-class African American experience. Stalking quickly across the stage in his self-proclaimed "stick and move" style, Rock is part boxer and part MC as he delivers punch lines with uncanny accuracy. While the rhythm of his walk often recalls the frenzy of rap concerts, his speech remains grounded in African American vernacular. Like the black sermonic tradition, Rock's speech acts in perfect harmony with his audience, dictating pace while responding to their reactions. The adoption of oral tradition allows Rock to signify on people or ideas in popular culture. His combination of cleverness, daring, and intelligence elevates him above many contemporary comics whose style, according to critics and older comics, has devolved into crassness. Though the same problems that have plagued both Pryor and Murphy in their movie choices have affected Rock, his experiences on television have yielded much better success in the expression of comic rage.

Rock's career shows us how artists can resist being assimilated into mainstream culture through the continued production of works of comic rage that challenge fundamental assumptions about race. The celebration of Rock centers on his 1996 HBO special *Bring the Pain*, specifically his segment on what he calls the "civil war going on in Black America." After identifying the warring factions—blacks and "niggas"—he hammers home his general point: "Every time black people try to have a good time, ignorant-ass niggas fuck it up!" This particular riff, along with criticisms of Marion Barry and O. J. Simpson, led many African Americans to see Rock as a "black conservative" and to silently question his allegiance to black America, while many whites celebrated him for saying what they often wished to say. Rock's message, however, is wholly in line with comic rage's tendency to criticize both whites and blacks, regardless of how it is received. Rock immediately understood the implications of his routine and began to take measures to prevent his work from being used to maintain stereotypical constructions of blackness.[1] His 1997 Grammy-winning comedy album *Roll with the New* retains much of the material from the HBO special, adding hilarious parodies of rap/R&B songs, an interview with O. J. Simpson and Ike Turner, and examples of bad phone sex. In a skit titled "I Love This Show," which purposely comes after his black-folks-versus-niggas routine, various well-wishers compliment a silent Rock on his show. All of the people, including a Latina, mention the "niggas and black folks thing." However, when the final well-wisher, who is clearly intended to be taken as white, confesses, "I hate fucking niggers too," a punch is thrown—presumably by Rock himself—and a brawl ensues.

Rock more explicitly addresses his objection to white usage of the term "nigger" in his 1997 book, the bestselling *Rock This*. After his famous "Who You Calling Racist?" routine, Rock's "Mommy? Can I Say 'Nigger'?" section seeks to address directly the impulse to take his own usage of the term as license for whites to appropriate it: "Any black person can say 'nigger' and get away with it. It's true. It's like calling your kid an idiot. Only *you* can call your kid that. Someone else calls your kid an idiot, there's a fight" (20). Rock goes on to say that whites frequently ask him why they cannot use the word. He relates how, when he asks one "white person" why they would even want to use the word, he gets a response familiar to many African Americans: "I don't mean anything *bad* by it. I've traveled the world. I got a yacht. I fucked Raquel Welch. Now, if I could just say 'nigger,' everything would be complete" (20). Rock constructs an image of whites who believe that their privilege is limitless and should be accepted as such, even when they have an unhealthy need to use a word that is almost universally considered offensive. While more contemporary manifestations have found whites claiming their friend-ships with blacks as a pass to use the term, Rock's scenario remains accu-rate. In the book and on the album Rock characterizes whites who use the term as figures harboring a deep-seated need to rely on racist language as part of their discussion of race, but also as part of a larger sense of their identity. The relief that the white person on the album expresses and the desperation we can read into the white person in the book reveal both to be interested only in invoking their privilege to offend without conse-quences. Comic rage works to prevent Rock's rage from being expressed through actual violence. Rock's book approaches the routine according to the specifics of the medium. On the album, an extended explanation by Rock would be an incongruous fit. He thus parodies a brawl, not only to expose the offensiveness of the white person's comment but to connect to the rage of the audience. In both mediums, Rock prevents his own critique of "niggas" from becoming a part of the mainstream discourse and ultimately perpetuating stereotypical views of African Americans as "niggers."

Instead of the overt fixation on shock, sex, and vulgarity that many of his contemporaries depend on, Rock's work is more concerned with exploring political and racial questions that people refuse to publicly engage. Rather than turning celebrity news and scandals into comedy routines, like Murphy's stories about his ex-wife or Martin Lawrence's about marijuana abuse, Rock takes what Ralph Ellison might call Amer-ica's "national pathology" (108) and transforms it into cogent racial commentary. In his next stand-up special, *Bigger and Blacker* in 1999, Rock consciously addresses issues that challenge white national narra-tives about race. In the quote that begins this chapter, Rock highlights the pervasiveness of white privilege across gender, class, and sex lines. His confession that he is scared of "young white boys" also signifies on the rash of school shootings in the late 1990s, particularly Columbine. The routine directly responds to the practice of racial profiling and the historical fear of black male violence. Here, then, Rock's use of comic rage critiques whites, blacks, and even responses to his own success. Rock deploys multiple mediums to prevent the critiques embedded in them from being depoliticized and commodified into digestible pieces.

Although Bambi Haggins rightly places Murphy and Rock together in her examination of post-soul comic personae, I see their successes and failures as emblematic of why comic rage flourishes in particular mediums while falling flat in others. Certainly both actors move beyond the supporting or B-movie-quality film characters played by Pryor, but Murphy clearly emerges as the preeminent comic film star. In contrast to Murphy's string of 1980s blockbusters, Rock's films have never been economic powerhouses, critical touchstones, or cult classics. Murphy's comic persona seems to fit more easily within the mediums of television and film. Murphy, of course, relies on an updated version of the Comic Bad Nigger, one enriched by Murphy's gift for morphing into multiple characters. Murphy has thus achieved the crossover appeal that Haggins discusses, while Rock has been less successful in the big-budget buddy films that Martin Lawrence and Will Smith perfected in the 1990s. Even Haggins points out, "Murphy and Rock represent two strains of black humor that converge stylistically but diverge significantly in terms of ideological content and their performance of blackness. As Rock himself notes, his humor bears a closer kinship to the socially relevant comics of a previous generation (Gregory, George Carlin, Pryor) than it does to Murphy and his Def Jam progeny" (97). Rock's connection to comics like Gregory and Pryor manifests itself not only in his groundbreaking style but also in his rejection of the more formulaic content—with explicit references to sex, obligatory comments about the differences between blacks and whites, and plenty of appropriation of the Comic Bad Nigger's aggressive tone—that saturated African American comedy's entrance into the mainstream via Russell Simmons's HBO laugh-fest *Def Comedy Jam* in 1992–97. As Haggins notes, "One might even argue that Eddie's stand-up is fundamentally about Eddie—his celebrity, his sexuality, his experience of media. . . . the post-*SNL* comic persona of Murphy, while being a significant comic annunciation of black masculinity and machismo, arguably, speaks not to the black experience in broader sociocultural terms but rather to the black superstar experience—with a certain brand of observational humor that is descriptive rather than prescriptive" (97). While Murphy and those that have followed his blue-print often use personal anecdotes as a way to depict a take-no-prisoners attitude toward whites, blacks, and sex—in an ironic twist on Freud's incongruity theory of humor—Rock prefers only brief references to his life growing up in Bedford-Stuyvesant to interrogate and critique white supremacist hegemony and its byproducts. Rock embodies comic rage's versatility to move nimbly between a progressive critique of white su-premacy and a conservative politics of personal responsibility, from his "Niggas vs. Black Folks" routine to "Tired of Defending Hip-Hop" to "Rich vs. Wealthy."

In discussing Rock, Haggins believes that his "comic persona is built around sociopolitically informed articulations of blackness and serves as the post-soul era's logical reconstruction of Gregory's comedic dis-course—in a slightly less transparent ideological frame" (97). In these routines Rock moves from a Cosbyesque critique of behavior (one that is not class specific) to an observation on the limits of rap to the build-ing of black wealth. Here, then, we see Rock moving beyond simplistic stereotypes or counter-representations of blackness. He avoids Gregory's struggle to balance his political commentary with the stand-up format as well as Bill Cosby's failure to place his critique of poor and working-class African Americans within a larger context. His nuanced perspective, his willingness to challenge all of his audience, and his overt re-visioning of form have made his stand-up shows and comedy albums the foundation of his popular and critical acclaim, while his starring roles in film have been limited to sometimes underappreciated, inconsistent fare. Rock has become perhaps the most famous employer of comic rage in the post-civil-rights moment. The attempts to transfer their comic personas to the screen reveal how Murphy's appropriation of Pryor's *style*, if not his content, have proved more palatable than Rock's embrace of an array of styles—Cosby's storytelling, Carlin's wordplay, Pryor's character render-ings—that together do not translate to film, especially in the representa-tion of blackness. Not surprisingly, Rock's comic persona has worked best in mediums where he has almost complete control and is rarely censored. Rock's limited success in film has been in those where he has significant input as a writer, as in gangsta rap parody *CB4* (1993), or as the director in films like *Head of State* (2003), *I Think I Love My Wife* (2007), and *Top Five* (2014). On television *The Chris Rock Show*'s 1997 premiere on HBO avoided the problems that preceded it (in Richard Pryor's show) and that followed its 2000 finale (Dave Chappelle's show's abrupt cancellation).[2]

Recently, Comedy Central's *Chappelle's Show* would seem to have demonstrated that Pryor's television failure was the result of a television world—especially one pre-cable—not prepared to cross the lines that Pryor so willingly dismissed. The show and its star become a cultural phenomenon, adding any number of catchphrases to the popular lexicon on a weekly basis and pushing back against a tide of African American humor increasingly formulaic and devoid of cogent racial analysis. Chappelle's parodies are reminiscent of Murphy's best work, with Chappelle's wildly popular Rick James skits becoming a more demented, drug-fueled version of Murphy's memorable channeling of James Brown, and Chappelle's note-perfect performance of Prince reminding audiences of Murphy's similarly good mimicking of Stevie Wonder. Yet while Chappelle's work is often unprecedented in its conception—a blind black white supremacist and a white family called the Niggars are particularly good—they often do not produce a cogent racial analysis. Instead there is a spirit of ridicule, one that highlights the differences between the races and the privilege that whites enjoy but rarely traces those differences to the fundamental inequality that continues to plague the country. Thus we see Chappelle going undercover to expose that whites are actually musically inclined when given the right music, that giving blacks reparations will result in irresponsible spending, and a racial draft may be necessary to permanently end the controversy over multiple races' claiming of certain celebrities. Of rage there is virtually nothing.

"Like Pryor," Carpio declares, "Rock gives voice to that rage almost always in relationship to controversial contemporary topics, such as the current debate over reparations, while Chappelle plays it out through charged fantasies regarding slavery, involving not only reparation but also retribution" (108). Chappelle's return to stand-up suggests that much of his discomfort was alleviated by once again being in a space where he maintains complete control. Stand-up, a medium in which Rock has been critically and popularly more celebrated than Chappelle, is the vehicle through which the artist's vision, and thus comic rage, can be most fully realized.

In *Never Scared*, which won a Grammy for Best Comedy Album of 2004, Rock engages in a fully realized comic discussion of national issues. The album pulls from his HBO stand-up special in Washington,

D.C., as well as a stand-up routine from Philadelphia that covers much of the same material. In directly addressing affirmative action, for instance, Rock situates his discussion in the history of slavery, much like Pryor's final routine. Using the dynamics of the classroom, he cogently expresses the inequality he sees affirmative action responding to: "That's all America is, a nation of B and C students. But let's keep it fucking real. A black C student can't be . . . the manager of Burger King. Meanwhile the white C student just happens to be the president of the United States!" Rock's reference to George W. Bush's lackluster performance in school and his admission to Yale based on his father's alumni status points to a fundamental opportunity gap between whites and blacks. Rock's repetition of various phrases like "The government hates rap" or "It's all right 'cause it's all white" highlights his thematic foci. Like the black sermonic tradition, Rock's speech acts in perfect harmony with his audience, dictating pace while initiating and feeding off their reactions.

Where Rock's progression from Pryor's *Bicentennial Nigger* is most obvious is in the inclusion of various skits and parodies that augment his stand-up. In previous albums he included mock interviews with O. J. Simpson, Ike Turner, and Monica Lewinsky, substituting their voices with select rap lyrics from N.W.A., Run DMC, and Lil' Kim. In *Never Scared*, Rock's skits critique whites with the ironic "Tip Your Hat to Whitey," which mocks white economic exploitation from Jamaica to Mars. Yet *Never Scared*, like *Bring the Pain*, also criticizes African Americans who contribute to mainstream stereotypes. Where Pryor enacted a black minister, Rock is particularly interested in skewering the hypermasculine, overly violent images of blackness found in contemporary hip-hop. From "Thug News," which opens with gun shots and the intro "It's time to bust a cap in that ass!" to a "Real People of Ignorance" mock commercial that targets members of rap entourages, Rock's skits reveal a barely contained fury at the promotion of the "gangsta" culture that currently permeates rap music and has been taken by both blacks and whites as representing authentic contemporary African American culture. So while Pryor's employment of comic rage challenged middle-class representations of African Americans because they ignored the underclass, comic rage in Rock's work often critiques simplistic definitions of African American culture that are based on glorifying a specific segment of black underclass life. In either case, both reflect comic rage's resistance to narrow, ideologically based ideas of blackness.

Although he takes on a number of topics that are the subject of popular media attention, like the rape accusations against Kobe Bryant, they
immediately become secondary to the controversial Iraq War and post-
9/11 America. He dismisses other topics by arguing, "Don't let all this celebrity news fool you. Right now. All this stuff going on. It's just a trick to
get your mind off the war. . . . I think Bush sent that girl to Kobe's room.
Bush sent that girl in Kobe's room. Bush sent that little boy to Michael
Jackson's house. Bush killed Laci Peterson. Bush was fucking Paris Hil-
ton in that video. All to get your mind off the war." Rock also discusses
the "gang mentality" in America that separates individuals into various
camps that blindly embrace ideology while ignoring the complexity of issues and situations. In his assessment of post-9/11 America, he counters
a faux hypernationalism by proclaiming, "I'm not scared of Al-Qaeda, I'm
scared of Al-Cracker!" Expanding on the attitudes of the hillbilly in Pry-
or's album, Rock exposes the disturbing correlation between American
national identity and hostility toward minority ethnic groups.

In a country with a diverse history of ethnic groups, assimilation into
America is still dependent on the adoption of mainstream ideologies of
race, particularly as regards African Americans. Rock's comment, then,
is reminiscent of "What America Would Be Without Blacks," when Ralph
Ellison wondered aloud, "Perhaps this is why one of the first epithets
that many European immigrants learned when they got off the boat was
the term 'nigger'; it made them feel instantly American" (111). Rock's discussion of the Iraq War reflects the ambivalence many African Americans
expressed after the terrorist attacks on September 11, 2001. Although
most, if not all, shared in the shock, outrage, and pain that the rest of
America experienced, Cornel West reveals in the foreword to *The Paradox of Loyalty* that those feelings were not new to him or other African
Americans. As he argues, despite his success, "I was still a 'nigger' in
America. To be an American 'nigger' is to be unsafe, unprotected, subject
to arbitrary violence and hated. I concluded that 9/11 had initiated the
painful process of the 'niggerization' of America—we are now all unsafe,
unprotected, subject to arbitrary violence and hated" (xii). In *The Paradox
of Loyalty*, many of the authors express frustration that African American perspectives in the War on Terror have been virtually ignored, except in providing hymns and spiritual rhetoric. Rock's expression differs,
and his use of humor provides white audiences with a perspective that
they are often unfamiliar with, in a manner that does not alienate them.

Simultaneously, African Americans respond to Rock because he provides the rhetoric necessary for a community seeking to effectively express dissatisfaction with racial inequality. Rock's use of comic rage thus becomes an important successor to Pryor's by effectively transmuting into popular culture African American critical voices that challenge popular American narratives. So while Rock's routine on "niggas and black folks" may seem like an endorsement of the black conservatism one finds in the rhetoric of Clarence Thomas, Shelby Steele, and John McWhorter—rhetoric that is the toast of many white Americans prepared to absolve themselves of responsibility in the "race problem"—Rock is merely challenging extremist ideologies that do not include the role of African Americans in securing their own equality.

Conclusion

On Being Pissed Off to the Highest Degree of Pissivity

Save for Langston Hughes, Ralph Ellison, George Schuyler, Zora
Neale Hurston, and a select group of others, the defining characteristic of the African-American writer is sobriety—moral, corporeal,
and prosaic, unless you buy your black literature from the book ped-
dler standing on the street corner next to the black-velvet-painting
dealer next to the burrito truck: then the prevailing theme is the
ménage à trois.

**Paul Beatty, Introduction to *Hokum: An Anthology
of African-American Humor***

Comic rage has become significant, especially since the transformation
of Pryor, in the mainstream because of its versatility for a diverse, segregated audience. For white audiences, African American humor provides a perspective that they are often unfamiliar with—willingly or
not—through the centralizing of African American attitudes. For African Americans, humor often provides the rhetoric necessary for a community consistently seeking to effectively express dissatisfaction with
racial inequality. In avoiding the historical categorization of both African American humor and militancy, comic rage fuses the two in order to
maintain a sustained resistance to simplistic perceptions of blackness.
Its lack of concern for a white audience is evident in its adoption of references and language that are familiar in African American culture and
thought. Artists' works become abjections to white notions of race that
permeate the mainstream as well as African American representations

that are equally destructive because of their simplicity, either in their militancy or their definition of authentic blackness.

So, in Percival Everett's 2001 novel *Erasure*, Thelonious "Monk" Ellison's obscure and experimental novels find virtually no success. As a writer who sits outside the expectations of a "black" author, Ellison is frustrated by the success of *We Lives in Da Ghetto* by an author who, like the black Ivy League college students in *The White Boy Shuffle*, appropriates an idea of blackness in direct contrast with his own middle/upper-class experiences. In a fit of rage, Ellison adopts a moniker, Stagg R. Leigh, based on a popular black folk hero and pens a novel in the tradition of *Native Son* called *My Pafology* (which he later changes to *Fuck*). The writing of the novel comes from a fury that Ellison's humor does not conceal, and it drips throughout his novel and his performance of Leigh. When the novel becomes a popular and critical success, Ellison begins performing Leigh as reclusive, antisocial, and "streetwise," which many see as normative. Everett's novel, like other works of comic rage, stands in opposition to the contemporaneous literary moments from which it emerges. The popularity of Terry McMillan's novels and the underground success of "street lit" authors Iceberg Slim and Donald Goines led to an increase in popular contemporary African American literature. *Erasure* injects itself into the larger debate surrounding authentic African American literature in the last two decades of the twentieth century. The novel destabilizes assumptions by both blacks and whites and uses its comic lens to lambaste attempts at exoticizing African American experience and pathologizing African American rage.

Beginning as a syndicated comic strip in 1999 and expanding to an animated television series in 2005, Aaron McGruder's *The Boondocks* openly challenges the post-civil-rights mainstream belief in the color-blind and currently sits at a vital place in American pop cultural and African American literary/cultural thought. McGruder's work interrogates the contradictions and tensions within African America, most notably through the ten-year-old Huey Freeman and his eight-year-old brother Riley. The two brothers on whom the strip centers spent their early years in urban Chicago but have been moved to the fictional almost-white suburb of Woodcrest. The strips and episodes explore the brothers' relations with each other and their white neighbors as McGruder examines how contemporary, even conflicting, ideas of blackness operate and adjust to whites in a post-civil-rights context. The strip gained national attention soon after 9/11, as McGruder began addressing the terrorist attacks on September 24, less than two weeks after the deadly events. The *New York Daily News* pulled the strip almost immediately. Many of the 250 newspapers in which *The Boondocks* appeared either pulled the strip or moved it to the editorial pages as the *Dallas Morning News* did. McGruder's three aptly named post-9/11 comic strip collections—*A Right to Be Hostile* (2003), *Public Enemy #2* (2005), and *All the Rage* (2007)— not only reveal an escalating comic rage but see McGruder broadening his comic critiques to consider white supremacy through the prism of terrorism, faux patriotism, and fear. Mainstream sentiment toward the possibility of post-racial America threatens to censor, if not erase, voices that critique the inconsistencies or hypocrisies in America's racial narrative. In an interview, McGruder contends that humor is an effective way to negotiate the minefields of race: "it allows people to sort of let their guard down—and rethink some issues. Certainly, it's been done effectively by stand-up comics. I mean Chris Rock and Richard Pryor, you know, have—have addressed race in a—I think in a very effective way" (*Rage* 135). I contend that McGruder's reference to Pryor and Rock situates his work with theirs as moving beyond traditional forms of African American humor to enact expressions of comic rage.

In stand-up, I contend that Wanda Sykes has established herself as one of the newer and most consistent voices in comic rage. She emerged as the most distinctive voice from *The Chris Rock Show*, winning an Emmy for writing in 1999. She builds on Rock's explicit topicality as well as Goldberg's interrogation of the intersection of race and gender. Haggins situates Sykes among a more populous tradition of black female comics: "Sykes's comic persona with its candid conversational and contentious sociocultural critique has the edginess of Goldberg's early work, but the ease of delivery is strangely reminiscent of Moms Mabley's when she took on the role of storyteller as truth-teller" (175). As with Mabley and Goldberg, mainstream popular culture has frequently marginalized Sykes because she resists easy categorization and generally refuses to temper her acerbic wit, even when hosting the annual Correspondents' Dinner in the presence of President Barack Obama in 2009. Not surprisingly, she has failed to find leading roles in film and television, although she has frequently appeared in supporting roles, including a recurring role in the Julia Louis-Dreyfus comedy *The New Adventures of Old Christine* (2006–10). Her stand-up had already served as her most effective site for the expression of comic rage. Yet when she officially came out as a lesbian in 2008, she began an interrogation of sexuality that added an important layer to our racial discourse. In the tradition of James Baldwin, Audre Lorde, and E. Lynn Harris, Sykes explores the intersection of race, gender, and sexuality. Her first HBO special after coming out, *Im'a Be Me* (2009), finds Sykes openly confronting not just racist oppression and misogyny but the hostility toward gays and lesbians that she finds across the country and in the African American community. Her show breaks down multiple assumptions and wades into unprecedented comedic waters as she considers whether being gay is more difficult than being African American and her consideration of what it might be like to "come out" as black lambastes our dependence on artificial and reductive stereotypes. The evolution of Sykes's work reveals the increasing significance of comic rage in our discourse about race, identity, and nation. The need to establish new ways of critiquing white supremacist hegemony has only increased in the second decade of the twenty-first century. A backlash to the election of President Obama, fueled by fear of the deteriorating power of white privilege, resulted in the election of Donald Trump on a wave of rhetoric that expressed open hostility to minorities and women. While the belief that Obama's election had led to post-racial America was a claim some voters used to justify voting for Obama and then Trump, the post-fact environment has made nontraditional forms of discourse and resistance crucial to black cultural expression. The presence of comic rage in Sykes's work, as well as the others I have discussed here, seizes on a tradition that tears down the post-racial veil and exposes the continuing pervasive presence of hegemonic oppression with the "biting ridicule, blasting reproach, and withering sarcasm" for which Douglass calls.

The works of comic rage that populate this book deploy Douglass's criteria at critical moments when traditional forms fail or embrace one-dimensional portraits of black life. They achieve a balance that aggressively challenges attempts to simplify or ignore the gulf between the promises of America and its practices. So while humor prevents rage from becoming consumptive, nihilistic, or destructive, the presence of rage rejects perceptions that humor should only serve as entertainment. As Beatty suggests, "Humor is vengeance. Sometimes you laugh to keep from crying. Sometimes you laugh to keep from shooting" (16). Comic rage expands the possibilities for expression and examination of one of the most controversial subjects in American history and society. The increasing appearance of works of comic rage across literary and cultural lines testifies to its importance as a response to oppression. Although I see comic rage as neither the sole nor the preferred form of humor or rage, this project seeks to demonstrate that, in a post-civil-rights America increasingly hostile to overt critiques of the impact of white supremacist patriarchy, comic rage can act alongside other cultural responses as a form of resistance that allows audiences to engage in subjects otherwise taboo, to speak the unspeakable with a smile.

Notes

Introduction: A Joke to the Eye

1. Watkins argues that the short stories in Chesnutt's popular and critically well-received collection *The Conjure Woman* (1899) "revolve around Chesnutt's Uncle Julius, a character who bears some surface resemblance to Joel Chandler Harris's Uncle Remus but is actually a sly trickster whose obsequiousness masks his efforts on behalf of other slaves" (409). However, almost immediately after the success of *The Conjure Woman*, Chesnutt would turn to addressing issues of race directly.

2. Here Pryor's inclusion of a broad range of emotions becomes important as it highlights an important distinction between this work and recent works, specifically Mel Watkins's groundbreaking *On the Real Side: A History of African American Comedy* (1999) and Darryl Dickson-Carr's phenomenal *African American Satire: The Sacredly Profane Novel* (2001), that discuss African American humor and are vital to my work's genesis.

3. Dustin Griffin notes in *Satire: A Critical Reintroduction* that Menippean satire can be understood through Bakhtin's vision of the "Menippea," which includes "its bold use of fantastic adventure; inserted genres and styles producing a multistyled and multivoiced discourse; a presiding spirit of 'carnival' in which ridicule is 'fused with rejoicing' and orthodoxies of all kinds are freely challenged; and a 'philosophical end'" (32). As a result, *Black No More* is able to explore the pervasiveness of racism in ways that the novels of Griggs and Chesnutt are not.

4. Among the traditions Griggs accurately portrays is the use of humor for resistance to oppression. The novel humorously discredits the idea of education as the ultimate solution to ending racism. In *Mythic Black Fiction* Jane Campbell believes, for instance, that "Griggs rejects the myth that education necessarily

serves as a tool by which blacks can achieve material success in white society and replaces this notion with an emphasis on education as a process that should develop critical and creative thinking so that blacks can alter oppressive conditions" (50). In the novel we can see the maintenance of African American humor as a way to demonstrate the hypocrisy of racism and discrimination. Robert Fleming, in "Sutton E. Griggs: Militant Black Novelist," views Griggs's "use of broad comic scenes which ridicule the exaggerated dignity of the white master race" (75) as a significant part of his writing.

Chapter 1. (Re)Viewing Ellison's *Invisible Man*: Comedy, Rage, and Cultural Tradition in an African American Classic

1. I define signifying, also referred to as signifyin', as a central form of black cultural expression that involves verbal wordplay and that leverages the ambiguity in language generally—the literal meaning of a word versus the context that impacts the meaning a word has to individuals or groups—and in African American speech acts particularly. Many have come to see signifying as representing black vernacular itself. Like John Edgar Wideman, I see signifying as "serious play" that combines the critique, humor, and creativity necessary for African Americans to simultaneously adopt and subvert the Standard English—and the accompanying Western values and ideologies—imposed on African slaves. Frequently traced to African folklore and myth, the black American manifestation of signifying appears through the figure of the Signifying Monkey, a trickster who uses verbal wit and cunning to engineer the beating and ridiculing of his enemy the Lion. Henry Louis Gates's seminal 1988 work *The Signifying Monkey* sees signifying, which he traces to the Yoruba figure Esu-Elegbara, as a type of formal revision, particularly of literary predecessors and linguistic and cultural practices. Gates situates signifying at the center of African American literary tradition from the slave narratives to Alice Walker. The revision, or repetition with a difference, sometimes critiques certain destructive or stereotypical tropes and sometimes celebrates constructive or liberatory ones. As I focus on the latter, Ellison's *Invisible Man* and Ishmael Reed's *Flight to Canada* serve as crucial works here. Their presence in both Gates's book and my own emerges from the infusion of signifying both aesthetically and substantively. Additionally, both writers attack and ridicule multiple targets literary, cultural, and historical on both sides of the color line.

2. The novel was hailed by Alain Locke in "Reason and Race: A Review of the Literature of the Negro for 1946" as "a novel without ulterior good intentions, other than the best of artistic intentions to tell the truth vividly, honestly and objectively" (21). Bell hooks sees this as emblematic of African Americans' inability to express and negotiate rage because of the elimination of options. At

one point in *Killing Rage* she suggests, "We do what Ann Petry's heroine tells us we must in that prophetic forties novel about black female rage *The Street*. It is Lutie Johnson who exposes the rage underneath the calm persona. She declares: 'Everyday we are choking down that rage.'"(12). In addition to the placement of the act of violence at the end of the novel, *The Street*, as we soon see with the protagonist in *Invisible Man*, forges an undeniable connection with African Americans' search for and disappointment with the American dream.

3. Other authors sought to demonstrate how racist oppression resulted in an inevitable act of violence by African Americans against whites or other African Americans. Ellison's novel views rage as something controllable through the traditions established in African American folk/street culture. Therefore, it rejects the assumption that acts of violence are the only expressions of rage in the novel, a characterization that has helped maintain stereotypes of African American rage as a threat to American national and personal security.

4. Ironically, Ellison's separation of rage and violence also reveals that the novel continues in the Wright school's tradition of exposing racism as a central factor in the second-class status of African Americans. Unlike many of those novels, *Invisible Man*'s presentation of the various modes of resistance and articulation of rage mirrors the multiple avenues African Americans were taking during this time in order to agitate for equal rights. The novel in many ways is responding to the 1943 sit-in by the Congress of Racial Equality (CORE) and Jackie Robinson's entrance into Major League Baseball in 1947 and anticipates the Martin Luther King–led Montgomery bus boycott and the emergence of the Student Nonviolent Coordinating Committee (SNCC). In "*Invisible Man* as Literary Analog to *Brown v. Board of Education*," among the many similarities Alfred L. Brophy sees—such as the treatment of people as individuals—an important connection is that "both address *the malleability of history and its contribution to dissembling*. Invisible Man recognizes the power of history and Ellison presents two versions of its operation in the novel—the real versus the mythic, or the true way of seeing versus the self-delusional way. The legal framework contends against how people behave within it" (131). The novel's connection to the *Brown* case—in addition to demonstrating how legal challenges would act as another method of articulating dissatisfaction during the civil rights movement—highlights the importance of history in exposing the shortcomings in the execution of American democracy as well as the myriad paths African Americans attempted to use in response to discrimination.

5. Even in the epilogue, the narrator informs the reader, "Here I've set out to throw my anger into the world's face," and while he feels he has failed because "now that I've tried to put it all down the old fascination with playing a role returns, and I'm drawn upward again" (437), in truth it serves as an example of

rage acting as a stimulus for social action. Also, while rage may be the driving force, the telling of the story has brought other experiences, ones that the narrator benefited from and possibly enjoyed, that prevent his rage from boiling over into destructive action. As a result, the rage that paralyzed him and drove him underground is, instead of neutralized, tempered by other responses into an effective response to oppression. It is because of those other experiences and paths that the narrator does not kill the nameless white man in the prologue.

6. Ellison's discussion of the trickster is important because he reveals a common misconception. The figure of the trickster and the figure of the con man are frequently collapsed, transforming trickster characters into an image that fits into traditionally stereotypical constructions of African American criminality. For example, in discussing the character Rinehart, Gayl Jones describes him as "a preacher, gambler, lover, numbers runner, a symbol of chaos and 'dangerous freedom'" (148). Rinehart seems to be the only character that is completely free, and as such he is a much celebrated and admired figure by many in the Harlem that the Invisible Man inhabits. Yet Ellison believes that "one could extend this list in the manner of much myth-mongering criticism until the fiction dissolved into anthropology, but Rinehart's role in the formal structure of the narrative is to suggest to the hero a mode of escape from Ras, and a means of applying, in yet another form, his grandfather's cryptic advice to his own situation" ("Change the Joke," 56–57). Rinehart's versatility, then, gets him noticed by the Invisible Man along with the revelation of a multitude of possibilities of resistance that were unavailable to the protagonist before. In order to gain access to these options, however, it becomes necessary to step outside the mainstream expectations of behavior to which the narrator has been faithfully subscribing. This versatility characterizes signifying and African American culture itself, which are often marginalized because of their frequent resistance to mainstream ideas and values. Consequently, while tricksters may exist outside mainstream expectations of morality and behavior, that should not make them tantamount with black criminals. In making the figure of the trickster and the figure of the criminal synonymous, the assumption becomes that the vernacular performances used are similarly dangerous and undesirable. More likely, the trickster is employing rhetorical strategies to invert the relationship that finds him powerless, itself an inherent protest of (white) mainstream values. Although criminals often use the same strategy, they pull from a tradition that surrounds them but that they did not create.

More troubling is the casting of the African American trickster/criminal figure as the sole user of black vernacular tradition. Alongside this, black vernacular tradition runs the risk of becoming part of the "darky entertainment"

Ellison feared, achieved primarily through critics who view the male characters' verbal performances as proof of trickster status. Put another way, many critics depreciate black vernacular tradition by subscribing to the notion that since most of, if not all, the male characters embrace black vernacular tradition, they must all be tricksters/criminals. Perhaps the clearest example in refutation of this is in my viewing of the narrator as the type of picaro that resembles Max/Matthew in *Black No More*. Both are Euro-African creations, even as Max/Matthew's amorality and greed contrast with the Invisible Man's guilelessness. However, while Max/Matthew limits his use of black vernacular expression to the sometimes trite conversations with Bunny Brown—a sign of Schuyler's disregarding of black vernacular's importance—the Invisible Man frequently pulls from black vernacular tradition or finds important clues in its usage by other characters. Yet the Invisible Man is clearly not a trickster. Therefore, because we can view the use of black vernacular tradition as separate from trickster status, as well as separating tricksters from criminal status, it becomes possible to recognize Ras, Rinehart, and Clifton as representative of a folk culture that employs language and behavior that is filled with complexity and contradiction and exists outside—even as it sometimes participates in—mainstream values as they achieve the "near-tragic, near-comic lyricism" that Ellison championed ("Richard Wright's Blues," 78).

7. Ellison's ultimate concern with self-identity—which, according to Robert Penn Warren in "The Unity of Experience" (1965), is based on Ellison's belief in "'The basic unity of human experience" and his "own early capacity to absorb the general values of Western culture" (24)—often trumps more explicit expressions of comic rage that might challenge the impact of American or Western culture. Additionally, in 1964 Stanley Edgar Hyman in "Ralph Ellison in Our Time" pointed out that Ellison "is reluctant to recognize the African elements in American Negro culture" (42). Indeed, Ellison's project is the celebration of the democracy of individual experience that includes complexities that strict associations with a group are unable to provide. The novel's constant return to and play off the Declaration of Independence and the Constitution is highlighted even further by the privileging of individualisms over the group identity from which African American cultural tradition often emerged. Thus the construction of the protagonist as an Everyman threatens to depreciate the novel's engagement with the contemporaneous debates and themes that surrounded its publication.

8. A clearer example of a white American reading of African American humor and folklore, as mentioned in the introduction, can be found in Joel Chandler Harris's Uncle Remus tales from the late nineteenth century. By contrast,

according to Watkins, "the John and Old Master tales reflect the trickster mo-tif" in African American folklore even as these "tales never matched the popu-larity of the Remus tales for mainstream audiences, however; the portrayal of a slave outsmarting his master was simply not acceptable to most non-blacks" (447). These tales, in which the slave John outwitted the "Old Mas" to gain his freedom, not only counter some popular post-Reconstruction notions that Afri-can Americans were happier during slavery, but they reveal an African American intellect that disrupted the images of minstrelsy during the late nineteenth and early twentieth century.

9. Just as sermons and the singing of spirituals are not solely a religious mode, signifying is not solely a mode for comedy and entertainment, despite what the mainstream contemporary example of signifying, the "Yo mama" jokes, might suggest. The sermonic tradition, along with others in African American culture, is a fertile expression from which we can view key tenets of African American orality, including improvisation and call-and-response. Ac-cording to O'Meally, the protagonist's "first speech as the Brotherhood's Harlem leader," which is itself improvised, is an example of how one mode contains nu-merous tenets, especially since the speech also "depends on shouted responses from the audience, as a black preacher does" (98). This, again, is reminiscent of the sermon at the beginning of the novel.

Chapter 2. Dick Gregory, Moms Mabley, and Redd Foxx: Bridging the Gap between Comedy, Rage, and Race

1. Moms Mabley, in Smith, *Mo' Funny: Black Comedy in America*.

2. Della Reese, in Smith, *Mo' Funny: Black Comedy in America*.

3. Levine recognizes the lasting importance of Johnson as the embodiment of the Bad Nigger in the early twentieth century: "Long after Jess Willard took Johnson's championship away by knocking him out in the twenty-sixth round of their 1915 fight in Cuba, stories of his physical strength, his great speed, his habit of publicly predicting with some precision the outcomes of his fights, and above all his ability to humble his white opponents and thwart American soci-ety still circulated in the black community" (432).

4. There are moments of the first in Schuyler's casting of black leaders as fraudulent and Ellison's parodying of Booker T. Washington, Tuskegee, and the African American elite. Both manifestations of attacks are seen in Foxx's routines, particularly his commentary on black preachers, the black church, and sex that is reminiscent of Zora Neale Hurston's novel *Jonah's Gourd Vine* (1934). Additionally in Foxx's act, he might respond to hecklers by proclaiming, "I would put something in your mouth but my zipper's stuck!" Eliciting howls

of pleasure from the audience, this response places the attention squarely on issues of sexuality, specifically perceptions of black male sexual dominance and size as well as the unenviable and powerless position, in the male heterosexual mind at least, of performing oral sex.

5. While Foxx may not have been the very first Comic Bad Nigger, his specific portrayal of the role would influence the aggressive style, uncensored content, and folk spirit found in comics like Dick Gregory, Rudy Ray Moore, and Richard Pryor. Levine acknowledges, "Reversal of roles through direct confrontation with mainstream whites rather than through trickery or the use of surrogate ethnic groups seems to be a more recent development in black humor, but the technique itself is a traditional one dating back to slavery" (308). Foxx's comic defiance would seem to be in keeping with the framework of an African American cultural tradition that expressed militant rage at certain points throughout history and was contained in various aspects of art, life, and ideology. Though most of Foxx's "descendants" would make their status as a Bad Nigger murky through a refinement of their acts, Gregory for mainstream success and Pryor in his creation of the Crazy Nigger, Foxx's routines unmistakably solidified his standing as one of the most influential Bad Niggers ever.

6. Dick Gregory, in Smith, *Mo' Funny: Black Comedy in America*.

Chapter 3. From *Absence* to *Flight*: The Appearance of Comic Rage in the Black Arts and Black Power Movements, 1966–1976

1. To be sure, Ward's play is not the first to use humor to address issues of race during this period. Ossie Davis's underappreciated play *Purlie Victorious* (1961) lays the groundwork for Ward's work as a hilarious send-up of race relations and a simultaneous call to arms for African American resistance. Described as a "comedy in three acts," Davis's play tells the exploits of Purlie Victorious Judson and his attempts to defeat Ol' Cap'n Stonewall Jackson Cotchipee, a classic white southern gentleman. Purlie seeks to receive his inheritance, protect the honor of Lutiebelle Gussiemae Jenkins, and establish an integrated church. In *Purlie*, Davis is unflinching in the use of comedy and the expression of rage. As Davis puts it, "What else can I do but laugh? It's absurd. The play is an attempt, a final attempt to hold that which is ridiculous up to ridicule—to round up all the indignities I have experienced in my own country and to laugh them out of his story delivered in a stunning example of African American fire and brimstone sermon, acting as another avenue for the constructive expression of rage" (Oliver 126). Davis's play eventually ends as a rallying cry for African Americans to mobilize in order to fight oppression. In this sense, the play is comparable to works of the early 1960s that called for definitive, if strictly nonviolent, action.

The play, unfortunately, does not possess the scope of Ward's racial vision, and his characters never develop enough to challenge the stereotypes they were initially constructed to subvert.

2. An important example is Reed's poetry throughout the novel, particularly the initial poem "Flight to Canada." Quickskill, no doubt speaking for Reed, claims that his poem "kind of imitates [Brown's] style, though I'm sure critics are going to give me some kind of white master. A white man. They'll say that he gave me the inspiration and that I modeled it after him. But I had you in mind" (121). The casting of Brown as a satirist and the constant revising of his narrative and novel reflects the novel's reimagining of history in its unyielding comic tone.

3. In fact, in 1969 a partially successful Day of Absence was carried out in New York City, where African Americans were encouraged to stay home instead of going to work. In the play as well, the absence of the black population highlights their presence in the life of American culture as loudly as the declarations hailing from Baraka's poetry. In fact, while Baraka's Black Arts Repertory Theatre would last only a year in New York, Ward's article resulted in the procurement of a Ford Foundation grant to start the NEC with producer-actor Robert Hooks and white manager Gerald Krone.

Chapter 4. Fury in the "Promised Land": Comic Rage in George C. Wolfe's *The Colored Museum* and Paul Beatty's *The White Boy Shuffle*

1. Newton's direct response to Cleaver's attack on Baldwin, as well as his rift with Cleaver over the direction of the Panthers, makes it reasonable to assume that he would differ with Cleaver over the image of homosexuals. In "A Letter from Huey to the Revolutionary Brothers and Sisters about the Women's Liberation and Gay Liberation Movements," Newton encourages his audience, especially its male members, to overcome their "insecurities . . . about homosexuality. When I say, 'insecurities' I mean the fear that there is some kind of threat to our manhood. I can understand this fear. Because of the long conditioning process that builds insecurity in the American male, homosexuality might produce certain hangups in us" (283).

2. For Miss Roj, recovering "the snap" is critical because music and dance have been co-opted, leaving snapping as perhaps the only viable option to access the power of the drums and, thus, African American oral culture and expression. As a way of resisting the deterioration of mainstream society, and signaling a strategy for others, she and her demons/contradictions "don't ask for acceptance. We don't ask for approval. We know who we are and we move on it!" (17).

3. The vignette cites that history as the tumultuous 1960s and 1970s, captured in Man's various buttons, "Free Angela! Free Bobby! Free Huey, Duey, and Louie! U.S. out of Viet Nam, U.S. out of Cambodia, U.S. out of Harlem, Detroit, and Newark" (34). The references to the Black Panther Party, including the humorous reference to Donald Duck's nephews, reflect the radical ideology fostered by militant rage and the contentious relationship between African Americans and the police, FBI, and CIA.

Chapter 6. Direct from a Never Scared Bicentennial Nigger: Comic Rage in the Work of Richard Pryor, Whoopi Goldberg, and Chris Rock

1. Thus Rock prevents his own critique of "niggas" from becoming a part of the mainstream discourse that might ultimately use the term to perpetuate stereotypical views of African Americans as "niggers." Rock differs from Bill Cosby's critiques of the language, behavior, and dress of young black urban America that began in 2004 and created a firestorm because of Cosby's failure to recognize the continued structural inequities—and the class warfare within black America—that heavily contributed to the younger generation's inability to fulfill the promise of *Brown v. Board of Education* (1954).

2. Of course, the efforts of his predecessors paved the way for *The Chris Rock Show*, Rock's weekly half hour on HBO in 1997–2001. Yet much was made possible by the presence of HBO. In a TV universe that has become increasingly less daring in its thematic content since the 1970s, with certain exceptions on cable, HBO's most significant contribution has been its willingness to engage traditionally silenced histories and uncompromising voices. Ranging from HBO films that bring to light underrepresented stories like *The Tuskegee Airmen* (1995) and *Unchained Memories: Readings from the Slave Narratives* (2003), to miniseries about the complexity of contemporary African America like *Laurel Avenue* (1993) and *The Corner* (2000), to biographical treatments, most notably *The Josephine Baker Story* (1991) and *Introducing Dorothy Dandridge* (1999), HBO has consistently produced dramatic tellings of African American life that move beyond dichotomous representations of black versus white and good versus evil. In these shows African Americans are not completely good, whites are not completely bad, or vice versa. There are times when African Americans contribute to their own oppression and times when whites work to help African Americans advance. What becomes most important is the revelation of previously untold stories told from the point of view of African Americans. To be sure, HBO is not the first or only television channel to produce such shows. But HBO has been unique in its willingness to present the full range of African American humor. Freed from the need to appeal to traditional network advertisers and censors,

HBO's content can often explore the country's most taboo subjects. The result is a space that has allowed the underground humor of African Americans to reach mainstream audiences on a regular basis. The weekly series *Russell Simmons's Def Comedy Jam* in 1992–97 introduced a plethora of black comics, including Martin Lawrence, Steve Harvey, and Bernie Mac. HBO's embrace of Chris Rock, who both appeared on and hosted *Def Jam*, resulted in Rock's breakthrough stand-up special *Bring the Pain* on HBO in 1996.

Bibliography

Acham, Christine. *Revolution Televised: Prime Time and the Struggle for Black Power*. Minneapolis: University of Minnesota Press, 2004.

Allen, Danielle. "Ralph Ellison on the Tragi-Comedy of Citizenship." In Morel, *Ralph Ellison and the Raft of Hope*, 37–57.

Andrews, William L. *The Literary Career of Charles W. Chesnutt*. Baton Rouge: Louisiana State University Press, 1980.

Baldwin, James. "Alas, Poor Richard." In *Nobody Knows My Name: More Notes of a Native Son*, 200–215. New York: Dial, 1961.

———. "Everybody's Protest Novel." 1949. In *Notes of a Native Son*, 13–23.

———. *Notes of a Native Son*. Boston: Beacon, 1955.

Baraka, Amiri. *See* Jones, LeRoi.

Barksdale, Richard K. "Black America and the Mask of Comedy." In Rubin, *Comic Imagination*, 349–60.

Barlowe, Jamie. "'You Must Never Be a Misrepresented People': Spike Lee's *Bamboozled*." *Canadian Review of American Studies* 33.1 (2003): 1–15.

Beatty, Paul, ed. *Hokum: An Anthology of African-American Humor*. New York: Bloomsbury, 2006.

———. *The White Boy Shuffle*. Boston: Houghton Mifflin, 1996.

Bell, Bernard W. *The Afro-American Novel and Its Tradition*. Amherst: University of Massachusetts Press, 1987.

Bennett, Stephen B., and William W. Nichols. "Violence in Afro-American Fiction: An Hypothesis." 1971. In Hersey, *Ralph Ellison*, 171–76.

Benson, Sheila. "Humor and Hubris: 'Hollywood Shuffle': Pungent Wit, Wicked Satire." *Los Angeles Times*, 24 April 1987.

Bergenholtz, Rita A. "Toni Morrison's *Sula*: A Satire on Binary Thinking." *African American Review* 30.1 (Spring 1996): 89–98.

Bier, Jesse. *The Rise and Fall of American Humor*. New York: Holt, Rinehart, and Winston, 1968.

Bigsby, C.W.E. "Three Black Playwrights: Loften Mitchell, Ossie Davis, Douglas Turner Ward." In *The Theatre of Black Americans: A Collection of Critical Essays*, edited by Errol Hill, 148–67. New York: Applause, 1987.

Black, Ray. "Satire's Cruelest Cut: Exorcising Blackness in Spike Lee's *Bamboozled*." In "Black Film and Culture," special issue, *Black Scholar* 33.1 (Spring 2003): 19–24.

Bogle, Donald. *Primetime Blues: African Americans on Network Television*. New York: Farrar, Straus and Giroux, 2001.

———. *Toms, Coons, Mulattoes, Mammies, and Bucks: An Interpretive History of Blacks in American Films*. 4th ed. New York: Continuum, 2001.

Boyd, Todd. "Put Some Brothers on the Wall! Race, Representation, and Visual Empowerment of African-American Culture." In *Shared Differences: Multicultural Media and Practical Pedagogy*, edited by Diane Carson and Lester D. Friedman, 149–64. Urbana: University of Illinois Press, 1995.

Braxton, Greg. "As Robert Townsend Sees It: He's Fighting Stereotypes with 'Meteor Man' and New TV Show." *Los Angeles Times*, 3 August 1993.

Brophy, Alfred L. "*Invisible Man* as Literary Analog to *Brown v. Board of Education*." In Morel, *Ralph Ellison and the Raft of Hope*, 119–41.

Brown, William Wells. *Clotel, or, The President's Daughter: A Narrative of Slave Life in the United States*. 1853. Bedford Cultural Edition, edited by Robert S. Levine. New York: St. Martin's, 2000.

Bruce, Dickson D., Jr. *Black American Writing from the Nadir: The Evolution of a Literary Tradition, 1877–1915*. Baton Rouge: Louisiana State University Press, 1989.

Bryant, Jerry H. *"Born in a Mighty Bad Land": The Violent Man in African American Folklore and Fiction*. Bloomington: Indiana University Press, 2003.

———. *Victims and Heroes: Racial Violence in the African American Novel*. Amherst: University of Massachusetts Press, 1997.

Butler, Robert. *Contemporary African American Fiction: The Open Journey*. Madison, NJ: Fairleigh Dickinson University Press, 1998.

Byrd, Rudolph P., and Beverly Guy-Sheftall, eds. *Traps: African American Men on Gender and Sexuality*. Bloomington: Indiana University Press, 2001.

Campbell, Jane. *Mythic Black Fiction: The Transformation of History*. Knoxville: University of Tennessee Press, 1986.

Carpio, Glenda R. *Laughing Fit to Kill: Black Humor in the Fictions of Slavery*. New York: Oxford University Press, 2008.

Chappelle, Dave. *Killin' Them Softly*. VHS. Urbanworks, 2000.

Charles, Nick. "The Suicide Hip-Hop." Review of *The White Boy Shuffle*, by Paul Beatty. *Nation*, 8 July 1996, 30–32.

Chesnutt, Charles W. *The Conjure Woman, and Other Conjure Tales*. 1899. Durham, NC: Duke University Press, 1993.

———. *The Marrow of Tradition*. Boston: Houghton, Mifflin, 1901.

———. *The Wife of His Youth, and Other Stories of the Color Line*. Boston: Houghton, Mifflin, 1899.

Chidester, Phil, and Jamel Santa Cruze Bell. "'Say the Right Thing': Spike Lee, *Bamboozled*, and the Future of Satire in a Postmodern World." In Hamlet and Coleman, *Fight the Power!*, 203–22.

Chidester, Phil, Shannon Campbell, and Jamel Bell. "'Black Is Blak': *Bamboozled* and the Crisis of a Postmodern Racial Identity." *Howard Journal of Communications* 17.4 (2006): 287–306.

Clark, William Bedford, and W. Craig Turner, eds. *Critical Essays on American Humor*. Boston: G. K. Hall, 1984.

Clarke, John Henrik, ed. *William Styron's Nat Turner: Ten Black Writers Respond*. Boston: Beacon, 1968.

Cleaver, Eldridge. *Soul on Ice*. New York: McGraw-Hill, 1968.

Cone, James H. *Malcolm and Martin and America: A Dream or a Nightmare*. Maryknoll, NY: Orbis, 1991.

Cooke, Michael G. *Afro-American Literature in the Twentieth Century: The Achievement of Intimacy*. New Haven, CT: Yale University Press, 1984.

Corliss, Richard. "The Shame of a Nation." Review of *Bamboozled*, by Spike Lee. *Time*, 1 October 2000, 108.

Cose, Ellis. *The Rage of a Privileged Class*. New York: HarperCollins, 1993.

Cox, James M. "Toward Vernacular Humor." 1970. In Clark and Turner, *Critical Essays*, 107–20.

Dance, Daryl Cumber, ed. *Honey, Hush!: An Anthology of African American Women's Humor*. New York: W. W. Norton, 1998.

Davis, Matthew R. "'Strange, history. Complicated too': Ishmael Reed's Use of African-American History in *Flight to Canada*." *Mississippi Quarterly* 49 (1996): 744–54.

Dickson-Carr, Darryl. *African American Satire: The Sacredly Profane Novel*. Columbia: University of Missouri Press, 2001.

Douglass, Frederick. *Narrative of the Life of Frederick Douglass, an American Slave, Written by Himself*. 1845. New Haven, CT: Yale University Press, 2001.

———. "What to the Slave Is the Fourth of July?" In W. Brown, *Clotel*, 253–58.

Du Bois, W.E.B. *The Souls of Black Folk*. Chicago: McClurg, 1903.

Duncan, Rozell Renée. "An Awakening of Black Consciousness as Seen in a Production of Douglas Turner Ward's *Happy Ending* and *Day of Absence*." Master's thesis, University of Akron, 1973.

Dunne, Sara. "Women as Children in American Comedy: Baby Snooks' Daughters." *Journal of American Culture* 16.2 (June 1993): 31–36.

Dyson, Michael Eric. "'Speech Is My Hammer': Black Preaching, Social Justice, and Rap Rhetoric." In *Open Mike: Reflections on Philosophy, Race, Sex, Culture and Religion*, 289–304. New York: Basic Civitas, 2003.

Elam, Harry J., Jr. "Signifyin(g) on African American Theatre: *The Colored Museum* by George C. Wolfe." *Theatre Journal* 44 (1992): 291–303.

Elam, Harry J., Jr., and Robert Alexander, eds. *Colored Contradictions: An Anthology of Contemporary African-American Plays*. New York: Plume, 1996.

Ellis, Trey. "The New Black Aesthetic." *Callaloo* 38.1 (1989): 233–43.

———. *Platitudes*. New York: Vintage, 1988.

———. "Response to NBA Critiques." *Callaloo* 38.1 (1989): 250–51.

Ellison, Ralph. "The Art of Fiction: An Interview." In *Shadow and Act*, 167–83.

———. "Blues People." In *Shadow and Act*, 247–58.

———. "Change the Joke and Slip the Yoke." In *Shadow and Act*, 45–59.

———. *Going to the Territory*. New York: Random House, 1986.

———. Introduction to *Invisible Man*, anniversary edition. New York: Random House; Vintage, 1982.

———. *Invisible Man*. New York: Random House, 1952.

———. "On Bird, Bird-Watching, and Jazz." In *Shadow and Act*, 221–32.

———. "Recent Negro Fiction." *New Masses* 11.6 (August 5, 1941): 22–26. Reprinted in Gates and Appiah, *Richard Wright*, 11–18.

———. "Richard Wright's Blues." In *Shadow and Act*, 77–94.

———. *Shadow and Act*. New York: Random House, 1964.

———. "What America Would Be Without Blacks." 1970. In *Going to the Territory*, 104–12.

———. "The World and the Jug." In *Shadow and Act*, 107–43.

Engeman, Thomas S. "*Invisible Man* and *Juneteenth*: Ralph Ellison's Literary Pursuit of Racial Justice." In Morel, *Ralph Ellison and the Raft of Hope*, 91–104.

Epp, Michael H. "Raising Minstrelsy: Humour, Satire, and the Stereotype in *The Birth of a Nation* and *Bamboozled*." *Canadian Review of American Studies* 33.1 (2003): 17–35.

Euell, Kim. "Signifyin(g) Ritual: Subverting Stereotypes, Salvaging Icons." *African American Review* 31 (1997): 667–75.

Everett, Percival. *Erasure: A Novel*. New York: Hyperion, 2001.

Fanon, Frantz. *Peau noire, masques blancs*. Paris: Éditions du Seuil, 1952. Translated by Charles Lam Markmann as *Black Skin, White Masks* (New York: Grove, 1967).

Favor, J. Martin. "'Ain't Nothin' Like the Real Thing, Baby': Trey Ellis' Search for New Black Voices." *Callaloo* 16 (1993): 694–705.

Feinberg, Leonard. *Introduction to Satire*. Ames: Iowa State University Press, 1967.

Fleming, Robert E. "Sutton E. Griggs: Militant Black Novelist." *Phylon* 34 (1973): 73–77.

Foxx, Redd. *The Best of Redd Foxx: Comedy Stew*. Audiocassette. Sony, 1997.

Foxx, Redd, and Norma Miller. *The Redd Foxx Encyclopedia of Black Humor*. Pasadena, CA: W. Ritchie, 1977.

Frazier, E. Franklin. *Black Bourgeoisie*. Glencoe, IL: Free Press 1957.

Fuller, Hoyt W. "Towards a Black Aesthetic." 1968. In Gates and McKay, *Norton Anthology*, 1809–16.

Gates, Henry Louis, Jr. *The Signifying Monkey*. New York: Oxford University Press, 1988.

Gates, Henry Louis, Jr., and K. A. Appiah. *Richard Wright: Critical Perspectives Past and Present*. New York: Amistad, 1993.

Gates, Henry Louis, Jr., and Nellie Y. McKay, eds. *The Norton Anthology of African American Literature*. New York: Norton, 1996.

George, Nelson. *Hip Hop America*. New York: Viking, 1998.

Gleason, William. "Voices at the Nadir: Charles Chesnutt and David Bryant Fulton." 1992. In McElrath, *Critical Essays*, 224–41.

Goldberg, Whoopi. *Fontaine: Why Am I Straight?* VHS. HBO Home Video, 1989.

———. *Whoopi—Back to Broadway (The 20th Anniversary Show)*. DVD. HBO Home Video, 2005.

———. *Whoopi Goldberg: Live on Broadway*. VHS. Lions Gate, 1985.

———. *Whoopi Goldberg Presents Moms Mabley*. DVD. HBO, 2013.

Gottfried, Martin. Introduction to *Day of Absence*, by Douglas Turner Ward. In Hatch and Shine, *Black Theatre USA*, 2: 264–66.

Greenlee, Sam. *The Spook Who Sat by the Door*. New York: Baron, 1969.

Gregory, Dick. *Nigger: An Autobiography*. With Robert Lipsyte. New York: Dutton, 1964.

———[Richard Claxton Gregory]. *No More Lies: The Myth and the Reality of American History*. New York: Harper & Row, 1971.

———. *Up from Nigger*. With James R. McGraw. New York: Stein & Day, 1976.

Grier, William H., and Price M. Cobbs. *Black Rage*. New York: Basic Books, 1968.

Griffin, Dustin. *Satire: A Critical Reintroduction*. Lexington: University Press of Kentucky, 1994.

Griggs, Sutton E. *Imperium in Imperio*. 1899. New York: Modern Library, 2003.

Haggins, Bambi. *Laughing Mad: The Black Comic Persona in Post-Soul America*. New Brunswick: Rutgers University Press, 2007.

Hamilton, Charles V. "Our Nat Turner and Styron's Creation." In Clarke, *William Styron's Nat Turner*, 73–78.

Hamlet, Janice D., and Robin R. Means Coleman, eds. *Fight the Power: The Spike Lee Reader*. New York: Peter Lang, 2009.

Hatch, James V., and Ted Shine. *Black Theatre USA: Plays by African Americans*. Rev. ed. Vol. 1, *The Early Period, 1847–1938*; vol. 2, *The Recent Period, 1935–Today*. New York: Free Press, 1996.

Hersey, John, ed. *Ralph Ellison: A Collection of Critical Essays*. Englewood Cliffs, NJ: Prentice-Hall, 1974.

Hill, Hamlin. "The Future of American Humor: Through a Glass Eye, Darkly." In Clark and Turner, *Critical Essays*, 219–25.

———. "Modern American Humor: The Janus Laugh." 1963. In Clark and Turner, *Critical Essays*, 91–99.

Hill, Herbert, ed. *Anger, and Beyond: The Negro Writer in the United States*. New York: Harper & Row, 1966.

hooks, bell. *Killing Rage: Ending Racism*. New York: Henry Holt, 1995.

Howe, Irving. "Black Boys and Native Sons." *Dissent*, Autumn 1963, 353–68.

Hughes, Langston, ed. *The Book of Negro Humor*. New York: Dodd, Mead, 1966.

———. "The Negro Artist and the Racial Mountain." *Nation* 122 (23 June 1926): 694.

Hurston, Zora Neale. *Their Eyes Were Watching God*. Philadelphia: Lippincott, 1937.

Hyman, Stanley Edgar. "Ralph Ellison in Our Time." Review of *Shadow and Act*, by Ralph Ellison. 1964. In Hersey, *Ralph Ellison*, 39–42.

Jackson, Blyden. "The Harlem Renaissance." In Rubin, *Comic Imagination*, 295–303.

Jones, Gayl. *Liberating Voices: Oral Tradition in African American Literature*. Cambridge, MA: Harvard University Press, 1991.

Jones, LeRoi. *Dutchman, and The Slave: Two Plays*. New York: Morrow, 1964.

———. *Home: Social Essays*. New York: Morrow, 1966.

———. "The Revolutionary Theatre." 1965. In *Home*, 210–15.

Kauffmann, Stanley. "On Films: Beyond Satire." Review of *Bamboozled*, by Spike Lee. *New Republic*, 30 October 2000, 32–33.

Kelley, William Melvin. *Dem*. Garden City, NY: Doubleday, 1967.

———. *A Different Drummer*. Garden City, NY: Doubleday, 1962.

Killens, John Oliver. *The Cotillion; or, One Good Bull Is Half the Herd*. New York: Trident Press, 1971.

———. Review of *Invisible Man*, by Ralph Ellison. *Freedom*, June 1952, 7.

King, Martin Luther, Jr. *I Have a Dream: Writings and Speeches That Changed the World*. Edited by James Melvin Washington. New York: HarperCollins, 1992.

Klawans, Stuart. "Amos, Andy, 'n' You." Review of *Bamboozled*, by Spike Lee. *Nation*, 6 November 2000, 34.

Klein, Marcus. "Ralph Ellison's *Invisible Man*." In *The Merrill Studies in "Invisible Man*," edited by Ronald Gottesman, 74–88. Columbus, OH: Merrill, 1971.

Kristeva, Julia. *Powers of Horror: An Essay on Abjection*. Translated by Leon S. Roudiez. New York: Columbia University Press, 1982.

Kroll, Jack. "Theater: Zapping Black Stereotypes." *Newsweek*, 17 November 1986, 85.

Landau, Saul. "Spike Lee's Revolutionary Broadside." *Cineaste* 26 (2001): 12.

Leab, Daniel J. "The Blue Collar Ethnic in Bicentennial America: *Rocky* (1976)." In *American History/American Film: Interpreting the Hollywood Image*, edited by John E. O'Connor and Martin A. Jackson, 257–72. New York: Frederick Ungar, 1979.

Lee, Malcolm D. *Undercover Brother*. Featuring Eddie Griffin, Dave Chappelle. DVD. Universal, 2002.

Lee, Spike. *Bamboozled*. Featuring Damon Wayans, Savion Glover, Jada Pinkett Smith. VHS. New Line Home Video, 2000.

Levine, Lawrence W. *Black Culture and Black Consciousness: Afro-American Folk Thought from Slavery to Freedom*. New York: Oxford University Press, 1977.

Limon, John. *Stand-Up Comedy in Theory, or, Abjection in America*. Durham, NC: Duke University Press, 2000.

Locke, Alain. "Reason and Race: A Review of the Literature of the Negro for 1946." *Phylon* 8 (1947): 17–27.

Lott, Eric. *Love and Theft: Blackface Minstrelsy and the American Working Class*. New York: Oxford University Press, 1993.

———. "Response to Trey Ellis's 'The New Black Aesthetic.'" *Callaloo* 12.1 (1989): 244–46.

Malveaux, Julianne, and Reginna A. Green, eds. *The Paradox of Loyalty: An African American Response to the War on Terrorism*. Chicago: Third World, 2002.

Marable, Manning. *The Great Wells of Democracy: The Meaning of Race in American Life*. New York: Basic Books, 2002.

Margolis, Harriet. "Stereotypical Strategies: Black Film Aesthetics, Spectator Positioning, and Self-Directed Stereotypes in *Hollywood Shuffle* and *I'm Gonna Git You Sucka*." *Cinema Journal* 38.3 (Spring 1999): 50–66.

Martin, Linda, and Kerry Segrave. *Women in Comedy*. Secaucus, NJ: Citadel, 1986.

Massood, Paula J., ed. *The Spike Lee Reader*. Philadelphia: Temple University Press, 2007.

McAllister, Marvin. *White People Do Not Know How to Behave at Entertainments*

Designed for Ladies and Gentlemen of Colour: William Brown's African and American Theater. Chapel Hill: University of North Carolina Press, 2003.

McElrath, Joseph R., Jr. *Critical Essays on Charles W. Chesnutt*. New York: G. K. Hall, 1999.

McGruder, Aaron. *All the Rage: The Boondocks Past and Present*. New York: Three Rivers, 2007.

———. *The Boondocks: The Complete First Season*. Directed by Seung Kim. DVD. Sony Pictures, 2006.

———. *Public Enemy #2: An All-New Boondocks Collection*. New York: Three Rivers, 2005.

———. *A Right to Be Hostile: The Boondocks Treasury*. New York: Three Rivers, 2003.

McWhorter, John. *Authentically Black: Essays for the Black Silent Majority*. New York: Gotham, 2004.

Moraru, Christian. *Rewriting: Postmodern Narrative and Cultural Critique in the Age of Cloning*. Albany: State University of New York Press, 2001.

Morel, Lucas E., ed. *Ralph Ellison and the Raft of Hope: A Political Companion to "Invisible Man."* Lexington: University Press of Kentucky, 2004.

Morrison, Toni. *The Bluest Eye*. New York: Holt, Rinehart and Winston, 1970.

———. *Playing in the Dark: Whiteness and the Literary Imagination*. Cambridge, MA: Harvard University Press, 1992.

———. *Sula*. New York: Knopf, 1974.

Moses, Wilson J. "Literary Garveyism: The Novels of Reverend Sutton E. Griggs." *Phylon* 40 (1979): 203–16.

Murphy, Eddie. *Eddie Murphy: Raw*. VHS. Paramount, 1987.

Nachman, Gerald. *Seriously Funny: The Rebel Comedians of the 1950s and 1960s*. New York: Pantheon, 2003.

Neal, Larry. "The Black Arts Movement." 1968. In Gates and McKay, *Norton Anthology*, 1959–72.

Newsweek. "A Sudden Turn for the Verse." 18 April 1993, 61.

Newton, Huey P. "A Letter from Huey to the Revolutionary Brothers and Sisters about the Women's Liberation and Gay Liberation Movements." 1970. In Byrd and Guy-Sheftall, *Traps*, 281–83.

———. *Revolutionary Suicide*. With J. Herman Blake. New York: Harcourt Brace Jovanovich, 1973.

Notorious B.I.G. *Life After Death*. LP. Bad Boy, 1997.

———. *Ready to Die*. LP. Arista, 1994.

Oliver, Clinton F., ed. *Contemporary Black Drama. From "A Raisin in the Sun" to "No Place to Be Somebody."* With Stephanie Sills. New York: Scribner, 1971.

O'Meally, Robert G. *The Craft of Ralph Ellison*. Cambridge, MA: Harvard University Press, 1980.

———. *New Essays on "Invisible Man."* New York: Cambridge University Press, 1988.

Peplow, Michael W. *George S. Schuyler*. Boston: Twayne, 1980.

Petry, Ann. "The Novel as Social Criticism." In *African-American Literary Criticism, 1773 to 2000*, edited by Hazel Arnett Ervin, 94–98. New York: Twayne, 1999.

———. *The Street*. Boston: Houghton Mifflin, 1946.

Price, Joe X. *Redd Foxx, B.S. (before Sanford)*. Chicago: Contemporary Books, 1979.

Pryor, Richard. *And It's Deep Too: The Complete Warner Brothers Recordings*. CD. Rhino, 2000.

———. *Bicentennial Nigger*. Audiocassette. Warner Brothers, 1976.

———. *Live on the Sunset Strip*. DVD. Sony, 1982.

———. *Pryor Convictions, and Other Life Sentences*. With Todd Gold. New York: Pantheon, 1995.

———. *Richard Pryor Live in Concert*. VHS. MPI Home Video, 1979.

Public Enemy. "Don't Believe the Hype." In *It Takes a Nation of Millions to Hold Us Back*. LP. Def Jam, 1988.

Reed, Ishmael. *Flight to Canada*. New York: Random House, 1976.

———. "Harlem Renaissance Day." In *Shrovetide in Old New Orleans*, 255–58. Garden City, NY: Doubleday, 1978.

———. *Mumbo Jumbo*. Garden City, NY: Doubleday, 1972.

Reid, Mark A. *Redefining Black Film*. Berkeley: University of California Press, 1993.

Rich, Frank. "Stage: 'Colored Museum,' Satire by George C. Wolfe." *New York Times*, 3 November 1986.

Riggs, Marlon. "Black Macho Revisited: Reflections of a Snap! Queen." In Byrd and Guy-Sheftall, *Traps*, 292–96.

———. *Tongues Untied*. Featuring Essex Hemphill. VHS. Strand Home Video, 1991.

Rock, Chris. *Bigger and Blacker*. VHS. HBO Studios, 1999.

———. *Bring the Pain*. VHS. HBO Studios, 1996.

———. *Never Scared*. VHS. HBO Studios, 2004.

———. *Rock This!* New York: Hyperion, 1997.

———. *Roll with the New*. CD. Dreamworks, 1997.

Roe, Jae H. "Keeping an 'Old Wound' Alive: *The Marrow of Tradition* and the Legacy of Wilmington." *African American Review* 33 (1999): 231–43.

Rose, Tricia. *Black Noise: Rap Music and Black Culture in Contemporary America*. Hanover, NH: University Press of New England, 1994.

Ross, Fran. *Oreo*. New York: Greyfalcon House, 1974.

Rourke, Constance. *American Humor: A Study of the National Character*. New York: Harcourt, Brace, 1931.

Rovit, Earl H. "Ralph Ellison and the American Comic Tradition." In Hersey, *Ralph Ellison*, 151–59.

Rowe, Kathleen. *The Unruly Woman: Gender and the Genres of Laughter*. Austin: University of Texas Press, 1995.

Rubin, Louis D., Jr., ed. *The Comic Imagination in American Literature*. New Brunswick, NJ: Rutgers University Press, 1973.

Rushdy, Ashraf H. A. *Neo-Slave Narratives: Studies in the Social Logic of a Literary Form*. New York: Oxford University Press, 1999.

Schechter, William. *The History of Negro Humor in America*. New York: Fleet Press, 1970.

Schuyler, George S. *Black and Conservative*. New Rochelle, NY: Arlington House, 1966.

———. *Black No More: Being an Account of the Strange and Wonderful Workings of Science in the Land of the Free, A.D. 1933–1940*. New York: Macaulay, 1931.

———. "The Negro-Art Hokum." *Nation* 122 (16 June 1926): 662.

Sloane, David E. E., ed. *New Directions in American Humor*. Tuscaloosa: University of Alabama Press, 1998.

Smith, Robert C. *We Have No Leaders: African Americans in the Post–Civil Rights Era*. Albany: State University of New York Press, 1996.

Smith, Yvonne. *Mo' Funny: Black Comedy in America*. Featuring Dick Gregory, Richard Pryor, Moms Mabley. VHS. HBO, 1993.

Smith-Shomade, Beretta E. "'I Be Smackin' My Hoes': Paradox and Authenticity in *Bamboozled*." In Massood, *The Spike Lee Reader*, 228–42.

Stowe, Harriet Beecher. *Uncle Tom's Cabin; or, Life Among the Lowly*. Boston: Jewett, 1852.

Styron, William. *The Confessions of Nat Turner*. New York: Random House, 1967.

Sykes, Wanda. *Wanda Sykes: I'ma Be Me*. Directed by Beth McCarthy-Miller. DVD. HBO Studios, 2010.

Townsend, Robert. *Hollywood Shuffle*. VHS. MGM, 1987.

Travis, Dempsey J. *The Life and Times of Redd Foxx*. Introduction by Dick Gregory. Chicago: Urban Research, 1999.

Vaidhyanathan, Siva. "Now's the Time: The Richard Pryor Phenomenon and the Triumph of Black Culture." In Sloane, *New Directions in American Humor*, 40–50.

Walker, David. *David Walker's Appeal to the Coloured Citizens of the World*. 1829. Edited by Peter P. Hinks. University Park: Pennsylvania State University Press, 2000.

Walters, Ronald W. *White Nationalism, Black Interests: Conservative Public Policy and the Black Community*. Detroit: Wayne State University Press, 2003.

Ward, Douglas Turner. "American Theater: For Whites Only?" *New York Times*, 14 August 1966.

——. "Being Criticized Was to Be Expected . . ." *New York Times*, 1 September 1968.

——. "The Goal Is Autonomy." *New York Times*, 2 February 1969.

——. *Happy Ending, and Day of Absence: Two Plays*. New York: Dramatists Play Service, 1966.

Warren, Kenneth W. *So Black and Blue: Ralph Ellison and the Occasion of Criticism*. Chicago: University of Chicago Press, 2003.

Warren, Robert Penn. "The Unity of Experience." Review of *Shadow and Act*, by Ralph Ellison. 1965. In Hersey, *Ralph Ellison*, 21–26.

Watkins, Mel, ed. *African American Humor: The Best Black Comedy from Slavery to Today*. Foreword by Dick Gregory. Chicago: Lawrence Hill, 2002.

——. *On the Real Side: A History of African American Comedy*. Chicago: Lawrence Hill, 1999.

Weixlmann, Joe. "African American Deconstruction of the Novel in the Work of Ishmael Reed and Clarence Major." MELUS 17.4 (1991): 57–79.

West, Cornel. Foreword to Malveaux and Green, *The Paradox of Loyalty*, xi–xii.

——. *Race Matters*. Boston: Beacon, 1993.

Wiggins, William H., Jr. "Jack Johnson as Bad Nigger: The Folklore of His Life." In *Contemporary Black Thought: The Best from the Black Scholar*," edited by Robert Chrisman and Nathan Hare, 53–70. Indianapolis: Bobbs-Merrill, 1973.

Willett, Cynthia. *Irony in the Age of Empire: Comic Perspectives on Democracy and Freedom*. Bloomington: Indiana University Press, 2008.

Williams, Elsie A. *The Humor of Jackie Moms Mabley: An African American Comedic Tradition*. New York: Garland, 1995.

Williams, John A., and Dennis A. Williams. *If I Stop I'll Die: The Comedy and Tragedy of Richard Pryor*. New York: Thunder's Mouth, 1991.

Williams, Sherley Anne. *Dessa Rose*. New York: Morrow, 1986.

Wolfe, George C. *The Colored Museum*. New York: Grove, 1988.

Wright, Louis B. "Human Comedy in Early America." In Rubin, *Comic Imagination*, 17–32.

Wright, Richard. "Blueprint for Negro Writing." *New Challenge* 2.1 (Fall 1937): 53–65.

————. *Native Son*. New York: Harper & Brothers, 1940.

————. *Uncle Tom's Children*. 1938, 1940. New York: HarperPerennial, 1993.

X, Malcolm. *The Autobiography of Malcolm X*. With Alex Haley. New York: Grove, 1965.

Yarborough, Richard. Introduction to *Uncle Tom's Children*, by Richard Wright, ix–xxviiii. New York: HarperCollins, 1993.

Index

Terrence T. Tucker is assistant professor
of English and coordinator of African American
literature at the University of Memphis.

Printed in the United States
By Bookmasters